The Simple Gospel

Volume 1

by

Bishop H.C. Morrison

First Fruits Press
Wilmore, Kentucky
c2015

The Simple Gospel, Vol. 1 by Bishop H. C. Morrison

Published by First Fruits Press, © 2015
Previously Published by the Pentecostal Publishing Company ©1919

ISBN: 9781621711766 (print), 9781621711797 (digital)

Digital version at
http://place.asburyseminary.edu/firstfruitsheritagematerial/83

Morrison, H. C. (Henry Clay), 1842-1921.
    The simple gospel / by H.C. Morrison.
    2 volumes ; 21 cm.
    Wilmore, Ky. : First Fruits Press, c2015.
    Reprint. Previously published: Louisville, KY : Pentecostal
    Publishing Company, 1919-1921.
    ISBN: 9781621711766 (pbk.)
    1. Methodist Church -- Sermons. 2. Sermons, American. I. Title.
    BX8333.M6 S5 2015   252

Cover design by Jane Brannen

First Fruits Press

The Academic Open Press of Asbury Theological Seminary

204 N. Lexington Ave., Wilmore, KY 40390

859-858-2236

first.fruits@asburyseminary.edu

asbury.to/firstfruits

BISHOP H. C. MORRISON.

The Simple Gospel

BY
Bishop H. C. Morrison
Leesburg, Fla.

———

"For I am not ashamed of the gospel of Christ; for it is the power of God unto salvation to everyone that believeth."—St. Paul.

———

Pentecostal Publishing Company,
Louisville, Ky.

DEDICATION.

When twenty years of age I was called of God into the ministry. My now sainted mother was the first person to whom I made the divine impression known. Calmly and without surprise she said, "My son, I have been praying ever since you were born that God would call you to preach the gospel." Of this she had never given me an intimation.

To her sacred memory this book is affectionately dedicated by the author.

FOREWORD.

I have seen no carefully wrought analysis of those elements of power which have made the preaching of the author of this book notable in the South for nearly half a century. I therefore give my own impressions, as one who has had unusual opportunity to study, at close range, his rare and beautiful homiletic gift.

There are men in pulpits who are not preachers; but are primarily teachers or lecturers; sometimes, alas, they are ecclesiastical mountebanks. Perhaps they lack the public temperament. Sometimes we cannot define their lack; but they leave us unmoved. Their oratory is but a painted flame—it does not warm.

Not so with the author of this book. The moment he appears before you you feel that you are in the presence of a master of assemblies. A compelling magnetism establishes rapport between speaker and audience. Every eye is riveted, every attention fixed. This power of personality is one of the rare gifts of a preacher; and without this his words sometimes become "as a sounding brass or a tinkling cymbal." We hear with outward decorum, but inwardly

> "The heart says, 'Brother, go thy way,
> None shall ask thee what thou doest,
> Or care a rush for what thou knowest.'"

There is a *moral* and also a *physical* magnetism. The born orator, to whom God has given the birthright of golden speech, generally has also the physical magnetism; but if a speaker lack this

4

it cannot be acquired. Not so with the moral magnetism. It is born of moods; which in turn are born of the divine Spirit. The same man may have it today and be without it tomorrow. It comes of protracted "tarrying in the upper room."

Yet, it is not wholly the creature of transient states. Some men so constantly occupy their minds with thoughts of God, and prayer is such a fixed factor in the mental and moral life, that the holy mood becomes a holy habit; and like Fletcher, they carry with them "an awful sense of other worlds." This other worldliness we call moral magnetism because no force is more hypnotic. The humblest street-preacher, if he has it, will dominate an audience with irresistible power.

No preacher impresses two auditors precisely alike; but everyone who hears Bishop Morrison senses this quality. In his quiet deliverances it is felt as a pervasive influence; and in his more powerful moods it broods over an audience with an almost awful and oppressive power. Out of such preaching character is often re-conditioned with dramatic and startling suddenness; and sometimes whole communities are transformed as if by divine magic.

Another element of power which marks the author of this book is *unity* of character. In some instances the several elements of personality do not perfectly fuse; but our author has a perfectly unified personality; and this is always an element of power. The men who lack this element are but intellectual Hamlets halting between opinions and refining upon subtleties.

Truth lies before the author of "The Simple Gospel" straight as a highway in the sun. Without hesitation or reserve, he delivers his entire force, mental, moral and personal, upon the conscience of his audience; and the recoil is sometimes tremendous. He has never relied very much upon "the subliminal uprush." He has always been a hard student, seeking his material with a passionate avidity and rarely quoting the language of another. Given a suggestion or seed-thought, ideas of his own throng him with almost bewildering profusion.

His mental world is a world of order. We have heard great preachers whose appeal was more to the imagination than to the reason; and the effect was like lightning among mountains where landscapes form only to dissolve without leaving any definite impression. This is never true of the author of "The Simple Gospel." His clarity is a delight, and his sentences move to their objective straight as a sunbeam. He employs one central vertebral thought, and all the others are grouped about it. Every exposition, trope, or illustration clings to the central thought as steel filings to a magnet. And to this delightful lucidness, there is added zest. Sentences volley and explode with epigrammatic percussion. Simile and metaphor rise unexpectedly, as the covey of birds from the wayside copse.

There is nothing of the decadent or moribund; and the effect is to stimulate rather than depress.

Readers of "The Simple Gospel" will also discover a *versatility* which is very rare. Even great preachers sometimes repeat other men, and repeat themselves; but we have seen in the author's study, as many as eighty discourses in manuscript; and we doubt whether there is so much as a paragraph repeated.

A final quality which we note is *vitality*. We have heard discourses which suggested the gloom of the morgue, and the length of the coffin. But the contents of this book are delightfully humanized. Vivacity and spontaneity are here. The discourses crackle and sparkle with the electricity of life; and, the secret of this vitality is in the author's first-hand relation to God and His truth.

HENRY F. HARRIS.

Leesburg, Florida,
June the 13th, 1919.

CONTENTS.

8

CHAPTER I.

THE BEGINNING.

"In the beginning God created the heavens and the earth."—Gen. 1:1

This is the complete account of creation. The original language leaves out the definite article—"the"—and simply says, "In beginning God created the heavens and the earth." When that beginning was we know not. There is nothing before this verse, and it has no connection with the verses that follow. It is out to itself. The ark on the flood. The lone sail on the sea. The space of time between the first and second verses has never been measured. Creation is complete in this statement—heaven and earth, with all that constitute them as a structure.

THE BEGINNING OF HISTORY.—An erratic imagination may venture beyond this writing; but, like the raven let loose from the ark, it will wander away and be lost. Truth, like the dove, finds no resting place for her foot; and hence returns to find sure rest in this handwriting of God.

The vast reach of the text declares it divine. The birth of all being is announced in a sentence, and that as simple as childhood. Here are heaven and earth standing together at the threshold of history. New-born of the divine. Twins, and, like the Siamese, never to be separated; and now making their debut into the economy of God.

THE BEGINNING OF OUR KNOWLEDGE
OF GOD.—This is the aim in redemption. For
this Christ lived, suffered, and died; that He
might do what this text does, bring us to God.
This opening sentence is the type of the final coming together of God and man. The end expressed in the beginning. Here we meet God for the
first time. Here the endless acquaintance begins.
Here we meet Godhead, mystery, power. In the
beginning; when was that? God—who is He?
"Created"—what does this mean? Here is the
fountain head of thought and inquiry. Here is
food for eternal investigation. Here God is in-
troduced under a name that implies tri-unity. The
"Elohim;" the three one. Here we learn the
name of the Father; and after the lapse of time
we come nearer and see the Son; and still later we
have the Holy Ghost come and dwell in us. God
in hearing. God in sight. God in us.

This text presents God as "past finding out."
The mystery and simplicity are evidence that it is
from God. The way of life is so plain that "the
wayfaring man, though a fool, may not err
therein;" and other portions of Scripture so deep
and strange that the philosopher must needs kneel
and confess. "Thine, O Lord, is the wisdom."
Here we see God at the extremes. In the simplicity of salvation, and in the darkness of His
own counsels. God revealed, and God past finding
out.

THE BEGINNING OF FAITH.—Faith begins
here. Where God meets us faith begins. When

we walk with God we walk by faith. The little child is not anxious as to where it is, and where it is going; only so its father is holding its hand. So faith is not anxious to know of the beginning or the end; only so it knows that God is with it. Hence faith is satisfied with this text, not because it understands it, but because God is in it. All beginnings are mysterious. The beginning of life, consciousness, love, thought. All mysterious; but faith is satisfied because "God is in all."

LEARNING TO BE A CHRISTIAN.—This is not like learning to spell, read, or reason. Faith has no A. B. C. to lead the heart by gradual induction. The Bible doesn't begin that way. Had it been a system of science it would have begun in that manner. But it is a system of faith, and faith has no need of such a process. Its first lesson is as difficult as its graduation. The soul is tested at the beginning. Abruptly and without preface you are called to believe that God is, and that He did create; that He did absolutely make something out of nothing. Not a mote or an atom, but a heaven and an earth. St. Paul states this test. "By faith (not science) we understand that the worlds were framed by the word of God;" (not arranged out of pre-existent matter, but created), "so that things which are seen were not made of things that do appear." Here is the test. If you can accept this first verse in the Bible, then you can believe all that is necessary to save your soul. The water in the stream of inspiration is as deep at the bank as in mid-current. If you cannot believe this text, then linger here and pray "Lord, increase my faith." Linger until He helps you to believe; and this will be your beginning of faith, love, life and immortality.

THE BEGINNING OF MANIFESTED LOVE. —Not the beginning of love; but the beginning of its manifestations. Labor is proof of love. Your continued and unflagging toil for your loved ones is proof of your love for them. God was here at work, not to build for Himself, for He inhabiteth eternity; but to build for another. Here is God's grand lesson in this wonderful text. Here we learn how to be co-workers with God. How to exalt our labor and make it worthy of the sons of God.

This was the daybreak of love. Creation creeping up from primeval darkness and unfolding her glory. This was the daybreak of divine love. I cannot see what is beyond the sunrise; but I see the light is there; the glory of the morning filleth the far-off abyss. I cannot see what is beyond this text; but the light is there, and I see the glory gleaming from beyond it. The beginning of that endless day of love that shall ever be rising and yet never reach its noon.

The new-made heavens and earth were the heralds coming up from eternity's wilderness crying, "Prepare ye the way of the Lord." Christ had for His forerunner a solitary seer in rude raiment. Adam had for his herald creation in all the mystery of the morning song of time.

THE TWO POLAR POINTS.—These are where

God's love seems to culminate. Points where the horizon closes down and beyond which we can take no reckoning. Creation and Crucifixion. In creation we see how high He could exalt man; in the crucifixion we see how low He could humble Himself. Creation tells what He did for us at first. Crucifixion tells what He suffered for us at last. Paradise and Calvary. Man living amid flowers —God dying among thorns. These are the extreme points of our vision. Eden's light and Gethsemane's gloom. The beauty and the blood. His work and His suffering can show us no more. All beyond is known to Him alone.

BEGINNING OF RELIGION AND SCIENCE. —Here is God and what God has created. To know God is religion. To know what He has created is science. Both begin here. They have an even start and should always be kept even. But the mistake is, while religion believes and worships and rests in the Creator; science digs, and doubts and struggles with the things created. This is fatal when the man fails to know God, and shuts himself down to a simple knowledge of creation. The man who knows the world, the things created, and loves, and lives in them and for them, is an eternal mistake, a sort of homo-swine—"Satisfied with snout of groveling appetite, to grub his happiness from the dirt."

THE PRIMER OF HUMANITY.—This life is the primary of eternity. We live on earth to study toward heaven. Earth is full of index hands pointing that way. Sometimes we come to a prov

idential problem that we cannot solve. We turn
it over, and around, and look at it through our
tears; but all in vain, there is no solution. But
heaven and earth were made by the same God,
and at the same time; always connected and
never in conflict. Hence these hard readings are
right if we could only read them aright.

How often when in school have you tugged, and
perspired, and fretted, and despaired, over a hard
problem in mathematics. You tried again, and
again, until your head ached; and still the answer
would not come like the answer in the book. And
when the kind teacher solved the problem for you
you were amazed at your own conclusion.

How we wrestle with the strange providences
of God, and try in vain to understand them! We
study them with moist eyes and heavy heart, and
sometimes conclude that they are wrong in the
Book. That God has not directed this, and has
nothing to do with it.

Heaven and earth can never be separated: God
hath joined them together. This life and the other life are connected. Paul speaks of the "Whole
family in earth and in heaven." His providences
are only the golden chains that connect the two
worlds. Here we can only feel our way. We can
reach the golden links only for a short distance.
We know to what they are fastened here; but we
cannot see the fastenings on the other side, nor
the hand that is drawing them. But after a time
we shall exchange worlds. We shall go up and
stand at the other end of the providence chains.

Then shall we see how graciously those chains worked in the dark, how they drew the dear ones, that were in danger, up and out into eternal safety; how they drew those things gently out of our hands and possession which were becoming a snare and an injury. Like the faithful nurse amid the little ones in the nursery, catching away from the little hands that which might wound or hurt, the angels of God, the "ministering spirits," are watching this old world's nursery, catching away, so strangely, so sadly sometimes, the things that would be hurtful.

We try now to read the other life through the experiences of this life; but all in vain. The light is too dim. Sin has dimmed our eyes. The letters get mixed; the reading is broken and incorrect. But when we come to read the other way; to read this earth from heaven's light; when we stand in that light, where "there is no need of the light of the sun;" when we read earth from heaven, then the reading will be all clear.

What a joy! Amid the restful surroundings, on some sweet hillock, hard by the River of Life; to sit down and quietly re-read our own history. What a revelation! To see how I was watched, guarded, pulled back from destruction. How I fretted and chafed when things were taken from me, things that would have wrought my ruin. We will read and rejoice. Then read again and shout, "Thanks be to God, who hath given us the victory," and brought us safe home at last!

CHAPTER II.

A SEPARATION ON THE FIRST DAY.

"And God divided the light from the darkness."—Gen. 1:4.

"I am the light of the world."—Jno. 9:5.

"THE PHYSICAL CREATION ILLUS-TRATES THE MORAL."—The infant earth was born blind and "darkness was on the face of the deep." The first necessity was light. And God said "Let there be light; and there was light." The human soul—like the infant earth—is born blind. Darkness is on the face of the deep. A depravity which is hopeless and helpless. Like the new-born world, there is no life. But it abides in death until God says again, "Let there be light." That same "Spirit of God" which moved upon the dead waters, moves upon the dead soul and it awakes to see and know its condition. And under this light of conviction and the moving of the Holy Spirit there comes order out of moral darkness and chaos. And the soul is born again; born from the dead; born from above.

"God saw the light that it was good." So the new-born soul when it sees the light of salvation, it shouts because of the goodness of that light, and rejoices as the angels in the morning-song of Creation.

TIME OF THE SEPARATION.—It was the first creation day on which "God divided the light

18

from the darkness." Light and darkness are incompatible and cannot dwell together. The first
thing that God did after He made the light was to
put a division between it and the darkness. This
division was not only the first, but an all-essential
one. And in this God has given us the great lesson to learn and practice in the moral and religious life. To divide between the light and the
darkness. The very first lesson for the young
convert is to learn to distinguish between what is
of God and what is of the world: and then to
make the division—make it clear and distinct—
and never to be reunited. God said when He instituted marriage, "Whom God hath joined together let not man put asunder." So when He
divorced the light from the darkness, it was forever. What God has thus put asunder let no man
join together. And as the very existence of the
day depends on this divorce, and upon keeping the
darkness out of it; so the clear, bright Christian
life depends upon its entire divorce from the
world. A separation as definite as when "God
divided the light from the darkness."

THE TWILIGHT LIFE.—This is a kind of
truce between day and night. What a multitude
trying to be Christians and yet unwilling to give
up the world; clinging to its customs and its
follies. These things darken their spiritual skies
and rob them of their joys: while they find that
as the light departs the darkness thickens. And
when the light that is in them becomes darkness,
"How great is that darkness!"

God divided between the light and the darkness before He proceeded with His work. Let us admonish you to follow the example. Follow the divine plan—separate between Christ and the world; because Christ is the light of the world."

Christ divided in the moral world as clearly as is the division in the natural world between light and darkness. "Whoso loveth the world the love of the Father is not in him." "No man can serve two masters." "He that is not with me is against me."

LIGHT IS THE EMBLEM OF CHRIST IN HIS PURITY.—He said, "I am the light of the world." That is the *moral* world; just as the natural light is the light of the physical world. And the natural light is the emblem of Christ's purity.

Sin has brought the world under the power of corruption and death. "By sin came death." However healthful the human form it contains the seeds of death. The flowers fade and the fruits only mature to rot. The earth is full of death, and death and corruption reign everywhere and over everything.

But the light, like the Master, is not in bondage to corruption. And, like Him, it "Shall never see corruption." It walks a conqueror through the grave-yards of the universe; too pure for contamination. It will go into the abodes of filth; creep through the crevice into the dark dungeon; stay all day in the contagion of the hospitals and pest-houses; find its way through the casement into the sick-room, and kiss the lips of the hopeless sufferer; and when the burial vaults are opened it goes down and creeps over the dust and bones of the dead; and yet withal, remains as pure as when it issued from the fountain of light at first.

Such is Christ in the moral world. Unaffected by sin and beyond its power of contamination. He stands the only one in the universe exempt from sin. Pure in life, in work, and teaching; yea, His very grave pure. Like the light, He went everywhere with impunity; too pure for contamination. He ate with sinners, suffered the sinful woman to caress and bathe His feet with her tears, touched the loathsome leper, mixed the clay and spittle for the eyes of the blind beggar, stood at the open grave and breathed the air from the four days dead, and yet remained as pure as when the shepherds gave Him welcome: and even when in the tomb, corruption, with hideous form, did not venture to tread the precincts of that tomb.

LIGHT IS A UNIVERSAL BLESSING.—God wrapped the young universe in a garment of light. He did not create the light for only a part of the world, but for all creation. For the pauper as well as for the prince. He did not light the sun to "put it under a bushel," but on the great solar candlestick and upon the center-table of the universe. Hence it "giveth light to all who are in the house."

Such is the universal light of Christ. Not the light of the Jew only nor the Gentile alone; but "The light of the world." Just as God wrapped the light about the new-born earth, so He wrapped His promise about the new-born race. "The seed of the woman shall bruise the serpent's head." God gave them a covering of skins for the body and a covering of promise for the soul.

And though it was hard for them to leave their Eden home and go out among the thorns, yet they could go anywhere and endure anything when wrapped in God's promise. So we can go from prosperity to poverty: from affluence to indigence; and even "glory in tribulations," when wrapped in the promises of God.

THE LIGHT HAS A LIFE-GIVING POWER— The natural light is the element which the flowers breathe. If you would stop the breath of your favorite exotic you have only to set it away in the darkness of the cellar and it soon has the pallor of death.

Christ declares, "If ye believe in me ye shall have the light of life." And we have spiritual life in proportion to our proximity to Christ. When we turn from this light and crawl into some worldly cavern to hide treasures, or into some den of selfishness where we may evade duty or escape responsibility, then like the flower in the dark cellar, we are soon at the point of spiritual death.

Nothing is more detrimental to health than living too close to the ground. And nothing is more hurtful to the spiritual health than living too close to the world. What the church needs is light and sunshine. She needs to come up higher.

To leave the basements and darkness of the world and come into the higher and purer altitudes where the spiritual life—like the flowers in the sunlight—can live and flourish. If you would be strong and healthful Christians remember that "Prevention is better than cure." To keep clear of religious chills we must keep on high ground and live above the world.

WHAT SCIENCE HAS CONTENDED.— While light is friendly to health and is essential to life, some have contended that it has healing properties and power to cure disease. And about forty years ago, it was thought that science had discovered the process for extracting the healing properties of the light by means of blue-glass. Some of you remember the "blue-glass craze" that swept over the country. The papers were filled with the wonderful accounts of the healing property of the light when brought through blue-glass. Many homes had one window filled with blue-glass; and the heart of many a sufferer beat with high hope, only to meet with sore disappointment. The sensation passed. The blue-glass disappeared from the journals and front windows, leaving the sufferers still to suffer.

But in Christ—the light of the world—there is healing power. The "Sun of Righteousness" has not only light, but healing in his beams. And God has revealed what science could never discover, that is, how we may extract the life-elixir from the divine sunbeams. Not with blue-glass, but with the glass of the gospel. "Now we

see though a glass darkly." Not by the natural
light, but by the light of the Holy Spirit. This
light comes to us through a crimson medium. It
is red with the precious blood of Christ. And the
divine Spirit, shining through it, throws a crimson glow and glory over our race. It is the blood
that saves and the Holy Spirit that applies. The
healing power of this blood-red light has been
tested for thousands of years and has never failed
of cure in a single case. The poor sufferer lay at
the pool for "thirty and eight years" without help
from that pool; the invalid carried in his easy-
chair and placed before the blue-glass window for
weary hours, only to be carried back in sad disappointment. But who ever placed himself before this gospel—this glass of God—looking
through it by the light of the Holy Spirit, and
failed to feel its healing power? This crimson
light is a light no cloud can obscure, no sorrow
can eclipse. It may be winter; the sun gone and
the heavens dark; loved ones dead and the home
sad; still you can read this blessed word, feel its
warmth and power, and shout for joy in its light.
Take it when you visit the graves of your dead.
And as you sit and sadly meditate, you forget the
dust that sleeps, while it shows you the resurrection and brings Jesus to you as He came to the
grave in Bethany; and you hear Him say, "I am
the resurrection and the life." "Thy loved and
lost shall live again."

Has He healing power? Ask the "four and
twenty thousand" at the throne—ask the millions

bivouacked under the sod and awaiting the resurrection—ask the multitudes marching heavenward on this God's foot-stool; ask the gray-heads in this congregation, if they have been healed by His power? They will tell you that "While the outward man is perishing the inward man is renewed day by day." May He evermore give us this light of life!

CHAPTER III.

THE FIRST LANGUAGE.

Text: "The heavens declare the glory of God."—Ps. 19:1

The language of the skies was the first and most simple speech, sublime as the Divine and simple as childhood. This is the first language learned by the little child. It asks about the heavens and the great God that made them. It takes its first lessons from the heavenly alphabet. It asks about the great sun and the beautiful moon, as if they were the capitals, and then about the stars, which are the lesser A B C's of the heavens. We learned something of this sky language before we learned our letters. We learned it because it was simple and pleasant.

You can teach a little child more in an hour with a map spread before it than in a day or a week without the map. God mapped the lesson on the velvet of the skies, so nicely adjusted to the sensibility of the eye. Its color never cloys. Study the heavens for an age and they never become commonplace. Other things lose their charm. The toy pictures over which we clapped our hands with glee have long since lost their interest, but the skies are as lovely to us now as when we first asked about them in childhood. Like the "old, old story" the heavens are ever new.

NOT A DEAD LANGUAGE.—We love the

26

speech that thrills; that eloquence which comes from an ardent soul thrilling through the words. There is life in the language of the skies. The sun warms His words into our blood and makes us feel what He says. The stars cause us to feel the far-away touch of that providence of which they silently speak. The balmy sky subdues the soul into a sense of its own sweet serenity.

Thus we are made to feel the great divine soul back of all these, speaking through them and thrilling our whole being.

A PERPETUAL LANGUAGE.—"Day unto day uttereth speech, and night unto night showeth knowledge." There is no cessation. The succession of day and night is an unbroken and continuous proclamation of the glory of God.

These appointments are not on the itinerant plan. No annual or quadrennial change, but they stand forever. The untiring old circuit riders of the heavens continue their rounds, while the stationed preachers of the skies stand in their lot, and the work goes on from the central city of the sun even unto the outpost of the universe.

We like the fearless fidelity of these heavenly heralds. They cater to nothing, but preach—not what we wish to hear—but what God directs, whether the sermon descend in the sunbeams, distill in the dew, thunder in the tempest, burn in the drought, or sweep in the flood. We may wish the burning summer gone or the dreary winter ended, but they pursue their course, doing their work to the glory of God. Is their fidelity due to

their position far above the world and close to
God? Then may we not by stubborn faith rise
to a like relation and proximity to Him and become fearless in every way?

PASTORAL CARE.—Those ministers of the
skies are not only faithful in preaching, "declaring the glory of God," but they exercise a personal pastoral care over us. There is not a day
in your history in which heaven has failed to senc
the light at early morning to your window and to
flash it along your pathway until nightfall.
Whether that light was used or abused, it has
come every morning to minister at your feet. No
weary evening has come in which heaven has not
been prompt to shut the blinds and draw the curtains and shut out the light and make the world
keep still and quiet while you slept. What is
nightfall, with fading light and hushing noise?
What means this general sinking of all things into
silence? It is but God, through nature, quieting
all things that His tired children may rest and
sleep. "Day unto day uttereth speech." Day by
day we have this pastoral care. Do we hear that
speech? Have we ears to hear what the heavens
are daily speaking? There is gospel enough in
a single passing day or gathering nightfall to lead
the soul to God.

A UNIVERSAL LANGUAGE.—There is no
speech or language where their voice is not heard;
not a mere dialect spoken by a single community,
but a language familiar to every nation under the
sun. Their line, or sound, has gone out through

all the earth. It is God's grand telephonic system, bringing Him into communication with all nations.

However obscure or degraded the intelligence, when it takes its place beneath the skies it comes into correspondence with God. Every dewdrop, sunbeam, or shadow, is an utterance declaring the grace and glory of God. That God has placed Himself in communion with this world at every point and with every creature is a fact of stupendous meaning. It gives vast consequence to life. We are now in a state which pulsates with the life of God. Those must be creatures of a mighty destiny who "live and move and have their being in him." It makes your home mean more since God is in it. Life means more to us since God has stooped down and is taking part in it—grand with the sight of His glory and vocal with the tones of His love.

TYPES THE GOSPEL.—Rather it is the gospel already proclaimed to every creature. But with all its glory it does not meet God's ultimate design. It fails to reach man's moral condition and to meet his deepest want. It is too far away and too cold. It is the Divine mind speaking to the human mind. It declares His glory grandly, continuously, but does not show us the Divine heart. There must needs be another gospel, a speech of God's heart to our hearts. Hence God went down to the depths of His own affectional nature and brought His only and well-beloved Son and sent Him to us as the expression of His love.

He incarpated the. language. "The word became flesh." He gave it a body, with heart and
blood, and human nature, invested with all the
fullness of the Godhead, and in this form and nature He came and dwelt among us. Now we realize that He is not far off; not behind the skies and
beyond the stars, but "Immanuel," "God with us,"
and touched with the feeling of our infirmities.

How different the two gospels! The one a picture the other a personality; one painted upon the
skies, the other living in our hearts and lives. One
is the beautiful yet lifeless portrait on the wall,
the other the living loved one with heart and voice
responsive to my own; the one is the shadow, the
other the substance, of love.

EASILY UNDERSTOOD.—Like the language
of the skies, it is adjusted to the child nature; the
one mapped out before the mind, the other
breathed into the heart by the Holy Ghost. The
child old enough to know the one can also know
the other. If it can know the natural sun it can
know the "Sun of Righteousness," for "out of the
mouth of babes doth he perfect his praise." Its
simplicity is its glory. The man with mind enough
to commit sin has mind enough to accept Christ.
The gospel at Pentecost was heard by every man
in his own tongue. It is heard now by every man
according to his own mental power, whether that
be mighty or feeble. I am not compelled to know
all the mysteries of astronomy before I can see
the sun and enjoy the blessings of the heavens. I
have but to lift my eyes, turn my face away from

the ground, and the everlasting panorama breaks upon my vision. So I am not forced to know all the mysteries of theology in order to know Christ. I have but to lift up mine eyes and turn my face away from the world, and His pardoning love falls upon my spirit as the sunshine upon the uplifted face.

IT IS TO BE UNIVERSAL.—When God spread the skies He measured the reach of the gospel. We are to spread the gospel as far as the heavens declare His glory. Then let the Church look up to the visible heavens and take her reckonings; throw out her lines until they have gone through all the earth; push the gospel until its saving message has reached "every creature" and its words are heard to the end of the world.

We are co-laborers with the sun, but ours is the more honorable ministry. The sun has warmed the world, purified its atmosphere, kissed away its dewy tears, painted its flowers, ripened its fruits, and matured its golden harvests; but it has never had the joy of carrying comfort into the home of poverty and kneeling at the bedside of dying widowhood or orphanage and whispering the story of "Jesus and his love." His light is only for a season and it will fade; but the light that we carry to souls in sorrow will burn on when the sun is forgotten.

Brethren, be as the stars in the firmament. Though one star is different from another star in glory, yet all alike are shooting their light into the depths beneath and mingling their beams to light the world in the night time. "Let your light so shine before men"—let all shine forth, both great and small, until the light of the gospel shall have gone out through all the earth and its words to the end of the world, until the Master shall say, "It is enough," and call the laborers, who shall return with shouting and with everlasting joy upon their heads, bringing an evangelized world to the feet of the Son of God.

CHAPTER IV.

THE SOURCE OF LIFE.

"Man shall not live by bread alone, but by every word that proceedeth out of the mouth of God."—Matt. 4:4.

Man speaks vocables, which die away on the air. God speaks things: heavens, earth, worlds, systems. His words do not perish. The sun, the sea, the wide-spread sky all tell us "We are his words which he spake in the beginning." "We are the proceedings from the mouth of God." The original language does not use the term "word," but uses the term, "Every proceeding from the mouth of God." God's utterances are not mere echoes in the air; they are substance. "The words that I speak unto you, they are spirit, and they are life."

THE SPIRITUAL IS INDEPENDENT OF THE PHYSICAL.—Life came first into the physical by the spirit. Man was made from the dust and did not live until God breathed a spirit into that dust. The spirit gave life to the body then and gives it life now. The body lives from the spirit, and not the spirit from the body. Organism is from life, and not life from organism. Hence, while the body cannot live without the soul, the soul can, and does, live without the body. Therefore death does not end all.

The body is so intensely mortal that it may be destroyed either from within or without. So manifold and delicate are its outward connections that damage or death may come unawares. Even when sleeping it may inhale the subtle poison that will render it no longer habitable and the spirit must move out. A friend of President Madison meeting him in the market, asked, "How is Mr. Madison this morning?" He replied, "Mr. Madison is quite well, but the house he lives in is much out of repair and Mister Madison will soon have to move out." Again there may come such pressure upon the spirit within, from which the body lives, as to force it to withdraw its support from the body; then death is the result. The overpressed spirit often fails to support the appetite and to give the body its required sleep and rest. Death comes as frequently almost from within as it does from without; as often through the soul as through the body.

How sad to see one dying from within. The Spirit shutting off the life forces from the body. The luster leaving the eyes, elasticity failing in the step, and the movement becoming tremulous and unsteady. The soul slowly killing the body; the body dying by hours and inches. To die from grief, mortification, or disgrace; to die from the inside. Strange, sad corporicide!

WHENCE DOES THE SPIRIT LIVE?— The spirit is as verily a creature as the body, and as absolutely dependent on something outside itself. If the body lives from the spirit, whence does the spirit live? We answer, the spirit lives from God. It is in Him "we live and move and have our being." Just as the body lives from the spirit, so the spirit lives from God.

Here we get back, and up, and away from the grosser and the material. We stand now at the fountain of life where we first lived; and the spirit life is strong or feeble in proportion to our nearness to God, and the inflow of the God-life into our spirit-life. Here is where the Master stood when He uttered the text and crushed the tempter. And we shall conquer in every conflict if only we be "filled with all the fulness of God" and using the weapon that Christ used.

FAITH IS THE CHANNEL FOR THE IN-FLUX OF THE DIVINE LIFE.—As the Panama Canal opened the way for the union of two oceans, so faith opens the way for the union of the human and the divine natures.

The divine life comes into our life by way of the thoughts, the sentiment, the imagination, and the affections. Faith keeps these powers open and receptive toward God, while his life permeates and fills the whole being.

With a feeble and intermittent faith the channels become clogged and the influx of the divine life is stopped. We allow "the world, the flesh, and the devil," to choke the channels; and sometimes we allow indifference to freeze and stop the inflow, as the bold streams are sometimes blocked with the ice gorge.

As a nation, a Christian nation, we have forgotten God far enough to allow worldliness, money-madness, and pleasure-madness, to clog the rivers of His benevolence and freeze the channels of His grace, until He is leaving us to melt out those things in the awful heat and horror of war. "There is a river, the streams whereof shall make glad the City of God." Oh, that the Church might cleanse her channels, until the God of life might fill our land, and the great heart of humanity turn back in consecration to Him!

THE LESSON.—God would teach us as He taught Israel. "He took them into the wilderness to get the nature notions out of them." And he carries us into life's desert places for the same purpose. He will take us away from Egyptian plenty and make us to hunger before we will learn much. Left at ease we never learn the higher things. Who would have believed the time would come in this God-favored Christian land when the government would make the allowance of what we should eat and should not eat? The material and the quantity that should go upon our tables. But strange as it is we see that day. And without a mighty turning to God, we shall see days of closer proscription and greater want. Give a man all prosperity and he will grow earthy; but reduce him, and he becomes teachable. In 1864 we carried some wounded soldiers to a hospital in Mississippi, expecting to return to the command on the next day. But the wounded men urged that we remain, and we spent two weeks in labor with them. There were fourteen conversions; and we did not see a man die without hope.

They were not only accessible, but anxious to

hear of Christ and His salvation. And we hear now of "revivals in the military camps," and the call for the word of God, and the hunger after divine things. Christ is having access to the hearts of the young men of this Republic, and a recognition in the broken home circles of the land, such as He never had in the halcyon days of peace and prosperity. Prosperity cannot feed the immortal nature. Only Christ can do that, and we can appeal unto Him or perish. "Without me ye can do nothing."

GOD'S PURPOSE WITH US IN THE WILDERNESS.—He led Israel to and fro in the wilderness for forty years, that He might teach them submission and how to be led by His hand. When He takes us into the wilderness we come out seeing as we never saw before. The "Baca valleys" make us to know God, and ourselves, in a deeper sense.

The hill-tops have most of sunshine; but the valleys have the richest soil and rarest fruits. We will find at last, that we have grown the best graces and made the richest parts of our character in the valleys; in the shaded places of life, and where the sunshine did not strike us much. When you come into a barren or wilderness place in your experience, it is that "You may know that man doth not live by bread alone; but by every proceeding from the mouth of God."

CHAPTER V.

THE FIRST RECORDED BURIAL.

Text:—"After this, Abraham buried Sarah his wife in the cave of the field of Machpelah, before Mamre."—Gen. 23-19.

This is the first registered burial. Sarah is the only woman in Holy Writ whose age is stated. Her age, death, burial, and the circumstances are minutely recorded. She occupied an important position while living and when dead her grave held a unique place in the history of her race.

This grave was the cradle of the Abrahamic kingdom in Canaan. Like the sleeping infant in which there is a great destiny, the dust of this sleeping Matriarch, cradled in the purchased sepulchre, was index to a wonderful history.

HER POSITION.—Historically she is the first woman in the Old Testament. There are two women in the two Testaments who hold the honor of a mighty motherhood. The two are counterparts. They fill similar positions and the hand of God was with them both. Sarah in the Old, and Mary in the New Testament. Both received Angelic messengers and both attained supernatural motherhood. Both were immortalized in the person of a son. But Mary's faith stands over against Sarah's incredulity. She responded to the heavenly message with a derisive laugh of almost mockery, ill-concealed: while Mary answered with that exultation which only faith can know. "My soul doth magnify the Lord." And yet, Mary with her perfect faith is not remembered in the sacred records nor is there any account of her last days and death; while the incredulous Sarah has her death and burial on the inspired register.

Why this? If Sarah finds record why not the more honored Mary? The answer is in their sons. Sarah's son was not greater than she and does not eclipse her; but such is the glory of Mary's Son that the personality of the mother is hidden in the luster of her child. Like Moses on the Mount, she is lifted up, but lost in the glory of the Divine presence. Sarah stands out in history co-equal with her supernatural son; while Mary with a beautiful humility hides her life in the life of her immaculate offspring.

THE SACRED SEPULCHRE OF THE OLD COVENANT.—There is something in the dust of the dead which holds a weird influence over the living. Voices from the tomb have influenced nations. Medina, where the Mohammedan Prophet is buried, is more honored than Mecca where he was born. Fifty thousand devotees make annual pilgrimage to worship about its precincts. This sentiment created the crusades in which millions of lives were sacrificed. The like sentiment makes Mt. Vernon sacred to us.

Sarah's tomb was the sacred sepulchre to the Israelites; and though a long while in bondage to the Egyptians, yet when Joshua led them back on that grand crusade into the Promised Land, they came again into possession of their mother's grave.

THIS GRAVE EXPRESSED ABRAHAM'S
FAITH.—God had promised to give this land to
him and his children. But there was no sign in
sight; no indication that it would be theirs. It
was owned by other nations, and himself a sojourner. No more likelihood of his owning Canaan
than there is now of a wandering gypsy owning
the State of Florida. Still he "staggered not at
the promises, but believed God." And now that
Sarah is dead he will bury her there in the place
destined by the promise of God to belong to him
and his children. He not only lived by faith and
walked by faith, but he buried his dead by faith.

Let political and national changes come, adverse or prosperous; let his sons be in authority
or in bondage; that tomb was to stand there resting on the promise of God; an imperishable monument to his unfaltering faith, the faith that this
land would one day belong to him and his children.
An Israelite could neither see nor think of this
grave without feeling the power of his father's
faith.

HAVE WE THIS FAITH?—A faith that will
stand monumental and impress those about us and
those to come after us? A faith that sets our very
tombstone in the Divine promise and chisels it
into the inscriptions to be read by our children
when they come to muse over our dust.

Graveyards should not be mere mourning places
where flowers are strewn and watered with tears.
We should go gladly to our graves to do our grandest work. The mightiest power of the true saint

is a post-mortem power. "Precious in the sight of the Lord is the death of his saints." The grave is the pulpit for the tenderest impressions, and the cemetery the place for the edification of the living.

THIS GRAVE BOUND THEM TO CANAAN. —They had absence from their country, bondage that was bitter, hard treatment and long servitude; but amid it all they held claim to Canaan by divine guarantee, and this was sealed to them by their mother's grave. But for this their own land had perhaps fallen out of memory.

There are places which we would have forgotten but for a grave we have there. A tiny mound it may be; but it holds the dust of an angel darling and we can forget it never. There is nothing that so fastens the heart and sentiment upon a place as to have a grave in it. Like the tomb of Sarah which held the sacred sentiment of her sons in their bitter bondage, there is many a mother who holds in the same way a wonderful and tender influence over her wayward boy who is in the bondage of sin; and wields that influence in the silence of her grave. Though his heart may be so hard that nothing else will touch it, still the spot where his mother rests has a silent power that penetrates his hardness and reaches his deeper nature. He grows serious in thought of it and tender as a child when he comes into its sacred precincts.

THE SEPULCHRE THAT ECLIPSES THAT OF SARAH.—Her tomb was the pillar of faith and the monument of hope to her captive children, and also the pledge of their final return and re-instatement.

But there is a tomb that holds a higher and more universal sway over the sentiment and faith of humanity; that is the empty tomb—not of Mary, but of Mary's Son. There was a three-days' gloom that rested upon that marble tomb. A darkness that could be felt in earth and heaven. But this was followed by a glory that no night-fall can ever dim or darken.

Our graves are as the "wailing places" at Jerusalem. It is there that sadness sits upon the countenance and memories come up moist with tears; yet, after all, the brightest place on this broad earth is a sepulchre. That empty one in Aramathea, where heaven's legatees beheld a victory that forever broke the power of sin and death. It is not the dawn, neither the sunrise; but it is the meridian noonday of hope and gladness. The glory of that empty grave goes out through all the earth, and the broken-hearted have but to turn to that center of hope and their sighs become songs and their tears pearls of peace.

CHRIST IS THE HEAD.—He is the head of the Church, while we are the body. But though this world be a vast cemetery, and a realm of sepulchres, His is the great Head sepulchre over all. Our graves are connected with His. He is not in union with the living and in disunion with the dead. "Because he lives we shall live also." His resurrection power shall be felt in every tomb, and earth's old bosom shall beat with life at every point; and "All that are in their graves shall come forth." That empty tomb is ever preaching. Abraham and Sarah, Mary and the others are in their graves and the doors are shut; but JESUS CHRIST IS NOT IN HIS.

The mouth of that sepulchre, opened by divine power on the third morning, began to proclaim the gospel of its risen victor, "Jesus and the resurrection." That note has never ceased. "Its voice has gone out through all the earth and its words to the end of the world." The most eloquent lips that ever preached Jesus are the marble lips of that open and empty tomb. The most unanswerable logic is the logic of an open grave. Infidelity may reply to our arguments, but it has no reply to that voice that comes from Aramathea.

Death exults in its dominion and holds sway over the dead millions; and now it is adding its millions almost in a month; but that dominion is not universal. There is one royal exception. One grave not under his reign; and that is the Great Head Sepulchre. The only Divine tomb. The only grave that ever held more than human ashes. The only grave that never "saw corruption."

It stands amid the vast empire of death, the prophecy and the pledge of deliverance of all from the power of death. As the tomb of Sarah was the guarantee to the bondsmen in Egypt that Canaan sould one day be theirs, so the empty sepulchre of the Son of Mary and the Son of God is pledge to us of deliverance from death and final return to the heavenly Canaan.

CHAPTER VI.

THE SCARLET LINE IN RAHAB'S WINDOW.

"And she bound the scarlet line in the window." Josh. 2:21.

There is majesty in the movement of men when God is leading. Israel is ready to pass into Canaan. The rapid restless Jordan is checked in its flow, its waters recede and stand mute and motionless, awaiting the passage of the hosts of God. Just beyond is the city of Jericho; and having passed over, they advance upon it. Not with bombs and machine guns, but with the ark of God and the rams-horn trumpets. Under God's direction they go round the city once a day for six days; and on the seventh day they go round seven times; and on the seventh round they blow their trumpets, and shout, and the walls of the city totter and tumble to the ground.

But yonder remains one bit of the wall unshaken, and upon it a house, single and alone in the midst of the ruin, and from its window hangs a scarlet line. That is the home of Rahab, who has not perished. "By faith Rahab perished not with them that believed not." That scarlet line is the expression of her faith, and the emblem of her deliverance.

HERS WAS A LIFE-RISK.—Marvelous rumors had reached Jericho concerning Israel: how the sea had separated before them, and how they had destroyed kings Sihon, and Og; and a great fear had fallen upon the men of Jericho. The gates were guarded, and strangers suspiciously observed. To conceal a spy was death without mercy. But in the face of all, and with her life in her hands, Rahab hid the spies and helped them to escape.

A mighty faith takes mighty risks. It takes the only son, and walks with steady step to the mount of sacrifice; it plats and plasters the bulrush basket, puts its babe in it and places it where the crocodiles crawl amid the river-flags; then rests as calmly as though each crocodile were an angel, and each flag an armed sentinel for its protection. Faith walks in places of peril, through dens of beasts, furnaces of fire, and amid death-valleys where shades and ghosts flit past; and yet it walks without alarm.

Rahab in conference with the spies is a scene for the hand of a Master. It is a star-light scene; they were upon the housetop and seated upon the flax, just a little above the city which is nervous with excitement and full of forebodings. In the face of death she is negotiating for the lives of her family and herself; taking an oath at their hands that while she protects them they shall save her and hers. As we look at this picture, we may well say, "O woman, great is thy faith!" Faith made her name immortal; made her worthy to be the mother of Boaz, the mother-in-law of Ruth, and the maternal ancestress of the Son of Mary.

The faith that saves us is a faith that takes

mighty risks; that swears allegiance to God in the midst of a God-hating generation; ready to hide the spies and help to bring humanity into captivity to Christ, though it cost criticism, ostracism, or even death; a faith that is seen by the night-stars, Rahab-like, upon the housetop and in conference with God for the salvation of its loved ones.

While the world sleeps morally, we must stand by the gospel windows, with firm and fearless hands on the scarlet lines—the saving influences —whereby men escape from the captivity of sin. It was a noble deed to let Paul down in a basket over the Damascus wall; a noble deed and noble words of this woman when she let the spies down and said, "Get you to the mountains." But it is a far nobler act to aid a soul to escape from the eternal ruin of sin, and bid it "Fly to the mountains and hide itself in the "cleft of the rock."

A PRACTICAL LESSON.—Rahab was not looking for the spies, and yet she was ready for them when they came. Her industry and diligence made her ready. Her flax was gathered, carried up and laid in order on the houstop; just ready for a hiding place for the spies when they came. And I dare say she knew just where to find that line when she needed it. It would have been an awkward affair had the flax been neglected and left in the field, and had she forgotten where she put the cord—nothing with which to conceal them, and nothing with which to let them down over the wall.

Yet this is the way with many good-meaning souls; always behind when opportunity comes. An unexpected opportunity comes to do a good thing; but the flax is in the field and the scarlet line is out of place. They have been improvident, slothful, wasteful; and now when God calls they have nothing with which to respond.

We waste enough in nonsense and needless self-indulgence, if it were only saved and laid by, to be ready for many a call of God. That is why the Scriptures mention Rahab's flax, and carefully tell us that "it was carried up and laid in order." God would teach us to be ready for His call though it come in the night-time and from a source we did not suspect. Whatever you have in goods or money, keep it in such shape that God can command it at any time. It is a good thing to have the flax and the line in readiness.

THE STYLE OF THE CONTRACT.—She did not attempt to dictate terms. If anyone ever had opportunity to have a contract her own way she had it. Their lives were in her hands and she had the finest opportunity to dictate the terms. Give some people her chance and they will negotiate for enough to make themselves and their kin comfortable, and to control the elections besides. But this woman makes but one demand. "That ye will save alive my father, my mother, my brethren, my sisters, and all that they have; and deliver our lives from death." True faith asks only its own: it seeks no commission from its opportunities. It never buys a widow's house for less than its worth because she is forced to sell; and never takes a poor man's home at under-value because it has a mortgage which he cannot lift; neither will it take the servant's labor at half its worth because he is forced to work at that price or starve.

SHE DID NOT ASK TO BE REMOVED.—It was a fearful ordeal she was to meet; to see her city destroyed and a wholesale butchery of its inhabitants; still she does not ask to be taken away from the dreadful scene. True faith does not ask exemption from the ills and evils common to life. It is willing to suffer and endure, only so it has the oath of God on which to stand. Rahab could endure all and witness the terrors, because of the oath that she and hers should be saved. How much we can endure when we feel God's promise beneath us! While we live in a land of uncertainties, the ground beneath and the skies above are doomed to destruction. It is a royal thought that God's oath is beneath us. Rahab-like, faith does not ask to escape tribulations, but only asks to feel its feet resting upon the oath of God.

Had Rahab asked only for herself and been willing to see her kindred perish, her act would never have been recorded. Its selfishness would have sunken it into oblivion. But she demands her kin, all her kin. Faith cries out for its kindred. It demands life for all, even the hopeless prodigal; and the faith that stipulates for less is weak and selfish. Have you stipulated for less? Have you closed the contract with God and left out a single one of your family? Then hasten back to the house-top, reopen the conference, put that one into the contract and open not the window nor let the Divine messenger go until you get assurance that the last one shall be saved.

SHE BOUND THE LINE IN THE WINDOW. —Thus she placed the protecting aegis over herself and kindred. This line was the symbol and guarantee of her safety. Israel was safe with the blood over their doors, for God had said, "When I see the blood I will pass over you." And when that blood-colored line is seen streaming from her window, she and hers are safe. The blood and the line represent the blood of Christ; the one, a protection to the Jew from the death-angel; the other, the protection of a Gentile from the hands of war-like men. How thorough and all-inclusive is the saving power of the blood! Whether a Jew in Gentile lands, or a Gentile on Jewish territory, all are safe under the blood.

The death-angel was duly instructed to "Trouble no house over whose door the blood was visible." Every soldier in Joshua's army had the order, "Protect the house that has a scarlet line hanging from its window." So the standing order of God has gone forth, and angels, men and devils understand it, "No harm is to come to the soul that is under the blood." "They that trust in the Lord shall be as Mt. Zion, which cannot be removed, but abideth forever.'

THE TAKING OF THE CITY.—We look upon Jericho on that fatal day only to shudder. The scene is awful. The walls lie in ruins; every house sacked and its inmates slain, the frenzied screams of wives and mothers, the piteous cries of bleeding children, the groans of dying husbands, and fathers, and the heavy heavings of butchered beasts—all is now over and hushed and still in death. Not a man, woman, child, nor so much as an ox, sheep, or ass, that lives. What a scene! But look! One lone house stands above the carnage and rests on a remaining bit of the wall. What preserves it? There is no bulwark round it, no armed men within it; only a defenceless woman and her helpless kindred occupy it. Why does that bit of wall stand as adamant beneath that house? Why are the inmates so serene and calm as they look out upon the awful scene? What is their defense? A simple scarlet line that hangs idly from the window and waves to and fro in the breeze. THAT IS GOD'S POWER TO SAVE.

THIS EARTH IS A JERICHO.—And it is doomed. "God hath appointed a day in the which he will judge it." His coming will be as the coming of Israel upon Jericho: "As a thief in the night." Have you bound the line in the window? Have you put yourself and family under protection of the blood?" Have you settled it with God that you and yours are to be saved in the final destruction? Are you ready for the falling of the walls? Ready for the crumbling of the earthly tabernacle and an introduction into the eternal world?

The same line which she used in saving the spies became the means of saving her and her family. She had doubtless platted and made that line, just as we plat and make our faith. The faith which is to save us at last is not a special kind, that has been laid up and kept on purpose to go to heaven on; like a special suit for a special occasion; but it is the same old tried, second-hand, well-worn faith, that we have been working with all the years. The staff on which Jacob leaned when dying was not a new and unused staff, cut and kept for that dying occasion, just as some queer people keep their coffins for years before they die. It was the same old staff that had propped him on his pilgrimage and perhaps supported him when he limped over the brook on a disjointed thigh; that staff was his prop, living and dying.

The same faith which, like Rahab, has been willing to risk for others, and has kept the soul's windows open, and the lines of influence reaching down to help others to escape from the ruin of sin—this, this is the faith that will support you in the last hour, when mortality's walls are falling; this is the faith that will keep you as serene in the final hour as she who looked from her window upon Jericho's ruin.

THE MEN SHE SAVED BECAME HER ESCORT.—The two whom she had saved received the order, "Bring out the woman and all that she has, as ye sware unto her." Those two were to bring her and her family out and escort them from the ruin and give her a home among their own people, and that because she had been faithful.

The all-conquering Christ, our own Joshua, will command those whom we have blessed to attend us in life's last hour. When this "earthly house is dissolving,' shall we not be met and welcomed by those whom we have loved and blessed in life? Is not this the last testimony of many of the servants of God? Have they not spoken to us of the presence of the departed when dying?

Then, if we are now making up our escort from this world, let us have a large one. I am not careful for a long train and a vast multitude to follow my dust to the cemetery; but I should love to see a white-winged multitude ascending with my tired spirit to its final home and rest.

Dear fellow spirit, candidate for immortality, see that "the line is bound in the window;" "for at such a time as ye think not the Son of man cometh."

CHAPTER VII.

JONAH'S GOURD.

Text: "And God said to Jonah, Doest thou well to be angry for the gourd? And he said, I do well to be angry, even unto death." (Jonah 4:9).

Here is the key to Jonah's character, and by using this key we find some ugly things in his make-up. But with it all he is a prophet of God. This may help some people to see what they never saw —how a man with weaknesses and ugly ways may be called of God to do His work. Some think that if a preacher is not perfect he has mistaken his calling and answered the call of someone else. Jonah's case answers this argument. He was full of defects, and yet God called him to be a prophet.

HIS INGRATITUDE.—Jonah was an ingrate, and the ingrate ranks among the high priests of meanness. God had selected him from all the men of his country to be His ambassador to one of the mightiest cities on earth, an honor that would perpetuate his name through all the ages. It was no excellency in Jonah that made him a necessity for this work. God could have found others fully as sweet-spirited and more obedient than he, who would have gone direct to Nineveh without all that round-about route toward Tarshish and into the whale's belly and through the paths of the sea. But He left them in obscurity while He immortalized Jonah by making him His messenger. But for this he would never have been heard of outside his own precinct. He owed all to his commission, and we hear of him today simply because "the word of the Lord came unto him." And here he is now, poor child of obscurity, in a desperate pout because God chose to glorify Himself and spare Nineveh as it lay in sackcloth and ashes at his feet rather than glorify *him* by sweeping the city into destruction.

Here we have a typical grouch. Every character in Holy Writ is representative. Jonah here portrays one well-known in pulpit and pew. Note those preachers who are always complaining that they are not appreciated, don't get the grade and promotion due them. You will find that they are like Jonah. They are men whom the Church has brought into notice, Church-made men. But for the reputation given us by the Church, some of us would never have been known further than the back of the garden or the pea patch. The pew also has its representatives in this class. The mutterers in the Church are generally those who owe their standing and prominence to the Church.

HIS DELIVERANCE.—His deliverance was the most wonderful in history, such as never was and never again will be. Yet he had so quickly forgotten it all! When those heathen sailors tossed him from their ship into the sea, to all human thought the hope of escape was folly. It would take the mad waters and the terrible sea monsters but a few brief moments to gulp or engulf the recreant prophet. But God was there.

Admit God, and you have the solution of every problem. You ask me how the sea separated and let Israel pass over dryshod and then engulfed their enemies? I shall answer, God was there. You ask me how I have passed the narrow junctures in life where no human help could reach me? I answer, God was there. God is the answer to every question in His providence or in human destiny. Admit God, and there is no further question. God rode in that tempest as it chased that ship. His hand was upon the slimy head of that great fish and shielded the prophet from its terrible teeth as it gulped him down unhurt. God was with him in that living prison as he went down to the bottom of the mountains, while "the bars of the earth were about him and the weeds were wrapped about his head."

His deliverance was as wonderful as his imprisonment. As he sat on the sand, fresh-belched from despair, and saw the monster sink back and disappear in the deep, it was no wonder that he shouted: "Salvation is of the Lord!" He thought then that he would never forget his deliverance. But, strange to say, it is not yet forty days when we see this same man in a terrible temper and wanting to die. And what is the matter? Just two things: the great city is still living and his pet gourd vine is dead.

Here is some of our moral ugliness. We have never been three days in the sea, but, like Jonah, we have been disobedient, and God has sent His agents after us to arrest us. When we were in dissipation, He sent nervousness and headache to correct us. When we abused our health, He sent disease to crush us down and pierce us with pains. When persisting in sin, He sent conscience with its double sting, and we have bled day and night under its torture. Again, without sin on our part, He has caused the waves and the billows to pass over us. A loved one was at death's door; you were in the deep, and the weeds were about your head and heart. You cried to God, and He sent deliverance and the loved one lived. You have cried to Him, and monster troubles have let you go and passed, like the monster from Jonah's sight, into the deep and, like him, you have thought you would never forget this deed of the Lord's; yet how often since that have you been thrown into a pout over some trivial thing and been ready to murmur and complain!

Had Jonah as he sat under his gourd vine compared his condition with what it was inside that fish, his pout would have ended in a shout. When we are half sour and ready to murmur, we have only to recall God's deliverances and remember that we are living only because he interposed in a close juncture; then will gratitude take the place of grumbling, and pessimism will give way to praise.

HE FORGOT GOD'S FORGIVENESS.—He had sinned egregiously in refusing to obey God's command, and yet God forgave his disobedience. This he had forgotten and also the hour when he looked back upon the watery grave from which he had

delivered him and shouted: "Salvation is of the Lord!" When God converted us, we thought we would never be done praising Him; yet how shamefully and frequently have we forgotten all this! When your soul is ready to write bitter things, pause and think of your conversion, and the bitterness will pass. A thought of pardoning mercy will cure every complaint. He has forgiven enough to have sunk us to hell, and the reason we are in the Church and not in hell is because He has pardoned and not punished. Let the complainer think of how God forgave him and hide his head for very shame.

HE FORGOT HIS SUCCESS.—I doubt if the preaching of any man since the world began was ever so successful as his. Noah's preaching was a failure compared with it. Even the ministry of the Master was not marked with such results. So soon as He began to preach the people began to repent. We have to preach for weeks to get a hearing and then preach a few more weeks to get the children and a few others to turn to God. Jonah hadn't preached three days before the king himself was on his knees in the dust. Then look at the city of six hundred thousand souls prostrate before God! The whole city was an altar of prayer and crowded with penitents. Everything was in sackcloth, from the king to the cattle. Was ever mortal man made such an instrument in God's hands? Now look at him in his booth watching the city on its knees before God, this illustrious mouthpiece of the Most High, there in

full view of his six hundred thousand converts and in a fume and a fret and trying to die about a gourd vine. Did Holy Writ ever paint another such picture? And yet it is only a picture of that delectable thing we call *"human nature."*

Many times have we sat for a picture like this. God has given you great and signal successes. In your suit for salvation Satan, the world, and your own evil nature were against you; but you gained the suit. God gloriously converted you. This was stupendous success. You brought a soul to Christ. This was success that an angel might envy. You reared your family in the fear of God. An archangel never equaled this. We have had a thousand successes; then we, after all, have often been ugly and fumed and fretted over the most trivial things.

THE QUESTION.—God said, "Doest thou well to be angry?" that is, grieved and vexed. Jonah's sensibilities were a little mixed, his feelings were a little hurt, and at the same time he was a little mad. He hardly knew whether to curse or to cry. He felt like doing both. Haven't you sometimes had that feeling? Then it was so trivial a thing, only a gourd vine, and that not his! God made the vine and the worm to kill it. It was God's vine. It stood only for a day, but that was enough to turn Jonah's head. He was just as well off after it was dead as before it grew up, but he did not feel so. Give us a day's success, let some providential gourd vine spring up and spread its shade over us for a day and a night, then wither and

leave us just where we were, and we get into a pout and almost wish to die. Some people never get over once being rich.

This gourd vine is typical. It pictures all our enterprises—a thing of comparative insignificance, like the things over which we do most fretting; little things in business, little things in society, little things in our fellow men, little things in everyday life. Such little vines are what we worry over most.

THE WORM AT THE FOOT.—The worm was there, but Jonah didn't know it; only an inch or so under the surface, but he did not suspect it. There is a worm at the root of every earthly enterprise, a worm at the root of every vine, put there by God himself to measure its life and mark its fall. We cannot see an inch beneath the surface. We sit and rejoice in our pet schemes and know not that they are being silently cut down. The man who builds lower than the skies builds upon a foundation that a worm may plow up.

"Doest thou well to be vexed for the gourd?" Thou whom God hath honored, whom God hath delivered from death, whom God hath so freely forgiven, to whom he hath given success, look back today over thy life, as the prophet looked over the city he had won to God, while we ask again: "Doest thou well to be angry and grieved over the petty affairs of this life, which grow up in a night and perish in a night?"

CHAPTER VIII.

A DANGER SIGNAL.

"Remember Lot's wife."—Luke 17:32.

A light in the middle of the street at night tells of danger, and we drive round it. The sea-light tells that the reefs are nigh, and in response to the warning ships keep aloof. God has placed warning lights at the danger points in life. This text is a danger-light—a warning bell above a reef. This woman stands out upon the morning horizon of history as a perpetual danger-light to the ages. And God bids us "Remember Lot's wife."

HER OPPORTUNITIES FOR A RIGHT LIFE. —Favored above the common citizen of Sodom. Although she lived in a godless city ripe for destruction, she had religious association. She was the wife of a godly man. With all his weaknesses Lot was a servant of the Most High God. Not a model saint, not the best specimen of what grace can make out of a man. Lot had an eye to the main chance, and when his uncle gave him his choice between "The well watered plains" and the poorer hill country, he took the rich bottom lands and let his uncle take the hills. He may have thought the highlands would be better for the health of his benevolent uncle. Lot also indulged in too much wine on one or two occasions; but after all, he believed in the true God and tried to honor and serve Him.

There are a great many Christians of Lot's order. There are lots of Lots in the ranks of the Church. Men who know a good thing when they see it; and will take care of number one at great hazards; yet they fear God and wish to do right. It is a great mistake to mark a man down as a hypocrite, simply because he is not perfect. Foibles and weaknesses are not always sins. We are not trying to enter an apology for Lot's sins, nor our own; but we submit that, because a man has weak points is no reason why he should be excommunicated, ostracised, and helped on to destruction.

GOD CAN USE INDIFFERENT MATERIAL. —We succeed in making a good thing when we have the best of material; and with bad material we can do just nothing. But God can bring out his strength through our weakness. He makes perfection out of material that we would not touch. He made heaven itself out of nothing; and now he is making out of us sinners, who are worse than nothing, the very saints who are to populate that heaven. Imperfection is the sin-mark on everything; and yet imperfection has noble sides. The best horse we ever owned was blind in one eye. His sight was imperfect, but his service was of the very best. I simply had to watch that blind side for him.

There are men with a one-sided view of things; not broad and universal; a sort of one-bladed men, and yet withal they are good men. We merely have to see for them on some sides where they cannot see.

A GODLY COMPANION IS A STRONG STAY.—Companionship with one who fears God is a perpetual tonic to the spiritual life. The companion may be far from perfection, and have as many faults and foibles as Lot had; still there is a reserve for God, and the life-trend is toward God.

The river channel is smooth in the main, though its smoothness is broken at times by the rocks, and its movement becomes roaring confusion, and its bosom too rough to reflect a single star from the heavens above it. But despite all this, that river comes to quiet again and holds its course steadily toward the sea.

Many a life has its weak hours, its times of tumult and confusion; moments when no feature of God is seen in the character; and yet that life holds its faith and comes to quiet again, and you can no more turn it away from God than you can turn the river from its channel. Lot's wife had such a companion, and in that a strong stay for a right life.

But to be the companion of one "Who neither fears God nor regards man," whose indifference meets and chills you at all points in life, is paralyzing and deadly. A cheerful fire will not be cheerful long when forced to burn up against the side of a huge iceburg. Then if you have a companion who fears God, know that you have an abiding benediction. Appreciate it, though that companion have the weaknesses common to mortals.

LOT'S WIFE HAD AMPLE MEANS.—Lot was a man of affairs; prominent and princely, and his wife had all the advantages that wealth implies. Sodom was not without its beautiful streets and elegant homes; and her home was, no doubt, on some fashionable street of the doomed city.

Wealth increases responsibility; and as Lot was a light among the men of his city, his wife should have led the women of Sodom in the ways and in the service of God. What power and influence in the hands of a refined and wealthy woman! Free from toil and care, servants at command, carriage at elbow, and her time all her own, such a woman is equipped to do work that an angel might envy. Then think of such an one living for luxury and personal pleasure, wholly absorbed in self.

Such I doubt not was the wife of Lot. No wonder it required the angels, and with hard work at that, to pull her out of the luxury of her Sodomitish home. And even the angels couldn't keep her from looking longingly back upon the ease and comfort she was leaving. Angels from heaven cannot prevent some women from doing what they set their heads to do. If we speak now to man or woman with time or means at your command, which you are not using to the honor of God; then we call you to "Remember Lot's wife."

SHE HAD SPECIAL DIVINE FAVORS.—She and her husband had scarcely gotten settled in their valley home, when some "confederate Kings" made war upon them; captured and carried them off with their possessions. But in place of slavish captivity, which they doubless expected, Abraham with his little army pursued, recaptured them and their goods, and re-established them in their home. Again, when their city was ripe for destruction and the messengers at hand, special favor is shown to her and the family. The angels lodged with them, protected them from the mob, and then led them out of the city before the fire fell from heaven to destroy it. Such deliverance should have produced implicit obedience; and yet this woman is not out of sight of the city before she breaks the command of God's messengers and falls victim to her own disobedience.

How special and frequent have been our favors! Aside from the common and daily blessings—whose very regularity and routine cause us to forget them—we have had special deliverances which should have produced perpetual obedience and praise in us.

Like the kings combining against Lot, things sometimes have combined against us. Misfortune, unexpected calamity, have taken us captive, and we were near to despair, when there came a turn in affairs. God sent some power—like Abraham rescuing Lot—to release and relieve us and put us back again in better condition than before.

You were nigh unto death; or your dear one was at death's door; but the angels were nigh and by a power unseen you were dragged back from the jaws of death, or your loved one was restored again to health.

Have not the angels pulled you back more than once from destruction? You have felt the saving grasp of a hand you could not see, you have had the warning, "Escape for thy life, stay not in all the plain:" and yet like the wife of Lot you have made but a feeble effort toward the highlands. Went a little way, but the lodestone power of the world was too great, and you halted and are now "looking back."

SHE WAS THE SUBJECT OF PRAYER.— Among the many mistakes on religious matters, is the mistake of concluding, "I will not be lost because someone is praying for me." A wicked and presumptuous resting upon the power of somebody's prayers. I knew a congressman who was accustomed to parry every approach on the subject of religion, by saying, "Wife prays enough for both of us." Lot's wife probably made this sad mistake. Leading a life of high-toned and decent morality, and at rest simply because she had a companion who feared God and prayed for her daily. She was the subject of prayer, so was Sodom. Abraham who was mighty in faith and the "friend of God," prayed earnestly for Sodom; stipulated and prayed again, and again; but Sodom went down in the fires of God's anger. Here you have the two awful illustrations of the folly of trusting solely in the prayers of others. Sodom, covered with Abraham's prayers, but sunken and seething in judgment fires; and in sight of this is the monumental "pillar of salt" where Lot's wife perished. A city and an individual, both prayed for, and both perish alike. Souls and cities likewise perish unless they repent.

SHE LACKED DECISION.—There was danger and she knew it. The urgency of the angels had convinced her of this, and yet she was reluctant to leave. She failed to keep up with her companion, but lingered half-regretful in the rear. Here is the point of danger. The difference between a military and a spiritual battle is the danger points. In the military, the further to the rear the safer. For myself, I would prefer to be about five miles in the rear. But in a spiritual battle, the danger point is reversed. The killed and the captured in Zion's war are those in the rear; and the further back the more dangerous. It was in the rear that Peter fell and Lot's wife perished. Had they kept well up, and been cheered by the others, perhaps neither of them had fallen. What power in the encouragement of others!

A house was on fire and a little child had been forgotten in an upper story. A ladder was thrown up to the window and a fireman was ascending when the fearful heat checked his ascent and he paused. The crowd below broke into a tremendous cheer which gave him heart to break through the terrible flames and the little one was rescued and both reached the ground in safety.

Your distance in the rear determines your danger. Tell us how far you are behind, and we will tell you your exact danger. Linger awhile longer in the dim distance; then perhaps you will conclude it is impossible for you to be saved. If you are near to this conclusion remember the words of Napoleon at the bridge. They were in a battle and the victory hinged on the destruction of a heavily guarded and fortified bridge. Napoleon ordered an officer to "capture and destroy that bridge." The officer approached and seeing what he had to meet, he returned to his commander and said, "Sire, it is impossible!" Napoleon turned fiercely upon him and vehemently shouted, "That word IMPOSSIBLE is not in the French language." The officer withered under the rebuke, returned and led his command to the destruction of the bridge, which turned the tide and gave victory to the French.

SHE LOOKED BACK.—The *will* governs the actions. There was doubtless a tumult in her feelings, a war between her judgment and her affections. But she was safe so long as she kept her face toward the mountains and her feet moving from Sodom. God, by the angels, had given the order, "Do not look back." But lagging, halting, losing resolution, she finally looked back, broke the command and perished.

THE FACE REPRESENTS THE WILL.—The face set toward a thing means the will is set that way. It means determination. Let the heart-battle be hot as it may, while the face is set toward God we are safe. With all her struggle Lot's wife had been saved if she had only kept her face toward the mountains.

No matter how fearful the heart struggle, how infernal the suggestions, how black and vile the thoughts thrust into the mind; though all hell come into the heart, with suggestions and impulses almost equal to the super-hellishness of a German commander, yet while the face—the will sets flint like toward God we are safe. The sky is clearer and the air purer after the most terrific storm. The life is sweeter and more serene after such a battle.

HER PUNISHMENT WAS SUDDEN.—"She looked back and became a pillar of salt." Divine judgment was as sudden as her act. There was but one thing between her and destruction, and that was her own will. So soon as she removed that the judgment fell. Next to omnipotent is the human will. *God cannot save until we consent.* The will is all that intervenes between many a soul and ruin. Influences, impulses, and sometimes desires, may all be leaning toward the world; but over it all, the will holds toward God and the right. Courage! Courage! Tried one, you cannot be lost until you give your consent.

She perished in sight of safety. This is the sad feature in the tragedy. So nearly saved and yet lost. Outside the doomed city, well under way and with Divine help at command, husband saved, herself in sight of safety, and yet she perished. How sad to see one perish when almost saved!

Men are hearing me now, who have seen wife saved, and children saved, and are themselves in sight of salvation. You are a part of the way toward God, and you have—as Lot's wife had—Divine help at command. All that you need is to set your will—your face—toward the mountains. "Escape for thy life!" Recall the points in this history, and in your own. And may God help you to know, and feel, the awful import of this warning. "Remember Lot's wife."

CHAPTER IX.

THE BIRTH OF CHRIST.

Text: "For unto us a child is born, unto us a Son is given, and the government shall be upon his shoulder: and his name shall be called Wonderful, Counsellor, The Mighty God, The Everlasting Father, The Prince of Peace."—Isa. 9:6.

"UNTO US A CHILD IS BORN." Had Christ come to us as He went away His mission had been a failure. Had He descended from heaven in full manhood we should have held Him as a stranger, a mere visitor. He would have been WITH us, but not OF US.

The announcement is not that unto us God will descend, but "unto us a child is born." Here our nature is met at once. The babe that is born into the home receives the homage of every heart in that home; and even the very grand parents are subservient to the infant king. He rules in the home by virtue of his innocence and helplessness. Thus Christ, in order to become our king, puts Himself in that relation which commands our hearts and our service. Hence His reign in the soul is the reign of true humanity; commanding what our own infant commands—a love that is unwavering and a devotion that will serve even unto death.

UNTO US.—In these words there is a breadth and all-inclusiveness that are divine. They bear a benediction to every heart and hearthstone. There are many homes where fortune smiles and wealth abides, that have never been gladdened by the gift of a babe. Homes where the sunshine of a child's face and the ripple of a child's laugh have never come. No tiny finger prints on the window panes, nor echo of a child's merriment through the silent halls.

Other homes there are where the little child was, but now is not. Naught remains save a tiny portrait on the wall, and the parents' eyes grow moist and a hush comes on the spirit as they pass through that room. We have seen such homes. But here in Bethlehem's babe—God's love gift to our race—we have a babe for every babeless home. Bereaved mother, He is yours. He is your Comforter, and takes the place of the dear "wee one" that went from your bosom back to God. This babe of Bethlehem will brighten every home where sadness has come and grief has found a resting place.

THE GOVERNMENT SHALL BE UPON HIS SHOULDER.—We have noted how nature wraps and hides her grandest possibilities. The bread of a generation may be shut up in a wheat grain. Ten thousand forests wrapped in an acorn. But grace displays what nature cannot—all the grand possibilities of the eternities wrapped up in an infant's tiny form. I look upon that form as it lies in its swaddling clothes in the cleft of the rock in Bethlehem's hillside manger; and then I read the Scripture, "The government shall be on his shoulder," the UNIVERSAL government; the grand enterprises of the Godhead in the ages past and to come; the destiny of all the dead, the living and the yet unborn; the unsettled issues of the ages; the resurrection call; the day of doom, and the march of the millions through the highways of eternity. The DIVINE government upon His shoulder! When we behold these stupendous issues, wrapped in this infant form; then—like the Magi—we kneel and worship. The soul brings its best gifts and lays them at His feet. Can it be that the eternal Jehovah, "whom the heaven of heavens cannot contain, "has embodied all the mighty interests that ever engaged his heart and thought in a human infant form, and laid them at our feet and said, "Unto you a child is born?" Unto you are all things given!

HIS NAME SHALL BE CALLED WONDERFUL.—Not merely because of the mysterious union of the two natures, the human and the Divine; for, this is a mystery before which human wisdom kneels in silence and over which angels bend in unavailing inquiry; but that name is wonderful in its influence upon humanity.

When King Saul's heart was troubled and he could not rest, he called for a young Hebrew harper, and under the music of his magic touch the King was soothed. It is so today with the great, aching, heaving heart of humanity. The name of Jesus is to it as the harp of David to the heart of Saul. The gospel, standing beside a world in unrest, is soothing it as it sings of that "name which is above every name;" and under its marvelous melody the raging seas of passion and pain, and the billows of sorrow and anguish subside; and "there is a great calm." Ten thousand times ten thousand hearts, which were as so many moral whirlpools "casting up mire and dirt," have heard the music of this Wonderful name and have become calm and restful. And, like the placid lake which mirrors the heavens, they now reflect the beauty of God. Christianity is recovering from the hoarseness of sin, and with purified power of song is everywhere hymning, "How sweet the name of Jesus sounds, in a believer's ears. It soothes his sorrows, heals his wounds and drives away his fears."

COUNSELLOR.—He has been with the father from eternity. He knows the eternal counsels of God; the aims and ends of every devisement for fallen man, and the weakness and wants of our race. He is familiar with the court and the prison, with the criminal and the judge; with the offended God and offending man. Who, then, is so well prepared as He to negotiate for the honor of the one, and the salvation of the other? What were his counsels with the Father we do not know; we cannot and may never know. One thing we know, and that is enough; we know His counsels were successful, and that through them we may be saved. And now He counsels us to yield our will and "Come unto him and be saved." Seeing, then, what His counsels have done—averting wrath, removing the curse and making salvation possible to us—well may we give Him supreme worship as "Wonderful Counsellor."

THE MIGHTY GOD.—Christ's power is equal
to His wisdom. He is wise to plan and Almighty
to execute. Had He been less than Omnipotent
He could not have executed His own counsels.
We hear of His POWER as soon as we hear of
HIM. It is as if God, from all eternity, would
guard the deity of Christ. When it is said "He
was in the beginning with God," it is added, "All
things were made by him," and further added,
"And without him was not anything made that
was made," and yet is added, "In him was life."

But we need no logic to prove Christ is God.
What would logic do in proving to us that the sun
is the light of the natural world? We would say,
"We want no such logic. We have the proof in a
far better form." We have it in EXPERIENCE;
the first and best form of evidence of any fact.
We behold His light, walk in it, enjoy it; it warms
our blood while we behold its boundlessness.

Thus do we know Christ the "Sun of Righteousness," the "Mighty God." "We see him by faith,
walk in his light and feel the warmth of his love."
That love flows—like heat in the veins—through
all the circulation of the immortal nature. Our
spirits all aglow with the life of the Divine Son;
and yet His grace and power are unexhausted
and equal to the lighting of other unfortunate
worlds.

THE EVERLASTING FATHER.—Here a new
relation breaks in upon us. How wonderfully redemption finds way into all our relations. We
have seen His wisdom as Counsellor, His power

as the "Mighty God," and now He breaks another side of His nature to us. He is the "Everlasting Father," and loves us well enough to execute His wise counsels by His mighty power.

It is here that our hope rests. Why did He love us and die for us? He did not need us. Why do you love your ill-formed and helpless child? You do not need it. It is just a tax upon your thought and your heart. But you say, "I could not do without my darling child. I need its love." And what is the secret of this? YOU ARE ITS Father. Then our heavenly Father has need of us. Deformed as we are by sin, and a continual tax on His loving kindness. Let your child be away from you and lost in the night-time, and you will suffer more than the lost one. So with our Father in heaven. He left the "ninety and nine" to come after us, because His fatherly heart moved Him to seek us. He is the exerlasting Father.

THE PRINCE OF PEACE.—It was separation from God that destroyed our peace. Then if in this babe of Bethlehem we find all that is needed to reunite us to God, shall He not re-establish in us the kingdom and the reign of peace?

With wisdom to plan, power to execute, and love to perform, it is through Him we have again that "peace which passeth understanding." Christ not only brings to us a GOVERNMENTAL but a PERSONAL peace. Find a man who belongs to Christ's kingdom and you find one whose heart and life are peaceful, despite all the storms that rage. Christ is the universal "Prince of

Peace." It was 740 years before His birth that the prophet announced Him as the "Prince of Peace;" and we stand now, nearly 2,000 years after His birth, and echo back the angelic annunciation, "Glory to God in the highest. On earth peace."

And the closer we and our enemies get to Christ the sooner will the horrid war, that sweeps our planet today, end in our victory and triumph over the wrong, and bring again that peace of which He is the universal Prince.

CHAPTER X.

THE KINGSHIP OF CHRIST.
(A CHRISTMAS TALK.)

"Where is he who is born king of the Jews? for we have seen his star in the east, and are come to worship him."—Matt. 2:2.

Christ's first worshippers were grand-masters in science. "Wise men from the east." A circle of scientists knelt about the infant form and placed the first wreath upon the brow of our Christianity. It was not ignorance, coming in stark astonishment; neither curiosity, with vague inquiry; but wisdom and devotion, coming with offerings of "gold, frankincense, and myrrh." "We know why, and whom, we seek." "We have seen his star in the east, and are come to worship him." The precise point from which they came is a matter of controversy; but they were of such dignity and importance as to command public consideration and produce a stir in court circles when they reached the Jewish Capital."

NOTE HOW THEY WERE LED TO LOOK FOR CHRIST.—They were doubtless astronomers and students of the heavens; and the knowledge of the Redeemer came to them through their familiar medium. "They saw his star."

Christ finds way to men of all vocations through familiar media. He came to the fishermen by the miraculous draft; and to the Samaritan woman by the water which she drew from the well. He reached the hungry by the multiplied loaves, and gained the hearts of the suffering by healing their maladies. He is, "Immanuel," God with us.

The preacher who connects the gospel with the personal interests of men, is the preacher who will win souls. Show the farmer, through his farming; the physician, through his profession; the invalid, through his suffering; and you link them by a living tie to the economy of grace. Religion is not a mere matter of sentiment or æsthetics. Occupation, profession, sickness, circumstances—all these are but gospel links to loop men on to the plan of salvation. The gospel world is the great Cæsar, to whom all worlds pay tribute. Astronomy, geology, mathematics, art and science, all are within the realm of the gospel, and the gospel commands them. "All things are yours."

HEROD'S INQUIRY.—The star seen by the wise men was perhaps two years previous to the birth of Christ. Evidently there was some time between the appearance of the star and the coming of the wise men. It required time. The distance was great, and these grave men would not come with the haste and excitement of the simple-hearted shepherds. Herod's action also proves this fact.

He first calls the chief priests and scribes, the men familiar with the prophecies, and demands of them WHERE Christ would be born? They say, "In Bethlehem of Judea." This question settled, Herod then calls the wise men privately, and inquired of them closely, "What time the star appeared." Now he has the two points. He knows where He was to be born, and what time the star appeared. Hence, in order to destroy the infant Christ, he gives the order, "Kill all the babes from two years old and under." As the star appeared two years ago, go back that far and leave none alive under two years of age.

THE QUESTION OF THE WISE MEN.— Their question was not as to His kingship, but His whereabouts. "Where is he?" Great characters can be graded in rank. Daniel was in high rank, but not king, in Babylon; Mordecai under Ahasuerus, and Joseph under Pharaoh; but Christ cannot be graded in rank or rulership—He is absolute in every sphere, never second, never subordinate. He can be nothing less than supreme. The wise men apprehend this fact. Hence they ask not for Him who is predicted, or claims to be king, but for Him "Who is *born* king."

John the Baptist questioned. "Art thou he that should come?" Pilate asked "Art thou a king?" The high priest said, "Tell us plainly, art thou the Christ?" But the wise men have this mighty truth beyond all question. *He is king*, and can be nothing less. His imperial dominion superrules all dominion. "His kingdom is to destroy (or absorb) all other kingdoms." And missionary effort is to this end. The restoration of the race and the emancipation of humanity will be complete only when the world accepts, acknowledges, and lives this tremendous truth—CHRIST IS KING.

HIS KINGSHIP SILENTLY ASSERTS IT-SELF.—"It comes without observation." Unlike earthly kingdoms which are established amid the thunders and carnage of war, His kingdom is the silent force of the universe. Christ silently measures the hours for earth's millions. The times, seasons, days, and years are named and numbered in His memory. The commerce of the earth bears His impress. Every note, and letter, from human pen; every column and communication from the daily press; every message flashed under the sea, or flying, spirit like, through the air bears date from the birth of the Nazarene. The note, the deed, the bond, the draft, is worthless without recognition of the universal KING. The infidel, writing a book against our Christianity, is forced to recognize Christ in dating his production.

CIVILIZATION IS A PERPETUAL GOSPEL. —Jesus Christ is engrafted into the very constitution of things—Practical, civil, social, domestis. The very onflow of life is a perpetual proclamation of His kingship. Like the ceaseless murmur of the waves, ever telling of the sea, the very babble of humanity's onflowing tide tells of His dominion. Strike Christ from human thought, allow men to indite no document, make no entry, and seal no contract that refers to Him, and you stop all commerce, unhinge all human activities, dissolve all organization, and leave the world a babel of confusion.

Drop any other character from human thought,

and the world moves on undisturbed; but strike out the Nazarene, and the KING is gone and earth is anarchy.

THE VISIBLE TYPES THE INVISIBLE.— Just as Christ rules the world by coming into its commerce, literature, and progress, so He comes into the invisible life of the soul, and asserts His kingdom with the same silent but divine power. He is to have place in all departments of the inner life. As He moves in the letter date, the cable or telegram, so He moves in all departments of the moral being; thought, affection, desire, conscience and will. Like the little home in Bethany—all departments become His delightful dwelling-place, while all the powers of the soul sit, like Mary, at His feet.

Christ cannot be less than king. A Christ in the life, who is less than king, brings no peace, "but a sword." He sets the man at war with himself. "His enemies are those of his own household." There is hostility between the carnal and spiritual natures. The carnal mind, rising in rebellion, refuses to have Christ reign over it; while the Holy Spirit, and conscience, come upon the scene and enter the struggle to subdue the beasts; lashing the lusts, rebuking the idolatry, murdering the pride and slaying the self-will, until the whole menagerie in the soul is slain, and the hiss and howl of beast and serpent have ceased, and all is surrendered to Christ, and He enthroned in the heart as "Lord of all." Then is there a great calm.

HOW CHRIST BECOMES KING.—He was BORN king of the Jews; and so He must be BORN king of the soul. Religion is not a legacy, neither a transmission, but a birth. Christ in the soul is not a matter of authority, but of life. He does not ascend the throne from without; but He is born in the soul, and thus gets possession and rulership over it.

The babe in the household is born to kingship the most real. By its very helplessness it commands all in the home. As the babe of Bethlehem, Christ commands the sentiment and service of the Christian world. He has taken hold of the great family of man as the babe takes hold in the domestic circle. He has filled the thought of the ages. He fills the sentiment of our Republic and of the Christian world today. He fills the thought of hoary age, and happy childhood this Christmas eve. He is humanity's rightful king. "To this end was he born." Regal alike in hovel and palace. In deep poverty, where Santa Claus never comes; even there Christ may reign as sweetly as in the chamber of the king.

GREATNESS OF THE CHANGE.—The coming of Christ into the world has changed the world more than all things else. And His coming into a human life changes that life more than all other things combined. And why? Because it is a change based upon the life. The great changes in us are not those of condition, or circumstances, or such as affect the tax list, but are those that touch the life.

If the companion die, or the child be taken, whose very being is incorporate with our life, then we are changed. Those things reach the base of our being, and we are never afterward the same. All great changes rest upon the life.

Thus, conversion changes us. A new life-current is turned into the nature. "Old things pass away, and all things become new." Paul was not the same after conversion; neither Luther, nor Bunyan, nor Wesley, nor yourself.

His coming changes all. He came into Peter's home, and the fever left the sufferer, and she arose to minister to him and his. He came into the home of the ruler, and the dead damsel awoke, and joy returned to the sad home. He came to Bethany, and the brother, four days dead, arose and joyful life came back to the cottage home.

Let Christ come into the Church, and deadness departs, indifference takes wings, while new life comes into all. Let Him but come into the heart, and that heart will rise above its sorrows—like the morning lark rising above the fogs to meet the sun—it ascends above its griefs to meet and sing the praise of God.

THE SUBLIME AND FINAL CHANGE.— This will be when "he comes the second time without sin, unto salvation." "The Lord himself shall descend from heaven with a shout; with the voice of the archangel and the trump of God. And the dead in Christ shall rise first." Then "we shall be changed in a moment, in the twinkling of an eye." The cemetery—the place of weeping—will be made to rejoice. I have never seen the face of joy among the tombs, or heard the echo of merry laughter amid the graves of the dead.

But His coming will change the charnel-house into cheerfulness. "Sorrow and sighing shall flee away." Mortality shall awake and live, and put on immortality, and shout, "Thanks be to God who giveth us the victory through our Lord Jesus Christ." The loud laughter of resurrection triumph shall echo through empty vaults, and glad Hallelujahs constitute the grandest jubilee since creation's morning.

GOD WILL HELP THE SEEKER.—Are you seeking Christ? Get the lesson from these wise men. They came to Jerusalem expecting to find the nation's king at the nation's Capital. How bitter their disappointment! But as they turned away, behold, the star they had seen again appeared, and "going before them, came and stood over where the young child was." They were sincere seekers; and heaven and earth combine to help the soul that is sincerely seeking Christ.

"Where is he who is born king of the Jews?" Where is He with us personally? Where in our creed? Is He Divine to us, the one true and living God? Where in our affection? Has He first place; or has some idol, or dear one, the place He should occupy? Where in our life? Can we say "For me to live is Christ?" Is He the soul's center about which all revolves?

WE ARE COME TO WORSHIP HIM.—This was their purpose in their long journey. So we have made the annual journey, and have come through all the dangers, difficulties, and disappointments of the year. Are we here now with "the gold, the frankincense, and the myrrh" of a sincere devotion? Has our life, through the year, been an effort to find and get near the king, that we may worship Him?

We stand today, just outside the enclosure where the dying year will be buried. Like those who cried, "We have no king but Cæsar!" Let us look up, by faith, to see His star, and shout in glad accents of undying devotion, "We HAVE NO KING BUT CHRIST?"

CHAPTER XI.

THE MISSION OF CHRIST.

"For the Son of man is come to save that which was lost." Matt. 18-11.

TO BE LOST IS TO HAVE NO SELF-STRENGTH.—Self preservation is nature's first law; and with all the strength a man has will he support that law. In battle, he will not recognize himself as lost so long as he can wield his sword. In the ocean storm, he feels that he is not lost so long as he has a spar to which he may cling. He hopes on so long as his benumbed and stiffening fingers can retain a feeble hold; and he never feels that he is hopelessly lost until his hands yield their grasp and he sinks dreamily into the sea.

So the sinner never feels himself lost until all self-strength is gone, and he realizes that "of himself he can do nothing." Dear sinner, have you been in hand to hand conflict with your evil nature, with your unholy tempers, unconquered appetites, and perverse will? Have you fought and fallen, time and again, until you have no power left? And are you ready to throw the rein on the neck of nature and say, "I am lost unless God saves me?"

Or are you still saying, "I can break off from my wicked habits and make myself all right?" If so, you are not lost in the sense of this text. You are in the ocean-storm trusting to the ship, or clinging to the spar, and still hoping, and hence not lost entirely. So it is not for you that "The Son of man came." If you can save yourself Jesus doesn't offer to save you. But give up every other hold and hope except the mercy of God; then we can say, "Jesus stands ready to save you." Throw down the sword, let go the spar, give up all self-strength, and sink down in the sea—the fathomless sea—of Divine mercy, and know how quickly and fully Christ can save!

THE LOST MAN DOESN'T KNOW WHAT TO DO.—If there is ever a time in life when one doesn't know what to do, it is when one is lost. In the depths of a dense forest, the day beclouded and his way lost, and the man at his wits end, he starts in one direction and is hedged in by swamps; he tries another way and is met by an impenetrable copse, and egress seems impossible. Night draws on, and he seems doomed to spend its dreary watches amid the darkness and dangers of the wild forest. If a man ever feels like praying it is at a time like this.

Dear sinner, have you a sense of this confusion and know not what to do? In trouble and no way of escape? Have you gone in all directions? Have you tried morality, good-works, paying to the church, baptism, and even church-membership? Have all these failed to bring peace and a sense of safety? If so, then you are the very one whom He came to save. He comes to you directly, PERSONALLY. His mission is to save

YOU! Try it for once, a simple trust in Him, and try it speedily. For the night draws on and "outer darkness" will soon envelop the soul, unless saved through the blood of Christ.

THE LOST CHILD.—A little child has wandered from its home and is lost in the woods. It comes to the consciousness that it is lost. Now mark its actions. It is excited, alarmed. It runs this way a little, then stops and turns back; then gives up in despair, and sitting down, begins to cry bitterly. And how piteous that cry! Sinner, "Except ye become as a little child ye cannot see the kingdom of God." Have you given up the struggle? Have you ever sat down to cry over your sins? Have you ever shed a single tear over your own soul, and like the little lost child, cried to your heavenly Father to come and save you?

Suppose you hear the cry of a little lost one and hasten to its relief. The helpless little thing is sobbing as if heart-broken. You take it in your arms, press it to your bosom, and soothe the little spirit, while your very soul runs over with sympathy and the tears come unbidden to your eyes; and yet it is not your child, but the child of a stranger.

How much more will the blessed Savior deliver His lost child, when He has come for that purpose, and its cry for help rises to Him. He will bear that one—as the lost lamb—in His own bosom of love.

There is joy among the Swiss highlanders when the signal gun is fired and the shout raised, telling of the lost child that is found. The echo rolls from hilltops and reaches through the valleys! "There is joy in heaven over one sinner that repenteth." What joy among the heavenly highlands, when the shout is raised that "The child of immortality, lost in sin for years and years, has been found." Oh! that the heavenly hills may ring, at this hour, with glad shouts over some lost soul returning to God!

TO BE LOST IS TO BE HOPELESS.—It is difficult to get the sinner to feel that he has no hope but in Christ. Sin in the soul, and consumption in the body, work alike. They flatter their victim to the very last, and carry him through death's door with a smile. You seldom see consumptives conscious of their condition. The brow may be white as marble, the cheek flushed, frame emaciated, and breath short and labored, and eyes almost glazed; and even then they will tell you "they are better."

So with the sinner; he hates to give up all hope and throw himself upon the mercy of Christ. He tries to think his morality sufficent. Tries to presume on God's mercy. Tries to believe God is too good to suffer one to be lost who has lived a moral life. How strange that the devil can delude a man and lead him steadily and directly on to hell, and yet keep him hoping all the time that he will be saved.

Like a poor fellow to whom we carried the death sentence in the Civil War. We carried him his sentence at nine o'clock in the morning, and he was executed at four in the afternoon. When first notified he began to look round as if hoping for someone to deliver him. And as the hours passed he continued to look, as if perchance someone might come to save him; and this continued even while we were in prayer with him. And when kneeling on the grave, in the last prayer, he gazed wistfully about for help; and when the blindfold was drawn over his face even then he tried to look for deliverance. He never gave up to die until the fatal volley sent his spirit into eternity.

Thus it is with many an impenitent sinner. They hope on, and continue to hope, until death hurls them into a hopeless and endless state. Oh, that you might, at this hour, realize that you are lost, and come crying, "Lord save or I perish!" And if you never intend to throw yourself upon the mercy of God, then you might as well be in hell now. It is only a matter of a little time. "He that believeth not shall be damned." These are awful words, but they are not mine, they are the words of Him who shed the blood of His heart for you. May the Holy Spirit sink them deep, and burn them lastingly into your innermost soul!

TO BE LOST IS TO BE IN DISTRESS.—To realize that we are lost is to be in consummate unrest and wretchedness. We shall never forget the feeling. In the sixties, when men carried their lives in their hands, I was trying to reach my home and receive a mother's kiss. It was a moonless night, and the forest dense, and I was lost; and that in the very midst of those who were thirsting for my blood. Fastening my horse, I lay down upon the ground and tried to feel composed, and thought I would sleep. But the "sweet restorer" fled from me. The owls hooted, the night-birds flapped their wings, while the winds sighed over me; and my loneliness became unbearable. I arose, and kneeling down I silently cried to God, and He led me out.

My unsaved friend, you are lost in the midst of your most deadly enemies, in the midst of those agencies which seek after your soul to destroy it—lost in an enemy's land. "This vile world is no friend to grace, to help us on to God." Are you conscious of your condition? Or are you at ease, and soundly sleeping on the very brink of eternal death, in the treacherous Niagara current and floating toward the falls, and at the same time dreaming of safety? Oh! that some gospel arrow might pierce your soul and quicken you from your deadness and danger and render you wretched, with that wretchedness which will drive you to Christ!

THE NEW GOSPEL.—We hear it now that, "The world-war has produced a new state of things which will require a new gospel." That "the soldiers returning from the war will demand a change." "That they must have a gospel of science, and sociology; and must be entertained when they go to church." Such talk as this is a slander of the soldiers, and an insult to their intelligence; and at the same time a blasphemy in the sight of God. They have been face to face with things eternal. They have had impressions not possible in civil life. And hence are prepared to appreciate a sound, simple, and saving gospel as never before. And they will feel a just and supreme contempt for the sycophant in the pulpit, who may offer any silly substitute for the blood of Christ.

FINALLY.—This is the glorious mission of Christ, "To save such as are lost." Such as have no self-strength and feel that they are lost. Such as know not what to do, and have no hope. Such as are completely wretched.

Dear dying man, if you feel thus at this hour, take courage! If you feel that you are not fit to join the church, not fit to come to the communion table, and fit for nothing but hell, then our message is to YOU. Of all men, you are the one to come to the fountain and be made clean: come to Christ and be saved! FOR YOU He is seeking. The greatest work of God is for you. Redemption is for you. He died to save sinners such as you; and gave a specimen copy of His work as He died, by saving the wretched and dying thief. Helpless, hopeless, powerless one, now in distress, give yourself to Christ! He lovingly waits to write your name in the "Book of Life." Come to Him NOW, with this text on your lips, and rest in the blessed truth that "The Son of man came to save that which was lost."

CHAPTER XII.

THE GOSPEL IN THE WIND.

Text: "The wind bloweth where it listeth, and thou hearest the sound thereof, but canst not tell whence it cometh, and whither it goeth: so is every one that is born of the Spirit."—John 3:8.

"Never man spake like this man." He makes that invisible and mysterious element that intervenes between heaven and earth, to set forth the mysterious work of the spirit on the soul, in preparing it to leave the one and become an inhabitant of the other.

The atmosphere is the life and breath of nature. Take it away and nature becomes one vast tomb without so much as a wind to wail over it. The Holy Spirit is the atmosphere of the immortal realm; the life and breath of the spiritual universe. Take it away and the moral world is left in hopeless death.

The atmosphere in motion we term "wind." The wind is only the air in movement. Here the Master makes the wind to show the movement and work of the Spirit. "The wind bloweth where it listeth." It was night time when He had this talk with Nicodemus. Perhaps the night winds were heard sighing or wailing without, giving suggestion which the Great Teacher used. "Thou hearest the sound thereof." Nicodemus, thou hearest it now; but thou canst not tell from whence nor whither. Wonderful Teacher! bidding the wisest of the age, "Be still and hear," while He should make the idle winds of the night to teach him the deep things of God.

FREEDOM OF THE WIND.—"It bloweth where it listeth," where it will. Essential freedom is its distinctive feature. It is unbridled. The untamed and untamable element in nature. There is no power to throw the lasso about it and to bring it into captivity. Its own caprice is its only law. The river is confined to its channel, and the ocean is bedfast and powerless to chase even a child; but the wind is swift-footed for the chase, and winged for the flight. It is alike at home on sea or land. Whether pursuing a recreant Jonah or bearing a triumphant Elijah to glory. All things else have learned submission. We disarm the lightning and turn it powerless into the earth. We bring the wild electric fire of the skies to its knees, and compel it to obedience, while it becomes the under-ocean carrier between ours and other nations. But the wind, like the human tongue, "hath no man tamed." It mock at man's weakness, and in its frolicksome freedom answers his efforts to harness it with its wild and taunting "Aha! Aha!"

The wind has its way with all alike. It toys softly with the ringlets of the little child; it vexatiously flaps and flutters the flounces of fashion on the public promenade; it rustles the rags of the beggar by the wayside, and dashes the dust into the face of royalty in the triumphant procession. It literally "bloweth where it listeth," caring naught for caste or rank—controlled by nothing save its own caprices.

Thus it is with the Holy Spirit. It is eternally free. Confined to no channel, bound by no cord. Everywhere present and everywhere free. The Psalmist understood this when he prayed, "Uphold me by thy free spirit." It will find out every man, whether he be fleeing from duty or pressing toward God. Whether his condition be one of pomp or poverty, whether a miner in the pit or a prince on a throne; God's Spirit will find him out. Nor can he escape it any more than we can escape the wind or the ever-present atmosphere. Some men take up life in fruitless attempts to get away from God's Spirit. They plunge into business, pleasure, society and sin, but in vain. Like Felix, bidding the Spirit "go its way," or like Jonah, hiding in the ship's hull, there is no escape.

Every man has felt its power as sure as you have felt the atmosphere or the wind. Reader, you have felt this power. Converted you may not be—convicted you have been, and you could not help it. "Whither shall I go from thy Spirit? Or whither shall I flee from thy presence?"

THE WIND IS RESISTLESS IN ITS POWER.—Though in its gentler and softer moods it suits its breathing to the delicate æolian strings, and the music be soft and sweet as the notes of a seraph's flute, yet in its wilder moments it becomes the king of terrors in the physical world. No other element dare dispute its sway. The earth that feeds its millions is powerless to resist it. The giant oak, the child of the forest, is torn in a moment from its place, and hurled heavenward by the passing cyclone, and earth's bosom left torn and disfigured. The city, made solid by the centuries, is caught and dashed as a child's toy to destruction. The ocean, the God-appointed and faithful old nurse of the earth, who has kept her arms about the world from the beginning; even she, when caught by the angry winds, shrinks back, falls into convulsions and staggers to and fro as a drunken man. The Arab leads his caravan, crossing and recrossing the desert for years, measuring its latitudes, wading its sands and braving its heat; then in an evil moment he sees the sand-cloud lifted by the merciless wind for his destruction. He has but time to turn his face to Mecca and commend his soul to Allah, when he and his train, like the first martyr, go down in their grave of sand.

Herein is a picture of the power of the Holy Spirit. Moving now in the terrible tempest, and anon in the "still small voice." Its gentle brooding over the dark, dead waters at the day-dawn of creation, giving life to the stagnant seas; hovering now over the dead sea of humanity to quicken it into life, the only power able to awaken a dead soul and bestir it from its sepulchre of sin. But its breathings can make even "dry bones" to live again.

The mighty revivals which have marked the different periods were but the movements of the

Holy Spirit. It is that power which has brought 150,000 in India to stand now at the door of the church pleading for admission. In these "violent movings" of the spirit multiplied thousands have been brought to Christ.

YOU CANNOT SILENCE THE WIND.— "Thou hearest the sound thereof." You hear, whether you will to hear or not. The wind in a winter's midnight may howl and wail without, and scream around the house corners as if demons were let loose, robbing you of your slumbers and tormenting you with unrest. But you are powerless to resist. You may wish the winds to silence, but in vain. You may turn your thoughts to other themes, trying to forget them, but anon in double terror their deafening roar breaks upon your ears. There is no escape save in the destruction of the sense of hearing. While that remains the sounds must be received, "Thou hearest the sound thereof."

So we cannot silence the Holy Spirit. The ears of the soul are greeted by its warning voice. Like the wind it "lifts up its voice without, and crieth in the streets." That voice breaks upon the cloudy elements of the guilty soul in terrible and tormenting tones. Oft in the silent night it brings wretchedness and unrest. The sinner may wish that voice silenced, but in vain; he may command it away, but as well may he try to command the winds; he may turn from it and seek to forget it in contemplating other themes, but anon it breaks in upon his soul with unearthly alarms. Sinner, your only escape lies in crushing your soul's receptive power—crushing the conscience—until it is seared, deaf and dead. The deaf are not disturbed by the howling of the night winds. The Holy Spirit has no alarms for the dead conscience. Therefore, if you do not feel the influence of the Spirit as you once did it is not because the gospel has lost its power to awaken, but it is because your soul has reached that deadness where the Spirit's voice can no longer be heard. What an awful state! A soul so dead that the Holy Spirit cannot awaken it!

NEITHER CAN WE AROUSE THE WIND.— We are as powerless to arouse it as to silence it. It is not in our power to move the self-willed currents of the air. We may be fainting beneath a tropical sun, dying in the stagnant heat, and feel as if we would give all for a cooling breath, yet we may perish in the very midst of the atmosphere because powerless to put its currents in motion. So with the Holy Spirit when it has ceased its movements upon the soul. We have no power to renew its motion. That was the fatal mistake with Felix, presuming that when it was "convenient to him" he could recall it. Here is the mistake of many. How many have wished for the Spirit's return, but alas! they might as well have wished for the moving of the wind. "Thou hearest the sound thereof." You hear it now. Blessed hour when this can be said! Sinner, hearest thou now the Spirit's voice? Heed the message! It may be bringing thee final farewell whispers of life and hope!

THE MYSTERY OF THE WIND.—"Thou canst not tell whence it cometh and whither it goeth." We know the general conditions of the wind, seasons, heat and other elements, but what know we of the origin or end of any current of air? It arises we know not where, and goes we know not whither. Here, doubtless, was a new thought to Nicodemus. He had marked many things in the old Scriptures, but had not observed this Spirit-wind. This Spirit current has come down mysteriously through the Old Testament ages, and is now going out with increasing volume over the whole earth, until every rational creature shall feel its power. It will ever be a mystery to the world and to every individual that feels its power. Hence, Nicodemus might well ask, as the world is ever asking, "How can these things be?"

MYSTERY IS THE GOD-MARK ON ALL THINGS.—The seal with which He stamped His own. Why shall we reject the works because we cannot read the God-stamp upon them? What matters it if the skillful physician marks his remedy with a name, or in a language, we cannot translate, only so we get its benefits, and regain our health? Mystery marks the origin and the end of things. "In the beginning God created—." But who knows when, how, where? "Of the end no man knoweth." But we are here between the two, walking the earth and breathing the air, which were made in the beginning and will endure to the end. So in redemption. In the beginning was the Word, "And the word was with

God." But we cannot understand the how, when and where? "And the Word was made flesh;" but who can read the mystery? And the Word shall come and call us to judgment. And here we are between the two—and as well pause to question the wind because you know not its origin or its end.

"So is everyone that is born of the Spirit." EVERYONE. Never an exception. Never one that understood the mystery. Heaven is filling up with those who accepted the truth and then went to heaven to learn the mystery. Faith gave them all the benefits, and heaven and eternity will give them time to study the philosophy. I think this will be no small part of my study, to find out and understand how God could save such a creature as I. "Waiting to understand." Waiting for what no man ever had and what you nor any other man will ever get.

Ask the Christians, one by one, and they will give the Savior's answer, "Thou canst not tell." The Spirit came. My sins were pardoned. The evidence given, and I have "peace with God, through our Lord Jesus Christ," but how I cannot tell.

Nicodemus never got answer to his question. But, accepting the truth by faith, he got his soul saved from sin; and he now has time, where "they know perfectly what we only know in part," to study the theme that he discussed with the master on that memorable night visit. May God give us faith to accept the saving truth which our feeble philosophy is now unable to master!

CHAPTER XIII.

THE FIRST MIRACLE.

"This beginning of miracles did Jesus in Cana of Galilee."—John 2:11.

This first miracle types the Master's entire work. He came to change humanity: to uplift and transmute it into the higher nature. This He typifies in this first miracle, by transmuting the water into wine. Raising the lower and the less into the higher and the better.

This is the effect of the divine touch. "I say unto thee arise." Christ never reduces, never depresses, never makes less. We may come in contact with men in such way as to be crushed by their dishonesty and unmitigated meanness, but contact with the "Man of Galilee" is always elevating and ennobling. The touch of His power lifts superstition into science, and heathenism into highest civilization. It is the touch of the divine intention that gives significance to man. It is what God intends for him; the Divine intention reaching down and touching man springs him into undying significance. God intends us for His own ultimate associates; to be pure enough, and wise enough, to think his thoughts, and "enter into his joys."

NOTE THE OCCASION.—It was a marriage, and it is specially stated "That the mother of Jesus was there." This ordinance carries an undying novelty and attraction. The missionary meeting may run down to six, the Epworth League to half a score, and the prayer meeting to a lone dozen, but the swell wedding will still pack the church and block the aisles. Just how much of the upper-tendom of the town was present at this marriage we are not told. The marriage party have died and are forgotten, and the site of the little town is now a question; but one thing immortalizes the occasion—Jesus WAS THERE.

There are days which never die out of memory. Occasions into which destiny seems to crowd itself. These are the days when we meet God. Moses at the bush, Abraham on Mt. Moriah, Elijah on Carmel, Jacob at the brook, and Saul on the Damascus road. These occasions were epochs in the lives of those men.

So with us. We have met God at the memorable points in life. You met Him in a dark providence, in a deep grief, in a glorious conversion. You have met Him in special blessings that raised you to a loftier experience. You have met Him in the sunshine and in the shadows of life. And like His coming to Cana to change the water into wine, your every meeting with Him has been a transformation. You were never just the same afterward. The water of life's common experience was changed into the wine of a richer spiritual life. How much it makes life mean—those meetings with God!

CHRIST WAS THE NEEDED GUEST.—His presence at that marriage not only sanctified the marriage ordinance, but it sanctifies the social joys of life, and is an abiding rebuke to that asceticism which hides itself away from society in the monastery or the trappis.

Christ also proved the guest above all others needed for that occasion. But for His presence the feast had ended in confusion and embarrassment. He is the needed guest in every home and in every life. Needed alike, in the sunny and in the shadowy seasons.

There was never a time since creation when Christ was more needed in the home than now. How we pity the Christless home at this time! So many homes with a vacant chair, and the loved occupant beyond the sea and facing death; when we know not the hour that the cablegram will bring the sad message, "Killed in action." And furthermore, we know not when the father will now be called to leave wife and little ones to face the same danger. Have you a happy home, and is that home without Christ? The loved ones growing up without being made familiar with Him who said, "Suffer the little children to come unto me and forbid them not." Oh, my friend, call for Christ to become the abiding guest in your home! Then, and only then, will you and yours be safe!

NOTE THEIR COURSE IN THIS EMERGENCY.—The moment was most embarrassing. The feast in progress and well advanced, when suddenly it is found that the wine is exhausted. If you, when acting as host, have felt fear of some element in your entertainment failing, then you can appreciate their condition. If you have ever undertaken to carve a very small fowl to feed a company of ten, or to carve a pound beefsteak to answer for twelve, then you know what deftness and tact it requires.

But there was one there who knew Jesus better than all others. "The mother of Jesus was there." And she knew just what to do. Going to Him, she stated the trouble in simple words, "They have no wine." Then turning to the servants, she said, "Whatsoever he saith unto you, do it." This was all.

This was a singular statement to make to a guest. But His great heart is so in sympathy with humanity that He feels what it feels. Hence, He took their case upon His own heart, and made their trouble His own. There was no other guest to whom they could go, and no other who could bring relief.

LIFE'S EMBARRASSMENTS ARE UNEXPECTED.—They break upon us at such times as we think not. Had they expected this failure they would have prepared a larger supply, and prevented the confusion. We come into unexpected embarrassments and trials which we cannot make known to a fellow-man, nor could he relieve us if we could. But there is no misfortune, or embarrassment that we may not carry to Christ. Here then is the lesson in the trying junctures. Go and state the case to Him, then wait. "And do whatsoever he commands you."

He is the God of the extreme hours. The present help in time of need. His omnipotence is to supplement our weakness. Where our strength ends there we touch His finger-tips. A widowed mother was in distress when she found the bread supply for herself and little ones almost exhausted; but one of the little ones said, "Mother, God will hear us when we scrape the bottom of the meal-barrel." That was a child's faith.

HIS RESOURCES EQUAL HIS BENEFI-CENCE.—This is not true with men. We find men with large benevolence and small means; and we find men with large means and small benevolence. There seem to be just two classes in this old world. One has the benevolence and the other has the resources. If we could only fuse the two, what a world we would have!

But Christ's resources and benevolence are without limit. Hence He not only sympathized, but He also relieved their embarrassment. He had been turning water into wine through all the ages. He had commanded the rains from heaven, and the waters percolated the soil, and found the grape-roots, and ascended through the vine and into the branches, and was transmuted into wine and bottled in the crimson clusters. He who had always been making wine through the chemistries of nature, could make it then through the water-pots in a moment. But you say, "This is a miracle." No more miracle than when He makes it in the vineyard. In one case, He uses time and nature. In the other, He works without either, and independently of both. He is Sovereign, and both alike are the work of His hand. But observe, Christ never made fermented wine. All the wine that He ever made, in all the ages, whether made by and through nature, or by miracle, was unfermented. Men take the grapes in which Christ has so beautifully bottled the sweet wine, and break the bottles—crush the grapes—and then make the fermented wine. If they would take the wine, just as it is made and put up in the tiny grape bottles, there would be no red eyes and red noses as the result.

HIS RELIEF INCLUDED FUTURE SUPPLY. —There were six immense vessels, holding more than a hundred gallons, but the feast is well advanced, and there is not so great a quantity now needed. One vessel, or a part of one is ample. But He bids them fill all of them, "and they filled them to the brim." He will not merely meet their present want, but will leave an abundant supply in the home. How lasting are His blessings. He blessed you with the pardon of your sins many years ago, but the memory lingers still, and you yet feel the refreshing of the hour.

Here in the first miracle, is that feature of FULLNESS that ever marks the divine hand. God does nothing by measure, nothing by the scant. He does not ask, "How much can you get on with?" "How much are you compelled to have?" But a royal fullness marks all that He does. When He made the light, He made it by the flood. He filled the sea to the full. He made the rivers to run for all time. When He fed the multitude, they took up "twelve baskets," and when He filled the fish-nets they were so many and so great, "that the net brake."

THUS HE DEALS WITH THE SOUL.—When He forgives our sins He forgives them all. When He fills the soul with His love, He fills it to the brim. When the church is filled with the Holy Spirit, she is "filled to the brim." "Fullness to the brim," is the divine measure.

We chafe under restrictions. This is a land of limitations. Broad as the globe is, the poor man is restricted to a few feet for his home, and perhaps to none at all. How the heart often longs to do what the limitations will not allow. Health restricted, we look into the face of the loved one, and see that the health forces are but half up; under depression, and but half alive. The very smile of this world is but half a smile, and it dissolves into the gloom of the grave.

But what must it be to get up, and out, of these limitations, and from this half-life; this land of leanness and hunger, and enter into that realm where all is fullness? Family—circle full—no vacant chairs like we now have. Health full! Heart full! Possessions full! And full for all eternity!

OUR LAW OF LIFE.—We have it in these words, "Whatsoever he saith unto you, do it." It is not ours to question with God, but to obey. Those servants might have questioned. Why this great labor at this late hour?. Why fill all these vessels when it is not needed? And why draw out water and bear to the ruler of the feast only to mock Him and meet His rebuke? But they simply obeyed.

Gideon could not understand why he should send back almost his whole army, and take three hundred men, with as many lamps and pitchers, and go to make battle with the army of Midian. But he obeyed. Let us surrender all to Him, and live by this rule. Let it henceforward be the law of life with us, "Whatsoever he commands you, do it."

THE CHARACTER OF THIS WINE.—Its excellency produced great surprise, and they declare the common order reversed, and "The good wine kept until the last." This is what Christianity does; it reverses the order of the world. This world gives the best first. Youth and its ardor, poetry, pleasure, and promise. But as life wanes and eventime comes on, it brings no comfort. No solace for sorrow, no light for the soul as it approaches eternity. Desolation and despair crown the evening of a worldly and godless life.

Have you seen a clump of lovely trees in full foliage, with birds making their branches vocal with their music, a picture of lovely life, when hard by stood an old leafless, branchless trunk, swaying to and fro in the wind, and waiting until some sudden gust should hurl it to the ground? That is an old sinner, in the midst of a Christian community, standing on the brink of life, and hopelessly waiting until the hands of death shall dash him to earth, when he shall enter the darkness of a hopeless future.

But Christianity gives the "best wine at the last of the life-feast." There is light at eveningtime with the child of God. There is no decline, but an increase of excellency. Like the ripe autumn fruit whose hues and tints are most lovely, and whose mellow fragrance makes the air redolent with sweetness, the beauty of Christian character is fullest and richest in advanced life. Foliage and bloom all perished, but full of the ripeness and flavor of perfection, and fit to be gathered to God.

CHAPTER XIV.

THE NEEDED SEPARATION.

"It is expedient for you that I go away; for if I go not away, the Comforter will not come unto you; but if I depart, I will send him unto you"—Jno 16:7

Twice already has the Son of God come into and gone out of this world. He came first by way of the manger, and went out by way of the Cross. He came the second time by way of the tomb, and went out through the cloud. He came first to bring life, and passed out to conquer death. His first coming gave light on human life from the cradle to the grave. His second coming gave light on that life which is beyond the grave. By His twice coming He has shed light upon both lives; and now He announces, "It is expedient for you that I go away."

HIS DEPARTURE WAS NECESSARY TO THEIR ILLUMINATION.—Spirituality is never derived from sight. Those who have worshipped visible gods have never risen to a spiritual plane. Idolatry with all its grossness lies in the visible; and materialism confines all to the low plane of the senses. It is a theology of the eyes, ears and hands.

Here is where Christianity joins battle and announces an interior, immaterial, and an invisible realm, and that illumined by the Holy Ghost. The divine Spirit enlightening the human spirit, and revealing that higher knowledge which is unknown and unknowable to the senses.

110

Christ must needs get personally out of their sight in order that the Comforter may come and lead them up and into that higher. knowledge Like the X-rays, penetrating the flesh and revealing the bones, that Holy Ghost was to pierce through the intellect and reach and fill the moral nature with a new and living light. They had been sight worshippers and without sentiment; vascillating, weak, and childish. Humble and teachable today, and tomorrow wrangling about "who should be be greatest in his kingdom." Now ready to "follow him to prison or to death," and again "swearing they did not know him."

It was necessary that Christ should get out of their sight, that the Holy Ghost might come and lift them out of the sensuous, and show Him to their hearts rather than to their eyes. And when they were thus uplifted and illumined they were filled with a holy heroism. No longer cringing cowards, but sublime and dauntless martyrs.

TO RECOGNIZE THE PRESENCE OF THE HOLY GHOST IS ALL-IMPORTANT.—He is as verily present with us as was Christ with His disciples. It is a mistake to think of Him as an INFLUENCE instead of a PERSON. We lost nothing by Christ's going from us. He declared it was "expedient for us." God the Holy Ghost is now our IMMANUEL, "God with us." We are not left alone. Let us not dishonor Him as an idea or an influence; but let us love Him, worship Him, and commune with Him.

He is to humanity what the atmosphere is to

the earth, or the sun to the universe. It is "In him that we live, and move, and have our being." Without Him there is no communication with God nor fruitful life in man. No petition reaches the throne, and no sorrow is ever soothed, except by the Holy Ghost. He connects the natural with the supernatural.

I wish to communicate with a friend beyond the ocean. I have the message ready, the cable-connection is perfect, but I can never send the message until a mysterious spirit-like element leaps from the battery, and catching my message flashes it across the deep. So I may be at the place of prayer, with this inspired cable connecting with the mercy seat, but I can never send my prayer-message until the Holy Ghost—like the electric current—shall catch and carry it to the throne. And how quickly we can tell when that message is heard. Who has not felt the glorious thrill from heaven's batteries when the Holy Ghost was helping our infirmities! We cannot pray without the Holy Ghost. Neither can we read the Holy Scriptures without Him. The sun-dial may be perfect, and all the hours distinctly marked, with a gnomon that casts an exact shadow; but if the day be cloudy and the sun not shining your perfect instrument is worthless; you cannot tell the time.

The Bible is the divine sun-dial. Its words, points, and marks, all correct and plain; but without the light of the Holy Ghost upon its pages it is worth little more than the sun-dial on a cloudy day. Men read the Bible and then go to destruction. But with the clouds of sin off the soul, and with the light of the Holy Ghost upon the word, to read the scripture is to "talk with God."

THE WORD AND THE SPIRIT MEET ALL OUR NEEDS.—Christ's personal presence is not now a necessity. He says, "The words that I speak unto you, they are spirit, and they are life." The divine life is in the gospel, and the Holy Ghost is present to give that gospel access to all hearts; and nothing more is needed. The word and Spirit are the agents for saving men.

And this gospel is absolutely interior in its appeal. It makes no "provision for the flesh," no adjustment to the senses, no panorama to charm, nor witching melody to enchant; but a simple appeal to the interior man, to the heart and conscience.

Man is *intellect, sensibility,* and *will.* This is the sum of man; and the gospel appeals to these *three* departments. Gospel truth in the intellect is received and believed like any other truth. If the evidence is sufficient it compels belief.

The gospel appeals to the sensibility—the heart. The Holy Ghost compels conviction here. It is a gospel of love, and it strikes the heart-chords in humanity. It is not dependent on language, but can put itself in tones, and touches, and a thousand gentlenesses. Hence the heathen is frequently converted under the gospel when he does not understand the language. Where love is the motive power even the inferior creation can recognize it. The horse, the dog, and the bird, are made to feel the power of love.

The inspired word and the Holy Ghost are the agents; and they will do their work. The word convinces the intellect, and the Holy Ghost convicts the heart. But the final appeal is to the *will*, the royal will. Here God pauses and waits, and says, "If any man will open the door—yield the will—I will come in." Right here our responsibility to the heathen comes to an end. "Carry the gospel to every creature." He that WILL accept and believe it shall be saved. "He that will not, shall be damned." Here the heathen finds his royalty. Finds that his own decision determines his doom. When the misionaries have brought the heathen thus face to face with God; then the responsibility rests upon them, and the missionaries may return to their own Christian homes.

THE SPIRIT GIVES POWER TO THE WORD.—He is a fanatic who enters the ministry or mission field without the conscious presence of the Holy Spirit as the source of help and the magazine of power. However well qualified and equiped, he is fated to fail if the Spirit be not with him.

The "Lone Star Mission" in India had labored on educational lines for more than thirty years, and was at the point to give up the field, when John E. Clough was sent of God to take up that forlorn hope. He did not try to affect the minds of the metaphysical Brahmins by educational processes, but went to the outcasts and began to preach "God so loved the world." The result was that "The Holy Ghost fell on all that heard the word," and more than two thousand were baptized in one day, and more than ten thousand were gathered in within one year. This changed the entire missionary policy of India.

The Holy Ghost will call, send, and guide those who carry the gospel to the "regions beyond." He also restrains. Paul and his companions were "forbidden to preach the word in Asia," and again, "They assayed to go to Bythinia, but the Spirit suffered them not.' Israel could make no mistake when "following the cloud." How confident we feel when we know that the Holy Spirit is leading us in our work! It is like heaven upon earth. Brethren, you cannot plan for the Holy Ghost, and announce "revival services at a certain time." Such announcements are next to blasphemous. But thank God, we can let Him plan; then we can "follow the cloud."

Young Judson had a call to Park Street, Boston, and against entreaties he turned from it and said, "My work is among the heathen." He went to Calcutta, only to receive orders "to leave the country." He went into France and waited, and came again into India. Once more they had orders to "leave their shores." With heavy hearts they fled to Rangoon, a place, as Judson thought, above all others unfit for a mission field. Here he found bonds and imprisonment, but did a work that made him immortal. Park Street is still a great church with a thousand members, but the church Judson planted in Burmah numbers thirty thousand besides those who have died.   The year after Judson was driven from India Barnabas Shaw reached Cape Town with plans to plant the gospel in Africa.   But the Dutch authorities ordered him away.   He bought a yoke of oxen and a cart, and with his wife and goods in that cart he headed the cattle toward the interior.   They journeyed three hundred miles, and on the twenty-seventh day, as they encamped, they saw a company of Hottentots halting near.   This band, headed by their chief, was en route to Cape Town to find a missionary to teach them "The Great Word" as they called it.   Here again, was Philip meeting with the officer from Ethiopia.   These examples prove that the Holy Spirit will direct.

Who then can doubt that He will guide and direct our armies in the present awful world-war, so long as they are fighting for the truths and principles which He commands us to hold sacred.

CHRIST MUST BE INTERIOR TO US.—He had to go away from the exterior that He might become interior to His disciples.   It makes a vast difference as to where we have our God.   The man has no power whose God is in his church, his preacher, or his denomination.   He may be ready for controversy and cavil, but he is not ready for toil or sacrifice.   But the man who has his God in his heart stands ready—like the emblematic ox on the Greek coin between an altar and a plow—ready for labor or for sacrifice.

In the higher and super-sensuous realm distance has no relation. The soul puts distance away when it looks out through the supernatural. How near and real things seem when we cease to think of them under the dominion of sight and sense.

A captive child was carried far away, and the mother almost lost her reason at the thought of its captivity and distance from her. But hearing that the child was dead she grew more quiet and no longer thought of the distance, because her thought went to the child in that higher realm where distance has no meaning.

Our view of Christ is broader and more glorious than if we saw Him through the senses. The Holy Ghost lifts us up from the sight-view to the higher view of faith. Thus He lifts the nations. He lifts the Indian above his "happy hunting grounds" to a heaven of internal and eternal joy. He raises the Buddhist above the semi-sensual, and the Mohammedan from his coarse and material heaven to a state of holy peace and rest with God.

SILENCE IS HIS MODE OF MOVEMENT.— The very silence of His work leads men to doubt His agency. They want to see, or hear, or touch something, before accepting that agency. But the kingdom of God comes like the kingdom of flowers, "without observation." The spring months bring the warm breath from the south, ere you are aware of it, "The kingdom of flowers is at hand." Field, and lawn, and meadow smile and send their fragrance heavenward on the air;

yet all is silence. Who has ever heard the noise of
opening rosebuds, or the foot-fall of approaching
butter-cups?

So there come springtimes to the church, times
when hearts grow warm and tender, and the
church grows large, liberal, and loving. New
graces bud, and the "beauty of the Lord" comes
upon His people; and all without parade or demonstration.

The Holy Ghost must speak to the sinner from
within, before he can realize the sinfulness of sin;
and he must speak to the church before she can
know her danger from lukewarmness and worldliness.

There are many things to drown this inner
voice. You cannot hear the singing of larks when
on a train, because the roar of machinery and the
clatter of wheels drown the notes. The voices
and bustle of the world about us prevent our hearing the command of Him who is here to "Lead us
into all truth." The songs of pleasure, and the
babble of business, how they drown the voice of
the Spirit! Oh, that the church could get quiet
enough, and quiet long enough, to catch His clear
command, GO FORWARD!

HE IS THE COMFORTER.—And comfort is
the need of the world. The child with aching
head needs no tyrant to scold, but a mother to
soothe. Humanity is "groaning and travailing in
pain" as never before. One universal sigh going
up from the hurting heart of the race. Never in
history did blood flow and hearts bleed as now.

The cry is for comfort! Divine comfort! And the Holy Spirit is brooding over hurting humanity everywhere. He is trying to deliver it from the curse of sin; even though He must lead it through flowing blood and unutterable groans. But wherever a soul accepts Christ, the Holy Ghost is there to lead that soul "into all truth."

CHAPTER XV.

THE PRAYER ON THE CROSS.

"Father forgive them; they know not what they do"—
Luke 23:34

This is the first of seven distinct utterances of the dying Christ while on the cross. His mission was one of INTERCESSION. In agony and ignominy He speaks forth that mission and aim of His Messiahship. "Father, forgive them." To this end was He born. For this has He lived, labored, and suffered. For this is He dying, that sinners might be forgiven of their guilt.

HERE WE SEE HIS DIVINITY.—His works, mighty as they were, did not more strongly proclaim His divinity than did His final suffering and death. And Christ is now seen more plainly in what men suffer for Him than in what they do for Him.

There is no estrangement or separation here between Him and the Father. He begins and ends His agony in communion with the Father. "Father, forgive them for they know not what they do," is the first; and "Into thy hands I commend my spirit," is the last echo from the cross, showing plainly that union and communion were unbroken between Himh and the Father through the entire agony. Had there been an hour, or a moment, when the divine was withdrawn from Him, then for that hour or moment He had been less than God. The tragic gush of agonized emotion expressed in the words, "My God, My God! Why hast thou forsaken me?" This certainly never meant that God had abandoned Him. There are times when the human soul loses consciousness of the divine support. Times when God's child will cry out in tones of despair. There is a moment in the souls agony in coming to Christ, the point where it makes full surrender, when it loses consciousness of divine help, and of hope itself, and in the cry of despair it breaks into the light of deliverance. The moment of supreme helplessness is the moment when it is nearest to God.

Such is the meaning of this strange cry of the dying Christ. "It was the tragic moment of the soul reeling out of life." The consciousness of the divine support overwhelmed in the magnitude of anguish. The voice of His baptism and His transfiguration spoke in audible tones, "This is my beloved Son in whom I am well pleased." But here that voice is heard in tones that make dead nature tremble and the dead to arise from their graves. This is My beloved Son in whom I have supreme delight! As the soul's cry of despair is the prelude to its triumph, this outcry of the dying Christ is the prelude to that triumph which broke forth at that hour and shall sweep and swell until humanity is brought back to its allegiance to God.

SUFFERING BEGETS SELF-THOUGHT.—Nothing turns our thought in upon self so quickly and effectively as intense pain. It is not in human nature to be wholly oblivious to self when in deep agony. So much as a headache, or sea-sickness, and we become indifferent to all sur-roundings. Even the mother in deep anguish becomes indifferent to the pleading of her helpless child. But here is one dying in agony that is beyond language, and yet He is in thought of others; in thought of His mother, His brethren, and His murderers; making no allusion to His own agony, save in the single utterance, "I thirst." Here is the only touch of the absolute human in all the six hours of anguish.

Can anyone stand with the old centurion and witness his death, and study that agony, and not see him divine? Every student of that tragedy is forced to confess, "Of a truth this was the Son of God."

HE ILLUSTRATES HIS OWN TEACHING.— He had taught most beautifully to "return good for evil." "Bless them that curse you." "If a man compel you to go a mile, go with him twain." If he take your coat, give him your cloak also."

"If he smite you on one cheek, turn to him the other." But will He practice what He has taught? It is easy to teach those beautiful precepts, but will He exemplify them now under this terrible test? His tormentors hold their breath and strain their ears to catch His words. Will those words be a curse for their crime and cruelty? Cruelty that should "turn the cheek of darkness pale." Nay! Nay! But the first utterance is a prayer—"Father, forgive them."

It was also present *insult*. Time is a factor in our experience. We may receive injustice and insult against which we revolt; yet after the lapse of time the keen edge of the wounded feelings wears off. Our asperities soften, and ultimately we reach a point where we can forgive the offender. But it is slow work with most of us. It takes years and sometimes a lifetime to forgive.

But here is one not under the memory of long past injustice and half forgotten mistreatment, but under present outrage, "mocking and wagging their heads," adding indignity to insult; and yet above the murmur of their mockery the prayer is heard, "Father, forgive them; they know not what they do." Can this be less than divine? "Socrates died like a philosopher, but Jesus Christ died like a God." Take His teaching, history and work from the world, and from human consciousness; let there be nothing known of Him save the six hours on the cross, and those six hours will convince the world that He is divine.

THE LESSON OF THE TEXT.—The first of these is a rebuke of harsh judgments. What is more common among the weaknesses, even of Christian people, than severe judgments of the motives of others? We receive a slight, a petty wound, or apparent indifference from someone, and instantly we adjudge his motive as the worst. We regard the offense as intentional, while it does not occur to us to change places with the offender and seek to find an apology.

Here is the sublime lesson against harsh judgments. The tormentors of the dying Christ had hounded Him to the death, and are now gloating over Him in such a spirit as might bring the blush to infernal cheeks. No apparent apology for their cruelty and crime. But the divine victim, with eyes of love, sees deep enough to find an excuse: "They know not what they do." They are not conscious of the enormity of their guilt. Can the Master find an apology for His murderers, even while His blood is still oozing? Then can we not find a mitigating feature in the wound received from a fellowman? Have we not so much of the Master's spirit as will pardon a petty fault? "If any man have not the mind that was in Christ, he is none of His." May this lesson, coming to us from flowing blood, help us to look more leniently upon our offending fellowmen.

IGNORANCE DOES NOT OBVIATE GUILT. —He did not say they were guiltless because they did not know; but He urged this as a plea for pardon. It was crime nevertheless; but their lack of knowledge mitigated the fearful deed and made it pardonable.

The sinner in rebellion against God, knows he is wrong, but he does not know the dreadful sinfulness of sin. He knows not what he does, until the Spirit of God convicts him of his sins and reveals to him his real condition. Hence there is ground of hope and room for pardon.

Mark this thought: He prayed for the rude rabble and the beastly Parthians and the Roman guard that executed Him, but did He pray for the false disciple and the bloody-spirited high priests? This prayer does not embrace them. The prayer is for such as sin through ignorance. There is no petition coming from His cross for such as sin against light and knowledge. Here is a thought at which the child of God may well tremble. Do we not know what we do when we willfully sin and crucify the Son of God afresh; when driven by temper, or led by lust, or hurled on by passion, we break His commands? What plea therefore can be made for us? He urges the plea of ignorance for those who drove the nails through His hands, but what plea can He urge for us when we tear open His wounds afresh and create new scars upon the scars from which He died? We do not say there is no forgiveness for willful knowing sin, but we do say, such are left out of this, His dying prayer.

HE ASKED FOR HIS MURDERERS THE CHIEF OF BLESSINGS.—This prayer was not merely asking that they might be pardoned by the state, saved from punishment by their commonwealth, but was a prayer ascending above all earthly favor and asking for them that pardon that carries its benefits through all eternity. That blessing, without which all other blessings are without value. This prayer comes up from the great deep of divine love, not only measuring up to the forgiveness of enemies, but asking upon His murderers the highest benediction within the gift of the Divine royalty. The Godhead in manhood stands out nowhere more grandly in all His utterances than in this dying prayer, "Father, forgive them."

HERE WE LEARN THE GREATEST GOOD WE CAN INVOKE UPON ANOTHER.—This first echo from the cross tells us to ask forgiveness, if we would invoke the greatest blessing God can bestow on our fellowman. We pray earnestly for friends and loved ones, when they are sick, or in trouble; and the soul sometimes aches for their deliverance; but never do we ask for blessing of such magnitude as when we ask for their pardon.

Let the criminal be under sentence and in sound of the hammer that is building his scaffold, and talk to him then of prosperity, health, or even of loved ones, and you only increase his anguish until he is pardoned. There is more music in that word PARDON than in all the melodies of the universe. So with the sinner, when convicted of his sins, and under condemnation before God. Tell him of other blessings, and you do but increase his wretchedness until God has pardoned his sins. It is our duty to pray for friends and enemies, and pray for all earthly good to come to them; but we rise to the true meaning and magnitude of prayer for them only when we use the language of the dying Messiah: "Father, forgive them."

CHAPTER XVI.

THE PENITENT THIEF.

Text:. "And he said unto Jesus, Lord, remember me when thou comest into thy kingdom."

Human nature responds to the tragic. That which jeopardizes life gets breathless attention. The bull-fight will draw forever, and the aviator attracts the upward gazing multitude.

The gospel is laid in tragedy for this reason, that human nature is responsive to the tragic. The crucifixion was a murder, although the victim volunteered to die. It was human malignity with Divine self-surrender. He had declared, "No man taketh my life from me. I have power to lay down my life, and I have power to take it again."

The victim on the cross never died under three days and sometimes lived for seven, but strange to say, Christ is dead within six hours. His final utterance is not a feeble gasp, but an outcry with full voice, showing he has full strength at the last. He laid down His life. No wonder that "Pilate marveled that he was already dead."

HIS LIFE WAS NOT TAKEN FROM HIM.— There were all the forms of malice and murder, but a tragic laying down of His own life. He might have laid down His life in the quiet of Peter's home, or in the restful cottage of Lazarus and his sisters where were only those who loved Him, but that life was laid down for the world, and therefore in view of the world. In sight of the mixed and murmuring multitude, and in the awfulness of tragedy that shocks the indifferent and stirs the stupor of mankind. Calvary will thrill so long as human nature remains the same and responds to the tragic.

OBSERVE THE SCENE.—It is Friday noon in the holy land. The Passover is at hand and the devout of the nation are assembled and there is excitement in the sacred city. An execution is transpiring without the gates; a boisterous multitude crowd the place and weeping women from a distant hill gaze sorrowfully upon the scene. Let us press through the throng and stand with the guards in the center.

Before us are three crosses and on each cross a victim suffers. He on the one hand is a sinner and he is dying. His history is dark, his destiny darker still. Standing on the verge of a ruined life he strains his dying eyes in a vain effort to look into an opening and awful eternity. The thunders of an awful doom break upon his conscience and, like every impenitent, his death pangs make him worse, and he breaks into cursing and railing upon the innocent sufferer by his side. The ungodly ever die as he died.

He on the other hand was a sinner when nailed to his cross, but his faith has changed his cross to an altar. The cross of death has become the altar of life. His crimes covered, nature's crysalis empty and broken, he is new-born in Christ. His spirit, blood-washed and ready poised for its upward flight, as he has caught the words, "Today thou shalt be with me in Paradise."

On one hand a criminal; on the other a convert; and in the midst the Savior suffers. Mark the awful meaning of this triple tragedy! An heir of hell, a convert of earth, and the Lord of glory; all dying for sin. Read here what sin means, as the three worlds thrill through their dying representatives with tragic horrors! You who look upon sin as a small thing, look upon these reeking crosses and read its meaning in blood. "The wages of sin is death," and here we have its awful proof.

What a pair of words! PENITENT AND THIEF. They are coupled together, but the one destroys the odium of the other. We think of his penitence and forget his thievery. Oh! if this word PENITENT could only be coupled with the name of every thief, and liar, and libertine, and murderer, and sinner of every sort. Then would there be a mighty moral revolution on earth and a jubilee in heaven!

PENITENCE CURES PERVERSENESS.— Neither logic nor learning will do this. Paul had as much learning when he helped to stone Stephen as when he stood on Mars Hill. He "breathed threatenings and slaughter" until a "light from heaven shone round about him." It is sin and only sin that can make wrong things seem right. Penitence is the only answer to the multitude of questions raised against Christ and the church.

When a man tells me "I cannot accept this or

that in God's economy" I tell him to "repent of
his sins." If he says, "I cannot believe this or
that in the Bible," I tell him to "repent of his
sins." Hatred of sin carries us round to where
we get right views. No man can see straight morally while he is in love with his sins. It is when
we are in high hatred of sin that the church
seems most lovely. It is then we are most forgiv-
ing, most charitable, most sympathetic.

Penitence raises no questions. We have seen
penitents by the hundred and more; but never
heard a true penitent raising a question. The
true penitent has but one question. "What must
I do to be saved?"

He is dissatisfied only with himself. God's
plans, judgments, providences are all right with
him. I am the wretch undone. "I indeed suffer
justly."

Dear sinner, do you want every question answered and all theology made satisfactory?
Would you have an answer to the question of fu-
'ture punishment, the necessity of conversion, the
possibility of apostasy, and all other questions
which have occupied your mind? Then, repent of
your sins and you will find them all answered.

A GLIMPSE OF HIS CHARACTER.—This is
all we have, but it means much. The body of the
little drowned child having drifted to shore and
buried in the sand, with only the tiny finger-tips
exposed; this will indicate its race, size, and sex.
This penitent thief, lodged here on the shore of
inspiration, with only a few finger-tips of char-

acter in sight, yet from these we get the moral measure of the man.

FIRST. He had reverence for moral worth. A reckless career, and perhaps blood on his skirts; still he had appreciation of the noble and the true. The majority of sinners have regard for a true Christian man; but there is little hope for the man who is without regard for purity and Christian worth.

SECOND. "He was in a degree unselfish." Although dying himself he could thing and feel for others. He did not forget his fellow-sufferers, but rebuking the one, he entered into sympathy with and justified the other, "This man hath done nothing amiss." There is hope of a heathen or highwayman, but who can have hope of the man who is wholly selfish? Selfishness is a sort of infernal malaria which throws every noble impulse into chill, producing the stupor of a hopeless paralysis.

It is the curse of the day as if hell had breathed upon humanity. There are exceptions to all rules, but too many men in business think only of ready and large profits. Men in office think of promotion more than public good. And, alas! men in holy orders are sometimes more in earnest for fame and favor than for saving the lost.

THIRD. "He had a fear of God." He feared to go into the presence of God and asked his fellow malefactor if he did not feel the same fear? "Dost thou not fear God?" There are men who have no fear of God before their eyes. Men who revel in sin and laugh at the idea of a future retribution. They have their prototype in him who is spending his last and dying hour in railing upon his Lord.

FOURTH. "He confessed his guilt." What more common than the culprit's complaint? The last words under the gallows are often words of bitterness; but there is no murmuring here, "no quarrel with the law, no cursing of the Sheriff," no complaint of jury or judge, but a frank and full confession. "We indeed suffer justly."

It is a fearful character which has in it nothing that is noble. Here is a man dying for his crimes, and yet we find in him a regard for moral worth, a degree of unselfishness, the fear of God before him, and the candor to confess his sins.

BUT THESE TRAITS COULD NOT SAVE HIM.—All his noble elements of character have no bearing with Christ. Near enough to him perhaps to touch him had the nails been withdrawn, but Jesus gives him no look of pity or word of cheer, until the faith of the malefactor rises up to call Him "Lord," and his dependence cries, "Remember me." Then the pitying eyes turn and the pale lips answer, "Today shalt thou be with me in Paradise." Saved! Yes, but not through his noble traits but by his faith and his cry for mercy.

Here is a typical conversion. This man would have gone down with his fellow-thief to destruction if he had not flung himself on the mercy of Christ. Every man who is saved, is saved like

this man; by an absolute trust in the Lord Jesus
Christ. There are men who have reverence for a
true Christian, who love the church and honor its
ministry; men who are in a degree unselfish, and
who fear God and confess themselves sinners,
and yet are going headlong to destruction simply
because they will not repent and beg for mercy.
It is sin—unrepented and unforgiven sin—that
damns men. God can save men in ignorance, in
weakness, in anything but sin,

"They parted at the cross." They had perhaps
been associates in crime, fellows in prison, and
walked side by side to the awful Golgotha; but
they parted at the cross. Families, friends, companions, part at the cross of Christ. The cross
is the great separator and is "set for the rise and
fall of many."

WHY IS HE BROUGHT TO VIEW?—He
comes as a witness for Christ. We see him but
once. He crosses the stage and utters a few
broken sentences and the curtain falls. But these
sentences are immortal and without them the inspired Book is incomplete. "Is it not true that
at this tragic juncture he is the only witness for
the dying Christ?"

His friends have lost hope; the disciples have
fled and Peter has sworn he "did not know him."
The only voice to call Him "Lord" is the voice of
this dying malefactor. What a place he fills in
the line of gospel testimony! What a link in the
chain of divine truth!

AN EXAMPLE OF FAITH.—Here is faith in

its full stature. The sublimest reach of faith ever made by mortal man or sketched on the canvas of holy writ. It was a mighty faith in Abraham, when he raised the cold steel to slay his beloved Isaac. A strong faith in Joseph, as he passed the weary years in Egypt's prison. A tremendous faith in Job, when on the ash-heap with property gone, children dead, and deserted by his companion, he lifted his voice, shaking the ashes from his brow, and cried, "Though he slay me yet will I trust in him." A mighty faith in Daniel, asleep in the den with head perhaps pillowed on the neck of the lion, and the arm of the great beast about him as though it had been the dimpled arm of his own child.

These are heroic examples of faith. But contrast them with the faith of this dying malefactor and they fade as the stars before the morning sun. "Faith is founded on testimony." These all had great ground for their faith, which this man had not. He is a criminal and under death pangs for his crimes. There is naught now to inspire faith in Christ. His followers have lost faith, his claims have seemed fanatical, he has become an easy captive and is now a dying victim, abandoned by those who knew him best.

Nothing visible save the bleeding form; nothing heard but the labored breathing of a dying man. Can this be God? Could you have believed it had you been present? How deep, how dark, how dense the cloud that now settles upon him!

Just then, the faith of this thief flashed out as a

gleam of light athwart the bosom of darkness.
Like the strong-winged eagle rising above and
defying the storm, this man's faith defies circumstances, darkness and death; and rising above all
and into the clear sunlight above and shouts, "Be
still, and know that this is God!" Beyond this
scene thou hast a kingdom; and when there enthroned, then "Lord, remember me."

Can you reach his faith? If so, then you may
wait for the dying hour to repent. He asked little
—only the boon of remembrance—but the answer
is much, "Today shalt thou be with me in Paradise."

THE WITNESSES.—Promptly and at the moment, this witness came forward, and his testimony is imperishable. Christ's witnesses now
are not confined to a single cross. Figures are
mighty and seldom stagger. Like the giant Cy-
clops, who "carried half a forest on his back and
jarred the earth when he threw down his burden
at the mouth of his cave"—figures have weighed
the planets and gauged the seas; but they stagger and fall back in the effort to tell the witnesses for Christ. Figures have to yield to divine
language, and we hear of "Hosts," "innumerable
companies," "clouds of witnesses." It now takes
these terms to tell the tally of the church.

Organized witnesses without number. Every
hospital, orphans' home, or house of refuge that
dots the earth, is a witness for Christ. Personal
witnesses fill every rank. Rulers from Melchize-
dek to Victoria; poets from Isaiah to Cullen

Bryant; scientists from Solomon to Lionel Beale; preachers from St. Paul to John Wesley and Enoch Marvin.

There are but three worlds absolutely known to be populated. Heaven, earth and hell. And this is the only world that has an infidel in it. Those in heaven know the truth of our Christianity by its happy acceptance. Those in hell know its truth by the awful consequences of its rejection. A man may start to hell an infidel, but he gets there a believer, and sends, or tries to send back word to his brethren that "They come not to that place of torment." Whether we accept or reject the truth while living, the light of eternity will establish that truth.

CHAPTER XVII.

THE BURIAL OF CHRIST.

"And when Joseph had taken the body he wrapped it in a clean linen cloth and laid it in his own new tomb." Matt. 27:59, 60.

The crucifixion and resurrection of Christ, the bloody cross and the empty sepulchre, are common pulpit themes. Between these is the incident of His burial which has little pulpit notice.

THE TIME.—"When the even was come." There is a profoundness in the calm which succeeds a storm; an oppressiveness in the silence on the field when the battle is over. It had been a day of storm, a day of battle. A strange confusion of elements. A storm without a cloud. A darkness without night. A day unlike all others.

The "ninth hour" has passed. The hush of evening is falling upon Zion and the shadows are long. The noise of the city is growing faint, the multitude has gone. Golgotha is deserted, save by its dying and its dead. At this hour the faithful come to the burial of the murdered Nazarene.

THE COMPANY.—It is not large. You may now measure a man's standing by the length of his funeral train. Five souls constitute the cortege of the Son of God. A greater than Solomon or Cæsar had died, yet is there neither pageant nor display at His burial. No lying in state until the magnates of earth may come to do Him honor; no lowering of national ensigns to half mast; no echo of funeral guns nor stately moving of crape-clad steeds with nodding plumes. Humanity gives no royal regard to its murdered Messiah. He had wept over the world, but the world has no tears for His tomb.

Nicodemus comes with Joseph and the two Marys; a small but honored company, who, in the hush of the twilight, lay Him to rest and roll a great stone before the sepulchre's door.

HIS BURIAL HAD BEEN ON HIS THOUGHT.—Of it He had made mention and commended what seemed in the eyes of avarice, "a great waste." "In that she hath poured this ointment upon me, she did it for my burial. She hath wrought a good work on me." He made her memory immortal and we have the perfume of this broken box unto this day.

Christ was not indifferent to the fate of His body after death. He did not suggest cremation or other improved and up-to-date manner of disposal. There is something revolting in the modern cremation idea. "Sell me the field and the cave, that I may have a place to bury (not burn) my dead." This was the appeal of the "father of the faithful" and the "friend of God." The illustrious of the ages have honored the dust of their dead by giving it back to its mother dust. When Moses died on Mt. Nebo and his remains fell into the hands of God, we are not told that God burned him, but we are told that "God buried him." Cremation has no recognition in holy writ, neither in the teaching of Him whose burial is the theme of this hour.

A WONDERFUL PROVIDENCE.—The presence of the Father was not more signal at His baptism than at His burial. God is in it all. His humiliation is complete and ended. He is dead. Dead on a cross. Dead between two thieves and under the jeers of a tumultuous mob; but no sooner is He dead than the scene changes. His agony and ignominy ended He passes from the company of criminals and from the gaze of the world into the hands of private wealth and affection. Joseph and Nicodemus come with the linen and the spices, and the tearful women with gentle touches, to aid in the last ministries. He is laid in the new and costly tomb, yet pure and undefiled, "wherein was never man laid."

How different His birth and His burial. Living or dead "he had not whereon to lay his head." Cradle and grave alike borrowed; but the one was borrowed from the beasts of the stall, the other from a nobleman of rank in his nation. He said, "It is finished!" Redemption finished. His humiliation finished. "He has his grave among the rich and not one of his bones is broken."

WHAT DOES THIS MEAN?—This care over His lifeless body? It means much to us. "He is the head, we are the members." As the lifeless Christ form was guarded, so will He guard ours, and the dust of our dead, until we shall awake in His likeness. His care is as verily over the silent narrow homes of our dead as over the happy homes where our living dwell.

HIS DEATH CHANGED HIS FOLLOWERS.
—There is that in His blood which transforms
men. Nicodemus had been fearful and had ven-
tured to come to Him only "by night." Joseph
was timid and had been His disciple only in secret; but they are now filled with a holy heroism.
The one comes fearlessly forward to do Him
honor, while the other, before the oozing blood
has congealed, stands boldly in the presence of
Pilate and asks the privilege of burying the body.
It is contact with that blood that makes men fearless. It is this blood-contact that transforms
men. A bloodless gospel is a powerless gospel.
Take the blood away and Christ is "weak and
powerless as another man." Your modern "advance thought" gospel, which makes nothing of
the blood, does nothing in the way of saving men.

"Conscience makes cowards of us all," but the
blood of Christ transforms cowards into heroes.
Find the soul if you can resting in this blood who
knows aught of fear. It makes men fearless alike
to live or to die. God has said, "When I see the
blood I will pass over you." Hasten, helpless soul,
to shelter in safety under that blood.

HUMAN POLICY.—What we call "prudence"
would have said, "Have nothing to do with that
lifeless body. Pilate is unscrupulous, the other
Senators were consenting to His death, the people are excited. You are in danger and can do
no good. It will cost you criticism and perhaps
your life." But it is the body of his Lord, and
Joseph will care for it cost what it may. Had he

faltered that body had, perhaps, gone down in disgrace to the "potter's field."

THE CHURCH IS HIS BODY.—Like the body on the cross, it is ever exposed. We are to care for it and keep it from dishonor at any cost. What have we to do with policy, speciously called prudence? That prudence which says, "Do nothing that will hazard your popularity or cost you a criticism." It was Joseph's heroism that saved Christ's body from disgrace, and our heroism is to preserve His church from dishonor. Policy will never risk Pilate's displeasure nor bring a yard of "clean linen" or a pound of "spices" to preserve the purity and honor of the church. Follow policy and the church goes down to find sepulchre in the world's potter's field. The two sink ignominiously into one common corruption and into one common grave. It is *moral heroism* we need in pulpit and pew, in mart and market. Aramathean heroism that forgets itself and its own reputation and popularity and, deaf to the world's Siren voices, sees only the exposed body of Christ. Heroism that stands boldly before the world's Pilates proposing to take care of the church at any cost. Heroism that brings its "spices" and "clean linen"—its love and its service—to promote and preserve the church.

HERE IS HUMILITY.—How expressive the words "He BEGGED the body.' Rich, prominent, Counselor; yet He regarded it a privilege and an honor to care for the murdered form. No pompous waiting to be asked and urged, but vol-

untarily, readily, anxiously, He comes and asks
this honor. No suggestion that "it was the duty
of another." No fear that He would do "more
than his part.'

That is a beautiful grace that comes asking to
do something for the church. There is a grace(?)
that will do something when it can have its way
and will quit when it cannot have its way. What
if Joseph had been of the quitting type? It was
a time of adversity with the Master. Judas had
betrayed Him, Peter had denied him, Thomas and
the rest had run off and left Him, and His enemies had killed Him. Nothing is now left save
the bloody and lifeless body, but Joseph begged
for that and gave it burial until it lived again.

Here is fidelity which clings to the church despite her reverses. Though others, and even the
leaders, desert her, though she be spiritually dead;
nothing left but the lifeless form; let us cling,
Joseph-like to that, and care for it until the spirit
returns and it shall live again!

HERE IS SELF-SACRIFICE.—These men
were servants of the public. They were burdened
with responsibilities and cares; but these are the
men for whom God has special work. He has little use for the man who has nothing to do and who
wants nothing to do. The "business man" makes
a mistake when he gives himself wholly to business, with never an hour save on Sunday, to give
to the church. Joseph and Nicodemus did not ask
"how much they ought to do." They saw the
need and met it according to ability. Some are
quite willing to bring "spices and linen," but hes-

itate when it comes to washing off the blood and binding on the spices. Willing to pay if excused from other work.

HIS BURIAL PROVES HIS FOLLOWERS IN-CREDULOUS.—Infidelity argues His disciples "credulous and weak," men who could be made to believe anything. His burial shows that His enemies were more credulous than they, and had more faith in His rising than did His disciples. The very fact of their embalming Him, and "coming early" to complete the work, is proof that they did not expect Him to rise again. Joseph placed Him in that "new tomb" to remain until the final resurrection. The other disciples had gone their way and didn't believe the women when they said, "He has risen." Thomas said, "he wouldn't believe it if he should see him and see the nail prints and the spear wound unless he could put his finger into the prints of the nails and thrust his hand into his side." These are positive proofs that they had lost all faith and had no hope of His rising.

Not so with His enemies. Their appeal to Pilate, the armed guard, the sealed stone, all show that they believed Him more than human, and had faith enough in His rising to fill them with fear and move them to every precaution.

Here at His grave, where all seemed lost, we find proof of His divinity and of the truth of our Christianity solid as the tomb of rock in which He rests. The lessons are sad and weird, but they are presented for our emulation and are mighty evidences of the soundness of our faith.

CHAPTER XVIII.

RESURRECTION OF CHRIST.

"Now is Christ risen from the dead."—1 Cor. 15:20.

Christianity stands or falls by this statement. Like a bridge that spans a chasm with but one massive pillar midway to support it—the Christian system bridges the abyss between heaven and earth and the resurrection of Christ is the central pillar that supports it. Take this out and all is wrecked. "If Christ be not risen, then is our preaching vain, and your faith is also vain."

WAS HE DEAD?—Did He die, or was it simply a case of suspended animation? Can His stay in the tomb be accounted for on some hypnotic principle? Let His enemies answer this question.

They nailed Him to the cross. They watched Him during the time. They came to hasten His death by breaking His bones as in the case of the other two who suffered with Him, but they said, "we found him dead already." A crucified victim never died under three days and sometimes lived for seven days; and yet He is dead in six hours.

But they would be sure of His death and hence made the crucial test. "A soldier thrust a spear into his side, and forthwith came there out both blood and water." Not blood alone, but water and blood. Scientific proof that He was dead. That old Parthian spear pierces infidelity to the heart, while that flood-tide of water and blood washes its foundations from existence.

HE WAS PLACED IN THE TOMB.—His body lay for three days under the power of death. That three days was not a time of carelessness on the part of his enemies. They sealed the huge stone before the door of the sepulchre with the Governor's seal, and placed sixty strong and fearless men to guard the grave.

Six hours on the cross, pronounced dead by His enemies, pierced to the heart by a huge spear, then wrapped and laid in the tomb and watched by these enemies for three days and nights. His death was so absolutely certain that those enemies have never called it in question.

THE BODY WAS MISSING FROM THE TOMB.—This fact has never been disputed. His friends say so, His enemies say so. Then how, and by whom, was the body removed? There has never been but two answers. Either the body was stolen from the tomb or He arose from the dead. One or the other is true.

The story made up to cover their chagrin was that "his disciples came and stole him away while they slept."

Let us see. Were the disciples the kind of men for such a feat? They were few in number, timid in spirit, and had forsaken Him in the face of the mob. The bravest and the leader, had

"thrown away his sword" and swore he "didn't

know him." Living they deserted Him; will they now hazard life for His dead body?

To make the attempt was death at the hands of the guard. To break the Governor's seal on the door of the sepulchre was to incur the vengeance of the Roman power. Besides, it was the feast, and the moon was at its full. The grave adjacent to the city and the vicinity thronged with people from every part of the land. Hence to perpetrate such a theft was simply impossible. Again, we ask what would they want with the body, and what could they have done with it?

THE GUARD.—Sixty trained Roman warriors on watch in the pure open air with nothing to make them stupid or sleepy, and the penalty death if they did sleep. Is it likely that one of them would go to sleep under such conditions? Would thirty of the sixty fall asleep? Would fifty out of the three score? Would fifty-nine out of the sixty be found sleeping and only one left on watch? Would this last sixtieth man go to sleep, and all be sleeping at the same time, and sleeping so soundly that the disciples could come in a company, and with all the noise of removing the great stone from the door and carrying away the body, not wake even one of the sixty armed men all sleeping under penalty of death? All these absurdities are true, or else "he is risen from the dead."

They were either asleep or awake. If awake, why did they allow the body to be stolen? If asleep, how could they know the body was stolen, or who did it? Why didn't they arrest the disciples and make them confess the theft? You say, "The disciples had run away?" They didn't run very far. They were preaching Christ to these very men in less than two moons from that time. Charging His blood home upon them. Matthew published the made-up story and they made no reply.

If He was a blasphemer and deserved to die, then there was nothing wrong in putting Him to death. Then why did not He go as the other two went? If He was not the Christ, then why hold a caucus, and fix the seal and place a guard? If He was not the Christ, then He was the prince of impostors and far worse than the two who died with Him. The answer to all this is found in the words, "Of a truth this was the Son of God." And "Now is Christ risen from the dead."

TESTIMONY OF THE DISCIPLES.—Infidelity says, "His disciples were ignorant, weak and credulous men, and were deceived into the belief that he arose from the dead." So far from this, His disciples were incredulous. Notably so. They would hardly believe anything. Jesus had upbraided them with this, "Oh, slow of heart to believe. How long shall I suffer you?" This was true while He was living, and after His death they became absolutely incredulous.

When the women told them that He had risen they did not believe it; but it was to them "as an idle tale." When they had all seen Him but one, that one would not believe all the others. No doubt he said "you are a set of fanatics. Someone has made fools of you. You say, you saw him and saw the nail-prints in his hands and spear-wound in his side. I don't believe it, and wouldn't if I had seen it all myself. Unless I put my finger into the prints of the nails, and thrust my hand into his side, I will not believe."

But the proof of His resurrection was made so strong, so overwhelming, that even the doubting Thomas, with all the others, became His witnesses and sealed their testimony with their blood. If any fact was ever made certain in this universe, it is the fact that "Christ arose from the dead."

WHAT CHRISTIANITY CAN DO.—It can turn out its last friend and shut itself in with its enemies and they will establish its truth. This is just what was done in the providence of God. As "his hour" drew near in the passion-week, His friends withdrew and His enemies form the circle about Him and give their testimony. First, Pilate's wife. "Have nothing to do with that just man; for I have suffered many things this day in a dream because of him." Pilate, with uplifted hands dripping with the water of innocence, "I am innocent of the blood of this just person." Judas, who betrayed him, "I have sinned in that I have betrayed the innocent blood." The thief, dying by His side, "We indeed suffer justly; but this man hath done nothing amiss." The old Parthian soldier in command of the squad that crucified Him, as his armor quivered as he saw the convulsion of nature, "Of a truth this was the Son of God."

Here is the testimony of His enemies. "Their rock is not as our Rock; our enemies themselves being judges." Thus at the time and place where He lived and died and rose again, and by the testimony of His enemies, and by that alone, Christianity is established. Well may we risk the soul for time and eternity on such a system!

HIS RESURRECTION IN ITS EFFECT ON MEN.—St. Paul makes this the pivot of personal destiny. "If thou shalt believe in thine heart that God hath raised him from the dead, thou shalt be saved." Christ's claims center here. However perfect in His teaching, and pure in His life, all is failure if He be not "risen from the dead."

Joseph's new tomb, and that empty, is the corner-stone of the Christian system. The tree of life strikes its roots down through the fissures of Aramathean rocks, while its body towers heavenward and flings its shadow ever over every nation, kindred, tongue and people.

"If thou shalt believe in thine heart." Mark the character of faith. It is a heart faith. Mere intellectual faith never saved anyone. It will save from heresy, because heresy lies in the brain. But it will not save from sin because sin lies in the heart. Hence it is with the heart that men must believe.

You believe a certain lady to be the wife of your neighbor, and that she has all the graces of the highest womanhood; but that has no influence over your life. You see your neighbor's child, proper and promising. You recognize another lady as being your wife, and another child as being your child, and with this intellectual recognition you have also a heart recognition which makes their lives one with your life. A relation which causes you to live for them, and if need be to die for them. It is the heart that makes the relation. Hence, to believe with the heart is to have that sort of. belief that gives you away to Christ as you give yourself to your wife or child. May you so take hold of this great truth at this hour!

IT TRANSFORMS SOUL AND BODY.—It transforms the life here and the body in the life to come. "If we be planted together in the likeness of his death, we shall be also in the likeness of his resurrection."

These flowers tell us of resurrection power. How were they produced? How do we rear a flower? We begin with a burial. We put the seed or bulb in the ground and leave it there until God shall touch it. There is no other way to make a flower. You may work a life-time and get a thousand people to help you, and you cannot make a violet. True we make pretty imitations and call them flowers, but they are only imitations. But to make a real flower we must get God to help us. Bury the bulb and leave Him to raise it from the dead. Then you have a real flower with fragrance because God has touched it. Carry such a flower into the sick-room, and the sleepless sufferer will tell you, "This is a flower of God's make because its fragrance has touched me." We can always tell God's work. The flowers He touches have fragrance, and the souls that He touches have virtues.

SHALL I KNOW MY LOVED ONES IN HEAVEN?—Do you know your flowers after God has raised them from the dead? They don't look like they did when you buried them. You buried it a little homely nut-brown bulb, but it has had a resurrection. God has touched it; and now it stands a bright and fragrant beauty. And you say, "My hyacinth is in lovely bloom." You buried it in dishonor. God has raised it in glory." "He giveth it a body; and to every seed its own body." This is the resurrection body of your flower; and yet you recognized it when you saw it.

Thus we carry our loved ones to the cemetery and lay them in the ground. "Earth to earth; ashes to ashes; dust to dust." But God will raise them as He raises the flowers, and you will know them as you know the floral beauties.

If you can say confidently, "this is my flower," how much more confidently will you say, "this is my mother; this is my father; this is my precious child; this is my baby brother who went away and left us so sad." But if the flowers be so much more beautiful when God has touched them and they stand in resurrection-life, how much more glorious shall our loved ones be when we see them in resurrection beauty and life?

THIS IS THE SOWING TIME.—Young and old, parents and children; all before me are but a handful of seed in the hand of the great sower.

We shall be sown broadcast over the earth; one here, another there. I shall sleep in one place and you in another. Families sleep in separate kingdoms. Oceans beat between the graves which are filled from the same home-circle.

But we shall not be forgotten. The time will come when no loved one will be living to bring the floral offering to your grave; but God will not forget. Abel's grave in the sand, is as fresh to God as that of the little child where the unused toys have lain—but a night.

"The Lord himself shall descend from heaven with a shout." We have heard the shout of an army in battle advance, as they charged the belching ramparts. There is in such a shout something unearthly and seemingly akin to hell itself. You feel your hair rise and your flesh creep upon the bones. But, "the shout of God." What can it mean? It is language unheard save this once in all the inspired Book.

We make our resurrection life. Character made here is immortal. Tell me how men live and look in time, and I will tell you how they will live and look in eternity. Heaven never retrogrades. Hell never advances. Are you willing to be forever what you are today?

CHAPTER XIX.

THE RISEN SAINTS.

Text:. "And the graves were opened, and many bodies of the saints which slept arose and came out of the graves, after his resurrection, and went into the holy city, and appeared unto many."—Matt. 27:52, 53.

Contemplate the text for a moment, and it brings upon you a strange feeling. Here we have a mysterious company numbered by the expressive word "many." "Many of the saints which slept arose." How great the number we are not told. The only company that ever came back from the spirit land to appear unto us. No other incident in the world's history like it. And this is mentioned but the one time in the Bible, and seldom noticed from the pulpit. But it is written for our learning and brings us nigh to the spirit world. Therefore let us consider it sacredly.

IT PROVES THE RESURRECTION OF THE BODY.—"How are the dead raised up, and with what body do they come?" This question has occupied the human mind through the ages and has often been a question with you. Shall these veritable bodies live again? and shall I recognize the form and features of my loved ones who are now under the captivity of death?

Here we have a living answer to this question. "By two or three witnesses every word shall be established." Here we have not only two or three, but many witnesses. Blood-washed and risen from the dust of death. Not raised with Christ, but the first to follow His resurrection. "Christ the first fruits; afterward they that are his."

Here they stand before us today. Not spirits merely, but risen saints—saints who have come out of their graves to appear unto many. Then there is no longer a question of the rising of the body. Though it is a mystery beyond human reason, yet God has spoken it. "The dead shall be raised incorruptible." And here before us are living witnesses to His word. Then with God's word, and the living proof before us, "Why should it be thought a thing incredible with you that God should raise the dead?"

I am glad that St. Matthew, under direction of the Holy Spirit, has brought this company of saints to the forefront as specimens of resurrection power and proof that we also shall rise from the dead.

THEY WITNESS TO THE POWER OF CHRIST.—He said: "I am the resurrection," and here is the evidence. There was no moment in the Master's history when He was without a witness. On Friday evening as He went down into the death valley, though forsaken by His followers, He still had one witness. Just as the darkness of death was settling upon Him the "penitent thief" lifted his voice to call Him "Lord." He had but the one witness as He went down, but He had many witnesses as He came up. Witnesses the most reliable because they were saints, and saints whom they knew and recognized.

Christ had proven His power over death before this; had spoken and death had obeyed. Resurrection power was witnessed by the multitude at the city of Nain, in the ruler's house, and at the tomb in Bethany; but Jesus had never before gone down into the territory of death. But now He has invaded the empire, conquered and subdued it; and on the morning of the "first day of the week" He came forth, the grandest conquerer in the universe; bringing this resurrection company, as captives liberated from the power of death, and as proof of His Deity. When He went out of the world and into Paradise He carried one redeemed spirit with Him—the penitent thief—as a trophy of His last battle and victory when He won the freedom of humanity. When He came back to earth He brought a multitude to proclaim Him victor over death and the grave. These were His first trophies and the living immortal proof of His power to save.

DOES THIS OPEN A LINE OF COMMUNICATION WITH THE SPIRIT WORLD?—This is what the world has always wanted, and spiritualism—since the days of Saul—has tried to produce. Here we have in our midst those who "are living and were dead." What now shall we hear from them? These spies who have been over and up into the heavenly highlands and have gathered the grapes and drunk the wine "new in the Master's kingdom." What do they tell us? How do they appear, and how do they act? How do they occupy their time among us? What of them?

Strange to say, there is not a sentence, or syllable, left on record in answer to these questions. "The graves were opened; they arose bodily from their tombs and went into the city and appeared unto many." This is all. Not a word of what they did or said. They "appeared" and were recognized, and that is all that we are allowed to know.

They glided among the other living, and along the streets of Jerusalem, on that memorable Sunday morning; were seen and known, and we hear nothing more. They pass before us in this text; it is but a glance and they are gone. They come to light nowhere else in the inspired drama. Matthew lifts the veil and we see them as they pass; but why this silence? Why has not the evangelist left us something by which we could find answer to the many questions which arise in our minds? Does not this inspired silence tell us in tones loud as Sinai and solemn as the sepulchre, that "Secret things belong to God?" Here is proof positive that God intends the living to know nothing of the dead save what is revealed in His word.

Had it been His will that we should know the spirit world, then He would have allowed the testimony of these saints to be taken and made a matter of record to be handed down to us for our learning. But while He is careful to give the fact that they arose from the dead, He is equally careful to record no word that will give insight into the spirit world, or even flash a ray of light along the foothills of eternity as we approach them. God has determined that everyone alike shall walk by faith when they walk through the doorway of time into the realities of eternity.

Men have made many and great discoveries, but they are all confined to this lower world. They have made no discoveries in regard to the endless beyond. So you and I will have no better insight into that future life than Abel had when he was thrust into it by the murderous hand of his brother.

FURTHER EVIDENCE.—Christ, who "spoke as never man spoke," and taught us of all our duties in this life and of God's will concerning us; who dealt in parables the plainest and most life-like; yet was careful to give no description of the spirit land.

The Savior's silence should keep us silent forever on this subject. He has told us that it is not a heaven of "meats and drinks." That they neither marry nor are given in marriage, but they are as the angels of God. That He "is gone to prepare a place for us, and will come again and receive us unto himself; that where he is there we may be also." This is enough for me. I can rest on this while I live, and risk it in full confidence when I come to die.

St. Paul, when caught up to heaven, witnessed scenes and heard words, but could not paint the scenes, and said, "It was not lawful—or possible —to utter the words." St. John, in the Patmos vision, tells of what he saw. But the imagery becomes bewildering in its gorgeousness and grandeur and the mind fails to grasp it.

Curiosity would rise up and ask, "What became of the saints?" The scriptures are silent here also, and hence we can only surmise or speculate. But we may well suppose that God would not have His saints pass the pangs of death the second time. Therefore we conclude that they ascended with their risen Lord and made a part of the escort on His triumphant entrance when "The everlasting gates were lifted up that the King of Glory might come in."

FINALLY.—This remarkable scripture not only opens to us thoughts of the spirit world, and is a pledge of our own bodily resurrection, but it is a living and literal picture of what we are to be spiritually. They were raised with Him bodily. We are to be raised with Him spiritually. The grand object of their rising seems to have been to stand as witnesses for Christ and His resurrection power. Here is the work of every child of God; to witness for His power to raise from the death of sin. "You hath He quickened, who were dead in trespasses and in sins."

Mark their manner. They went into the city, right among the multitudes who had recently crucified the Master, and among those whom they knew and who knew them. Here is our field for witnessing. Right among the multitudes of city and country. Those who are blaspheming His name and transgressing His laws continually.

Those whom we know, and who know us. Here is our place to bear testimony and win trophies for Christ. But take note. There is no "lifting up of their voices, no crying in the streets." Not a word did they utter which is left on record. But "they appeared unto many." It was their appearance that took effect on those who saw them. They glided among them, were recognized by those who had known them; but they were changed, and wearing the resurrection body. It was their heaven-like appearance and manner that made their influence so profoundly felt.

Here, brethren, are our teachers. Let us "become as little children" and sit at the feet of these risen saints and learn to be witnesses for Christ. Listen while they teach us that it is not by the voice, neither by noisome demonstration, but by our quiet Christian walk as we pass among men. It is by our "manner of life" that we wield the strongest influence for the Master. My brethren, men of the world know you. And if they see that you are different from what you once were; different from what you were before Christ raised you from the death of sin; if they see less of the world and more of Christ, then, like the people of Jerusalem, when the risen saints walked among them they will feel that they are in company with a citizen of heaven who is merely passing and on His way to the Eternal City.

And specially did their appearing affect those who knew them. Here is our first and best place for doing good. It is among those who know us personally. In our own home and family. My dear friends, allow me to ask, "Are you walking with the quietness and gentleness of a risen saint, as you go in and out before your family? Does the beauty of holiness, the quiet glory of immortality, rest upon your every day life?

May God, by His Spirit, deeply impress the thoughts, and as we return to our homes thinking of this strange, mysterious, risen and blood-washed company, may He make us more like them and prepare us for a final home with them!

CHAPTER XX.

THE INCARNATE WORD.

Text:. "And the word was with God. And the word was made flesh, and dwelt among us, full of grace and truth."—Jno. 1st chapter, 1st and 14th verses.

Christ is here called the WORD. A literal word is a vehicle to convey and express thought. This is the only use we have for words. A word formed in the mind is an unexpressed thought, or idea. We cannot think except through words; a word therefore in the mind is a thought ready for expression.

Here we have the suggestion that God ever intended to express Himself to humanity. The WORD was with God. It was in readiness for expression; and when that WORD was expressed, it was the expression of God. It was "God manifest in the flesh." Christ expressed to us all the qualities of God; the love, the beneficence, the gentleness, the justice, the compassion, the power, and all the divine attributes. "In him dwelt all the fullness of Godhead bodily."

Christ is not only the expression of God to us, but when we exercise faith in Him, He then communicates God to us, and we become "partakers of the divine nature;" insomuch that we then think in some sense as God thinks, and love as God loves, and become to some extent like the Divine One.

WE ESTIMATE WORDS BY WHAT THEY EXPRESS.—We place no estimate on the literal word; the estimate is upon what the word expresses. We buy the luscious fruit by the basket, but put no value on the basket. We speak of "eloquent words," "beautiful words." We mean words that convey eloquent or beautiful thought. Our estimate is wholly upon the thought expressed.

So with the divine WORD which was made flesh. Christ is worth to us just what He expresses. If He expressed nothing more to us than another man, then He would be worth to us no more than another man. Christ, apart from what He expresses would be like Samson apart from his locks. But for the fact that He manifests and communicates God to us He would be weak and powerless as another man. A mere word whose human echo would die away with the hush of dying history. But as the expression of God, He puts us on divine and undying ideas; moreover He puts those ideas into living form in His own life, and unites His life with ours, even as the vine with the branches, and we become one with Christ in God.

WE DO NOT CONSIDER THE MAKE-UP OF OUR WORDS.—Etymology is not a prime factor in the every-day affairs of life. The little child, and the majority of grown-ups, take their words by faith. They know little of their origin or organism. They do not know what elements make up their words, nor why such words are used. They cannot investigate their own words. The linguist can do this only in a partial manner.

The little child can know nothing of the word "Mother" in an etymological sense. It knows that word is the embodiment of all its needs. That word is a vocabulary to the little one; and having that word there are no perplexities to the child mind.

So we are not to be perplexed with the mysteries of the Divine Word, the "Logos." It is not for us to halt and stand waiting at the mystery of the great deep of the incarnation; asking of the "how of the hypostatic-union." But we are to "become as a little child" and take Christ as we did mother as the living embodiment of all we need.

When we undertake to investigate the Christ-nature and endeavor to find, and understand, the two-fold nature of His being; what it was that agonized and bore the burden for us, we get into water beyond our depth and end in confusion.

INVESTIGATING THE NATURAL SUN.—A man of inquiring mind and profound research is much exercised to know the constituent elements of the sun. There are divers opinions on this subject. One believes the sun to be a solid globe of fire; another regards it a gaseous globe, while yet another believes it to be the result of the contact of positive and negative electricity.

But this man proposes to understand this matter and know what he is doing before he will consent to receive any benefit from that sun. When he comes to know what the sun is, and to understand its processes, then he will be ready to receive a little sun-life into his blood. But he is too profound a man in his thinking to tamper with a thing which he does not understand. Whereas the pitiable dummy has lived from the life of the sun all his days, and would have been dead and forgotten but for the daily coming of the sun to perpetuate his life.

Here is the man demanding to know and understand the mystery of the Christ-nature before he can accept Him or any blessing at His hand, wihle his very possibility of eternal life is in the Christ-life. All that makes life of worth comes from that mystery of the Christ-nature, which is too deep for the human understanding.

So we have to "become as a little child," and accept Christ as we did mother when in infancy. "Except ye become as little children, ye shall not enter into the kingdom of heaven."

I DID NOT UNDERSTAND MY MOTHER'S NATURE.—That was not possible to me. I only knew her as the embodiment of all that my child nature needed. When hungry she fed me. When tired she rested me and rocked me to sleep. When my head ached she soothed the pain, There was no want that was not met in that word "Mother."

And now that mother has passed to the better land, I have found another word that meets all the wants of my nature; and I know Him as the impersonation of all my immortal nature needs. When the soul is hungry and faint, I have but to tell Him. Ofttimes tired, but He gives me rest. Wounded and bleeding in spirit, when no other cares for my pain, He binds up the wounds and hushes the sobbing spirit to rest. I found no want in my child-nature that my mother could not satisfy, and I have yet to find a longing in my immortal nature which is not met in Christ.

A student, pressing a line of thought, was annoyed by the singing of a canary in its cage in the window. The sun was shining on the cage. He thought, "it is the sunshine causing it to sing." So he arose and placed the cage in the shade, but the bird still sang. Looking again he thought, "it is because it sees the robin in its cage that causes it to continue singing." So he removed the robin out of sight; but still the little creature continued to sing.

It was not the sunshine nor the sight of the robbin that caused it to sing. It was in its nature to sing, and it was singing out of the great deep of its nature.

The world is full of unhappy souls who attribute their unhappiness to various causes. One says, "If my financial condition were only better I should be happy." Another says, "If it were not for my unfortunate domestic relations I should be perfectly happy." Another attributes his unrest to another cause. All alike are mistaken. It was not the sunshine or the robin that made the canary sing. It was its own nature. It is not the infelicities that cause your unhappiness. It is your deathless soul crying out after God, who alone can give happiness and rest.

CHRIST IS THE BREAD OF LIFE.—He is the bread of the whole being. There is a mind-hunger which no earthly thing can satisfy. The mind, like the silkworm among the mulberry leaves, is eating and ever eating, but never satisfied. We get a new book and read it with almost ravenous interest, and in place of being satisfied we are only made hungry for another. We enter a new field of thought, and pursue it to exhaustion, only to fall down more hungry in mind than before. Only give the human mind time enough and it will eat up the universe and then cry with hunger, as did Alexander, "for more worlds to conquer."

But Christ satisfies this immense mind-hunger. He lets God into the mind and sets it to feeding on the "Living bread." There is no exhaustion from thinking of Christ, but there is a satiety that gives rest. How the tired, aching brain finds rest when losing itself in him! And Christ, as the "bread of life" and the "water of life", is ever present.

In one place in Missouri, and near the great river the farmers do not carry water to their harvest field. They simply carry a bit of pipe and a tiny pump, and driving that pipe a few feet into the earth and attaching the pump they have an abundance of pure clear water.

But the water of life is more easily obtained. On the train, when running fifty miles an hour, I have but to draw down my hat-rim over the face, and turn my thought in prayer to Christ, and thus drink of the "living water," that water, "of which If a man drink, he shall never thirst."

CHRIST IS THE FOOD OF THE MEMORY. —Angels prepared food for the Prophet under the juniper-shade and he journeyed forty days in the strength of that food. The blessings of Christ in the past are strength to us now. We have had loved ones—a brother, sister, or companion—who were a source of strength to us as they walked life's way with us. But memory looks back to them only with a feeling of sadness. A faded portrait on the wall, a sweet voiced echo in the heart; this is all. They were not the "Living bread." But Christ in the memory is its life and joy. No shadow when we recall our meeting and our walk with Him in the past. But the recall of His blessings awakens new joy, and the songs come back like birds after the summer rain. We are stronger today from some blessings from Him in the years agone and, like the prophet going to Horeb, we can go almost to heaven in the strength of past blessings.

CHRIST IS THE WAY INTO THE REALM OF WORSHIP.—The imagination, in the highest sense, is the more nearly divine part of our nature that spurns all limitations and rises into the higher sphere and paints the ideals which we struggle to reach. That boundless unpolarized realm is the sphere of our worship. There is where poets place their heroes and heroines. It is only in that realm that we can worship our God.

A god that is only human cannot fill the sphere and meet the ideal. Again a god, apart from the human, who is pure spirit only, is a God we cannot apprehend. We must have a God who is human and more, who is divine and less; a God who is divine and yet human. Christ is that God. He said, "I am the way;" the way of God to us, and the way for us into the realm of worship. He comes into our nature and becomes our "elder brother." We take hold upon Him and rising into the realm of worship we find He fills that realm. He is "all and in all," He fills our whole being; He is all we want and all we shall ever want. "The Lamb which is in the midst of the throne shall feed us, and lead us to fountains of living waters."

Worship is the result of conscious salvation. "We love him because he first loved us," and we never worship until we are converted and realize that he loves us. I feared God in nature, but I never worshipped Him until He pardoned my sins and I felt His love, then my heart went back to Him in true worship.

On an Indian-summer afternoon in the antebellum days, a steamer was floating dreamily down one of the southern rivers. A gentleman sat on deck reading a magazine. Nearby stood a colored nurse holding in her arms a chubby babe, and yielding to the dreamy spirit of things she suffered the little one to leap from her arms into the river, but with a scream she caught the little cap from its head. The gentleman sprang to his feet, and speaking to a noble Newfoundland dog which lay near him, he lifted the little cap and pointed the way the little one had gone. Quick as a flash the noble brute plunged into the stream and in a moment was seen struggling to lift the little form above the water far out in the current. A boat was lowered and with a few strokes they were reached and dog and child taken into the boat. The frantic mother had to be held to prevent her following the little one into the stream, but when the babe was brought on deck and she saw it was safe, did she clasp it to her bosom and rejoice? Not so. But falling upon her knees, with arms about the neck of the noble animal that saved her babe, she poured out her soul in a genuine worship.

Take that idea up into the higher realm of worship and you will realize that worship is the result of conscious salvation.

"FULL OF GRACE AND TRUTH".—Full of divine elements. Full of love, sympathy, compassion, gentleness, mercy. "God manifest in the flesh." And He cannot be made manifest in any other way. He cannot be expressed by any formula of words. You cannot portray a *man* by any set of statements. You may put me to thinking of the man, and give me some idea of him, but to know him I must see him in person, look into his face, and read his living character.

Then if a man cannot be expressed in this way how much less shall God be thus made manifest. God has not put truth in this form, He put all truth into a person, and sent that person into our world, and into our nature, "Full of grace and truth." Truth, and all grace in human form, like the sun, is seen only by its own light. All the electric lights and incandescent lights in the universe could never enable us to see the sun, if he did not send his own light to help us to see him. It is not that which we find, but that which finds us.

It is the play of the light on the rose-bud that causes it to open and receive its life from the sun. Thus light and heat, by a mysterious chemistry, produce growth and perfection in the flower. Thus grace and truth, through Christ, come to the soul. Truth awakens, and grace works within, and the divine chemistry proceeds whereby the character is unfolded, beautified, and made perfect.

If you would awaken a sleeping babe you have but to part the curtains a bit and let the sunlight fall upon the infant eyes. Immediately the little eyes begin to quiver and twitch under the gentle irritations, and the little sleeper awakes to find the golden light. The light finds the babe and then the babe finds the light.

Christ, "Who is the light," first finds us. We do not find Him by our philosophy and logic, but He finds us by His grace. Grace brings the truth, and the truth irritates the eyes of the soul asleep in sin, and the sleeper awakes to find the "Lamb of God that taketh away the sin of the world."

May the divine sunlight come through the curtains at this hour, awaking every soul that sleeps in sin, that it may find the light of salvation!

CHAPTER XXI.

CHRIST IS GOD.

"In the beginning was the word, and the word was with God, and the word was God."—Jno. 1:1.

Inspiration records three CREATIONS. The Old Testament begins with physical creation, the New Testament begins with the INCARNATION, or spiritual creation, and Revelation closes with the third CREATION, "The new heavens and new earth wherein dwelleth righteousness." That is, the physical and the spiritual perfected.

THE PREHISTORIC PERIOD.—This text carries us back to where creation was not and only God was. A period of which we have no history; but Christ was then with the Father. The idle question as to "how the Godhead was employed before Creation, finds its only answer here. He was dwelling in society with the Eternal Son. But the beatitudes of that divine society, and the themes which engrossed the divine thought, are questions only of speculation. When we have been raised to think God's thoughts, and have entered into His joys, it may then be revealed to us that the pre-creation periods were taken up in plan and preparation for human redemption, and for bringing us into glorified association with Himself.

As Christ's human history is now filling the ages of time, may it not be that His pre-human history will fill the eternities? And will not our felicities be augmented as we follow on to know more and more of the Lamb which is to "feed us and lead us to living fountains of water?" Shall not that history be the Standard book of eternity? Will it not be our Bible in the cycles to come, as the old Book has been in the centuries of time?

CHRIST'S CREATIVE POWER.—The verses following the text declare the Deity and divinity of Christ, both by His co-existence with the Father and by His creative power. "By him were all things made." Then the following sentence declares that "Without him was not anything made that was made." This fixes Christ's relation to every atom in existence. There is naught in the universe which does not hold relation to Him. This places obligation upon all intelligence. If there were such a thing as a soul which had crept into being in some other way than by Him, then that soul would be under no obligation to Him.

Christ said, "I am the door;" the door by which all things came into being. The sun in the heavens, the sea, whose mighty tide-throb is the pulse-beat of nature, the endless sky, with its ever-marching army of orbs; all came through the door of His power when they came into being.

THEN WHAT OF CHRIST AS ONLY A MAN?—This entire first chapter of John, in common with the other scriptures, proclaims the extreme absurdity of that teaching which makes Christ only a mere man. "A good man, but *only a man*." If this be true, and He be only a man, then we have a man dwelling with God in the pre-historic ages; a man before the age of man— a man equal with God and who is called God. We have a man doing the creative work. A man making the heavens and the earth, setting the sun in its orbit, stationing the stars, spreading the seas, and touching the creative spring that set the universe in motion.

This monstrous absurdity, that Christ is not God, is not surpassed by the absurdities of heathen mythology. I can believe that Minerva leaped living from the head of Jupiter just as easily and intelligently as I can believe that this universe leaped into being at the word of one who was only a man.

HIS DEITY IS RECORDED EVERYWHERE. —There is an ingraining of His gospel in every created thing. There isn't an orb that circles the heavens, nor wing that cuts the air, nor fin that parts the water, nor flower that decks the earth, that does not testify to His Godhead.

Give up the divinity and Deity of Christ, and there is no gospel, and humanity would stand before the problem of life as Mary stood weeping at the sepulchre, saying as she said in despair, "They have taken away my Lord and I know not where they have laid him."

But the Holy Ghost, who indited the Scriptures, has been careful to establish the Deity of Christ. Then it is painted, and graven, and written, and etched into everything in heaven above and earth beneath;

The spacious firmament on high,
With all the blue ethereal sky,
And spangled heavens (a shining frame)
Their great original proclaim.
In reason's ear they all rejoice,
And utter forth a glorious voice,
Forever singing as they shine,
"The hand that made us is divine."

CREATION IMPLIES OWNERSHIP.—If you write a book, or invent an implement of value, you have complete and absolute ownership of them, and the laws of your government protect you in your possession so that your right may not be wrested from you. By this law all things belong to Christ, although Satan and men have unlawfully possessed themselves of much which they have appropriated to their own service. But the law of the divine government will arise to the rescue, and every element now in the service of sin shall be brought back to rightful allegiance to Christ. And every accountable intelligence now in rebellion against God shall return to its allegiance or be driven to destruction. "He that believeth not shall be damned." This is the motto on the banner of the gospel, and all the forces of the Godhead are behind that banner to bear it on to universal conquest. It is destined to wave over every soul and every inch of this fallen world. "Without him, that is independently of him, was not anything made that was made," and without Him, and independently of Him, shall not anything exist that does exist.

The present is a day of soft gospel. There is much plush and fine-fur theology now on the market, and the demand for the same increasing all the time. Men like to go softly on Sunday after the jolting and jostling of the week. To be made uncomfortable by an angular and orthodox sermon is not the most enjoyable thing in the world. The soft cushion seat and the soothing sermon are greatly preferred. But luxurious upholstering and splendid furnishing will not save the ocean steamer when doomed by the elements. The storms which howl above and the breakers that follow beneath have little regard for sinking magnificence. Thus is it with a soft and luxurious religion which is not in allegiance with Christ. After all the gentleness and long-suffering of the Christ nature, and the liberal teaching that "it matters very little what a man believes," there is a "wrath of the Lamb"—a hot displeasure against sin—which will gather into the tornadoes of eternity and sweep away every intelligent being that is out of harmony with Christ. Sinner, as sure as God made you, just that sure He will rule you, or you will sink into destruction!

"IN HIM WAS LIFE."—In Him was the "Zoa," the immortal life. Here we have an introversive view of Christ; the interior divine essence. "In Him was life, and the life was the light of men." The light that was in Christ was that pure, immortal, spiritual nature that man had before his fall. "All spiritual life is through Him." "He lighteth every man that cometh into the world."

As the grass and flowers that beautify the earth
arise out of a life within the earth, so truly do
all spiritual graces, and beauty of life and character come from the life of Christ in the soul.

"But this world is not a friend to grace to help
us on to God." There is now a typical conflict
in nature; it is the time of the swelling of buds
and the budding of foliage; the latent life in the
earth is pushing toward the surface; the early
flowers are beginning to peep and the tender
leaves are softly creeping out, but the elements
are unfriendly; the night frosts, with a million glittering spears, have pierced the infant
leaves and flowers through and through, and they
now lie withered and dead.

Such is the conflict with the Christ life in the
soul. The elements are unfriendly, and every budding infant grace is met with opposition. There
are forces waiting in readiness to frost and destroy every infant grace. The first thing with
the infant Christ was a flight from heartless Herod who sought His life. The first thing with us
is to learn to evade and escape the things that
would murder the spiritual life. Christ lived
by keeping out of Herod's way, and the infant
graces live by keeping aloof from things that are
unfriendly and destructive. Purity must never
listen to siren songs. Helplessness must keep
out of temptation's whirlpools. Let the eyes rest
upon nothing that kindles unholy desires; neither
let the thought dwell on what is displeasing to
God.

CHRIST'S RELATION TO SIN.—The verses following the text present this relation. "The light shineth in the darkness, and the darkness comprehendeth it not." The original language says, "Restraineth it not"; could not prevent it. Nothing is more antagonistic than light and darkness. They cannot dwell together; where the one comes the other departs. Christ has broken through and is shining in the darkness today. Sin has held the world in horrible eclipse for ages, but the eclipse is passing; the race is beginning to see the light, nations are rising from the dead, new influences are being brought to bear, and the darknes is retreating. The efforts to restrain the light are fearful; they are both human and infernal. Herod and the high priests never fought Christ more fiercely than modern infidelity, in its various forms and heartless imperialism, are fighting Him today. But the "light shineth in the darkness," the world is coming to the light. It is coming through blood, and such floods of it as never before were known, but it is coming through blood to get back to Christ.

Heartless imperialism is in its death agonies, agnostic institutions of learning are being swept from the face of the earth, the rum traffic is flying in search of a place of refuge, the Word of God is being called for, and is read by the millions, as never before, and the hungry heart of the world is "panting after God."

When the morning sun arises the darkness must retreat. Redemption's morning is opening upon the world, humanity is coming back to God, and Satan cannot prevent it. "The light and the life of Christ shall spread and prevail until darkness shall be no more.

This first chapter of the gospel of John is as deep as the Godhead. Here is Christ in eternity, in creation, in relation to humanity, in relation to sin, and in His final triumph over the powers of darkness.

CHAPTER XXII.

THE ATONING BLOOD.

Text: "When I see the blood, I will pass over you."—
Ex. 12:13.

"For the life of the flesh is in the blood." This statement stood for three thousand years before it caught the physiologist's notice. Draw out the blood and you draw out the life; close the wound in its own blood and it heals by first intention. Nothing has such healing virtue as the blood. The eternal life of all flesh is in the blood of Christ. Out of His blood creation is created anew. Out of His blood are the issues of everlasting life.

Salvation is wholly of God. The bleeding Christ is the divine substitute for man, while there is no substitute for his blood. Substitution is the aim of the age, to eliminate the supernatural, get God out of the Scriptures, out of the literature, out of the experience of men, and account for all things on natural bases.

One preaches Christ as divine only in a limited sense, another that the Scriptures are largely legendary, and with hell relegated, the judgment seldom mentioned, Sinai silenced, repentance unnamed, and sinners coddled and sung to sleep with love ditties and soft lullabies, while the real gospel message is wellnigh an offense. The man who dares offer it is a back number and deserves to be retired.

But over all the word of God stood good in Egypt. He provided the lamb and required its blood over the door. Nothing more was required, nothing less would answer. A Hebrew might have substituted anything else and his first born had died.

THE BLOOD NEGLECTED.—Yonder is the home of an eminent Hebrew who has neglected the blood, but his dwelling is of the true Israelitish style, with an altar on the housetop. Every environment tells, like the features of the Jewish face, that this is the home of a Hebrew. Then there is Moses himself standing sentry at the door, and over the door in glowing letters shining out upon the darkness, "This is a Hebrew's home." Surely this home is safe, no danger here, when lo! the death messenger on dark and noiseless wings halts before that home and looks in vain for the blood. He bids Moses "stand aside," and, passing into the home, the death gurgle is heard in the throat of the first-born, and the wail of grief goes up to an insulted God.

Nothing else will satisfy. Pious parentage, highest culture, most correct morals will not meet the demand. The outward life may be of the most approved Israelitish type, a man of renown in the Church, endowing universities, erecting hospitals, building homes for the helpless. God makes inquisition for none of these things He maketh inquisition for blood. If the blood be not on the heart's doorway, we shall perish under the death angel's hand.

Salvation is not by nice behavior in my way, but by the blood of Christ in God's way. "I do this, and don't do that." Do what we may or leave undone what we may, to ignore the blood is to be lost forever.

God demands its preeminence. It was not enough that the lamb was slain, but its blood must be over the door. Then the inmates would go neither in nor out without contact with that blood. "Out of the heart are the issues of life." Hence it is upon the heart that God requires the sprinkled blood. Then the thoughts, desires, and impulses which pass its doorway come in touch with the blood.

The blood in Egypt might have been set aside in a private place and the first-born in that home have perished. How many have a slain lamb set aside in their theory, a crucified Christ in their creed, while His blood is not upon their heart and life—Christ not visible in their character, God's requirement ignored and they exposed to destruction!

There is a legend of a Jewish girl who was ill and nigh unto death, who had a strange anxiety to know that the blood was upon the door. Her father assured her that he had given positive orders and that all was right, but she begged to be lifted from her couch and carried to the doorway that she might see the blood for herself. And, lo, when they came the blood was not there. Be the legend true or not it carries its lesson.

How many ungodly parents have been called

to look for the blood through the influence of a
dying child! It is not that men do not believe in
the blood; they simply neglect and ignore it. It is
in their creed and intention, but they wait until
some sad providence calls them, like the father
of the Jewish girl, to look and find that the blood
is not upon their heart and life.

The angel saw nothing but the blood, he did
not see the inmates, he knew not whether they
were old or young, feeble or strong; but he saw
the blood. They were sheltered behind it, and
that was enough. Miserable hut though it was,
with inmates on their beds of straw, yet they
were allied to God with His own blood seal over
their doorway.

What a night! The first born in every unpro-
tected home must die. Nevertheless, the obedient
Hebrew with blood over his door gathers his dear
ones within and sleeps as sweetly and safely as
if there were no death angel abroad. O the sweet
sense of safety under the blood!

GOD'S ESTIMATE.—This rests not on position, office, social prestige, or financial power. A
man may be master of millions, make his corner
on every commodity and upon the honest toil of
his fellow man; a few such may buy up a republic
and rob its myriads of their rights, but when they
come before God face to face, their power will fall
into paralysis. Even the gold standard will not
answer at the judgment, it cannot 'make a corner
on the atonement and put salvation into a trust.
It is a blood standard there, and nothing else will
pass.

Dives in diamonds is an offense, while Lazarus in rags is the object of divine favor; not because of his poverty, but because of his trust in the blood. The Pharisee before his altar in high self-esteem is an offense, while the wretched publican at the foot of the steps has God's pity and approval. And why? The one is thinking of himself, while the other smites himself and honors God. God will see nothing we can bring or boast, but He will see the blood. Nothing else will hide sin; but the blood will hide it. I say it reverently, God Himself can see no sin in us when He looks through the blood. It removes all sin. Then let us walk through no day nor sleep through a night without the blood on the doorway of the heart.

The blood has a voice. In contemplating this blood the soul may well put off the shoes from off its feet. It is holy ground; its mystery laps back into the life of God before he had formed the earth and the world. It was in His thought then, He eternally intended to unite His life with the life of man. This precious blood was to ebb and flow in a human heart, even if there had been no sin, and the awful fact of the coming of sin could not change the divine intention.

Again, there is that strange property in human blood that it cannot be hid. Cain buried the first blood ever shed, but it "cried unto God from the ground." Lady Macbeth could never wash its stain from her fair hands. Thousands have tried in vain to hide it. "Murder will out." Blood concealed still has a voice. It may be silent for decades, but some fortuity, some unguarded word, some guilty conscience on its death bed will part the curtains and let the world see the bloody hand.

The blood of Christ has more than human voice, it speaks with more than "the tongue of men and of angels." You hear it in Holy Writ, from the opening promise to the closing Apocalypse, from Paradise to Patmos. It speaks through millions of Bibles to the ends of the earth. Ten thousand presses clap their great inky hands, printing out the pages that tell of this blood. We hear it in trumpet tones from ten thousand pulpits, while the lips of childhood's millions sing it in the Sunday schools of the land. The Holy Spirit also speaks of this precious blood in sacred silence to millions more. "There is no speech nor language where its voice is not heard." God's eternal thought has become the world's universal anthem, and creation is vocal with the voice of "that blood which cleanseth from all sin."

THE POWER OF THIS BLOOD.—Jesus said: "If I be lifted up, if I bleed, I will draw all men unto me." The blood is the magnetic power of the gospel. The mob mocked Him until He died, then returned "smiting upon their breasts." This blood at Pentecost extorted the cry: "Men and brethren, what shall we do?" And three thousand were saved in a day. There was no substitute for the blood over the Hebrew door, and there is none for it in the pulpit today. It is the center and source of saving power. The pulpit is weak or strong in proportion to its nearness to the blood.

A bloodless gospel is an emasculated gospel. God save the pulpit from the lullabies that soothe and keep men asleep in their sins! Better to have them wake swearing than not to awake them at all.

Its efficacy is absolute, it saves the worst and saves to the uttermost. Sufferers seek the world's Bethesdas only to meet disappointment, but the soul that comes to the "fountain filled with blood" is made every whit whole. There is no other Siloam. "I cannot wash my heart, but by believing thee, and waiting for thy blood to impart the spotless purity."

The sight of the blood satisfies. His blood is the blood of peace. Since that awful tragedy the sun has not faltered nor the rocks rent, it gives peace on earth. Have I sinned, and is conscience warring against me? I fly to the blood and find peace and rest. Does Satan assail? I bring the blood and the devil leaveth me. He turns from this blood with loathing, as an Egyptian would turn from the bloody Nile. Have I grieved the Holy Spirit? I bring the blood, and then He bears witness to my acceptance. Is God angry because of my sins? I fly to the blood and hear Him say: "When I see the blood I will pass over you." Am I dying? Let me breathe my life out under the blood. Have I come to the gate of the eternal city? The sentry asks not my name, denomination, or nationality, but he sees the blood and bids me enter into the joys of my Lord.

This blood is God's ultimatum, it is *omnipotence in extremis*, the pouring out of God's life.

He can do no more than utter the tragic ultimatum: "It is finished!"

The world had caught glimpses of divine love in the soft sunlight, had heard it in the Aeolian winds, in the breathing of the flowers, and in the low music of the gentle rain, but they had seen only the surface of the love sea. There was a sea beneath the sea, a sea unseen and unthought; it was the gulf stream of this nether sea that broke upon the world in the tragedy of Calvary and showed the heart of God to men. It took God's *life* to tell his *love*. Here is love in divine exhaustion. Behold this blood and know the doom of him who slights or disregards it.

THE UNPARDONABLE SIN.—What is it? It is the disregard of the atoning blood. Abuse one of God's mercies, and He has a million more. Break all the commandments, and when the law springs its merciless guillotine for your execution you may fly to this blood and escape the stroke. But slight the blood, count it a thing of naught, and "there remaineth no more sacrifice for sin." God Himself canot help you then, He can do no more. Logically, then, is your sin unpardonable. There is no other remedy. Here then, is humanity's only hope. Out of this blood are the issues of life. The life eternal of all flesh is in this blood. Come under its crimson cover this good hour. Let the sinner fly to this refuge. Escape for thy life! God hath spoken and will keep His word: "When I see the blood, I will pass over you."

CHAPTER XXIII.

TITHING.

"I give tithes of all that I possess."—Luke 18:12.

This was the devout boast of a self-righteous Jew. He had complacency in the thought that he gave a tenth of what he had to the Lord. He tithed his "mint, anise, and cummin," but these fragrant herbs were not the products of self-denial, they were not produced by subsoiling the soul, they were a spontaneous growth, cost little, and yet were about as cheap witnesses as could be found to a Pharisee's devotion.

There remains to this day somewhat of that green herb godliness, vegetable Christianity. Many are more ready to give outward things to God than things of the heart. They had rather cultivate a mint garden for the Lord than cultivate their souls for Him. Working at the soul is hard work, and the majority of people do not work at their souls much, they study outward things—their surroundings, personal interests, and financial prospects—but fail to study themselves. May we have a period of introversive thought at this hour, and look for a time upon the inner self, and see if we can say, with this Pharisee, "I give tithes of all that I possess."

WHAT ARE OUR REAL POSSESSIONS?— To find these we must leave the mint-gardens and the outer world.   The things that are seen are temporal, evanescent, unreal. Bayard Taylor said when in the Mammoth Cave, "I have been twelve hours underground and have gained an age in a strange and hitherto unknown world."

Let us, by the light of the Holy Spirit who is our guide, leave the outer world and come for a time into the invisible soul-world.   The outer world is only its attendant for a time.   Now, with eyes closed, we are lost for the time to the visible, we are in the realm of the soul.

How vast! How wonderful! How strange! No Mammoth Cave can equal it in magnitude and strangeness.   Here are mental and moral powers —like mighty engines—hid away, but destined to work on forever; nothing is here that will ever perish.   Eternity is deep branded on all.   These ponderous powers we feel with the consciousness as Samson felt the massive pillars. We see them with our spirit-eyes as Paul saw things in heaven. Thank God for the touch of something solid, something imperishable! Seventy years have we staggered among the things that perish, but all is solid here! Oh, how we love to touch that which is to endure forever! It is as if we were getting out of the shadows and nearer to God, brushing the dew from the bushes along the banks of immortality!

HERE IS GOD'S DOMAIN.—"The kingdom of God is within you."   On these interior soul-powers, covered as they are with the mildew and corrosion of sin, God has written His name and

stamped His image, and it is from these He requires His revenue. The mint, the money, the
material things, are secondary; it is from the interior soul He demands His dues.

Are we giving tithes to Him from this inner
field, this territory which is unaffected by drought
or flood, this inner land which His eye alone sur-
veys, this soul-soil which alone can produce the
things that meet God's demands?

THE POWER OF THOUGHT.—No power less
than divine can equal it. The sun is the strongest
object in nature. He rules the heavens and lights
the by-paths that girdle the planets, but He has
no power like the power of thought. Electric fire
flows through earth, ocean, and air, and the flash
of its angry eye is instant death, but it has not the
power of thought. Growth is a power almost akin
to omnipotence; it drives the roots of the mountain cedar down through the fissures of the rock
until the granite mass is loosed and hurled from
its home of the ages, and yet it has no power to
equal the power of thought.

Thought is so mighty as to handle all these
forces. Thought made the glass that gathers the
sunbeams into flame, and the harness which the
electric currents wear. Thought makes men what
they are. Men grow up out of their own thoughts.
"As a man thinketh in his heart, so is he." The
nations of men stand up as the product and incarnation of their own thoughts.

HERE IS THE PLACE TO BEGIN TITH-
ING.—Your thought is your best power save the

heart-powers. It is one of the best gifts that you can give to your fellowman—better than gold or silver, or the fat of rams. God would rather have your thought than whole farms of mint and anise.

Are we giving Him His tenth from this indestructible thought-factory? The thought-loom is never still and never runs down. When the body sleeps we still think in dreams. Has God one-tenth of our thought or one-tenth of our dreams? Do we give Him day-thought sufficient to produce a dream of Him at night? It is a poor devotion that doesn't give thought enough to make a dream at night. Do you ever dream of God and His goodness? The ancient worthies met Him in their dreams, and the truly devout soul is apt to have its "Beulah visions" and its "songs in the night."

Our farms, factories, and stores may show a fair revenue to God and to the poor in the final judgment, but how will our thoughts show—the thought factory which ever ran at God's expense, throwing off bolt and bale of imperishable thought to be unrolled at the final day? The power that made your home beautiful and aesthetic, added constantly to your estate and put your children in the way of success in life. How will those thought-products show in the judgment hour? They will not, they cannot die; then, if we are to meet our thoughts there, may God help us to make them pure thoughts, and save us from meeting an army of thoughts to bring the blush of shame before an assembled world! Let us be as glad to meet our thoughts as to meet our loved ones who await our coming. "Cleanse thou the thoughts of our hearts by the inspiration of thy Spirit."

THE POWER OF MEMORY.—The thinking power is not confined to the present; we may throw the thought-rays backward and light up the past and see it all as we saw it at first. We are so made that what we see, hear, or feel, we can see, hear and feel forever. We may get away from a danger or horror, but we cannot get away from the memory of it—we carry that forever. Every grief that you ever felt you can feel now, every beautiful landscape that you have ever seen you can see now. The sweet voices of childhood may be hushed in death, but they have not died out of your mind, you hear them still.

What vast range life has! Living in every moment that we have passed, and each added moment making life broader. Blessed be memory! It is God's own recipe for preserving the past in all its sweetness and purity. It is the legacy of old age. When years and toil have made us tired, we sit down in the shadowy quiet of life's evening and live over again the sunny scenes and happy days of the past. How natural it is as we grow old, to turn and live again in the past, and sometimes it is like an old tune that you loved in the long ago; you say "its notes are sweeter than the songs they sing now." So the memories of age are often richer than the experience of the present.

Do we give God His tenth of our memories? In

living over the old scenes, do we dwell on the association we have had with Him? Do we think often of the day, and the joy, when we gave our heart to Him? Or of the time when the sea of sorrow got beyond our depth, and just as we were being overwhelmed, a hand unseen lifted us above the waves? Do you remember some season of special grace, when you dwelt along the Beulah borders, floating by day in a sea of love, and having "songs in the night-time;" and when you hardly knew whether you were "in the body or out of it?" Do we give to God His tenth of those reviews?

Do we love to sit down with an old friend and talk over the past? Is it not still better to talk over old times with God? Do all His past blessings mean nothing to us now? Are they to be forgotten forever? Jacob had a blessing by the brook, and it is on record and we hear of it now. Paul met with God on the Damascus road and never forgot it, but told it to rulers and kings, and held it as a tower of strength in all after-life. If Christian people would spend some time recalling past blessings—go back and sit down awhile with God, and live over in memory the pentecostal seasons of the past, there would be a rekindling of the old life and fire in the Church. God will meet us for such conferences, talk over the past with us, and make the review sweeter than the experience. Let us give Him the tenth of our memories, and as we walk through the past let us "walk with God."

THE POWER OF IMAGINATION.—This is the thought power turned toward the future; it is the "Imago," the image-making power—the painter in the soul. Everything in memory is second-hand, we have seen it before; everything in imagination is new and novel.

God is to have His part from this wonderful power. In every plan, conception, or calculation for the future, He is to be the prime factor. If we plan for gain, it should be settled that the proceeds shall honor God and bless humanity. In rearing and educating our children it should be the aim to make them helpful to their race. God should be first in every interest or undertaking; paint no picture, draw no plan for the future without a view to God's honor, "Whatsoever you do, in word or deed, do all to the glory of God."

This opens the way for God's blessings. Some men never carry their business to God, never consult or consider His honor in their plans, and yet He is the great Sun, whose light colors all with which we have to do. The natural sunlight falls of itself upon every uncovered face and unfolded flower. The waking daisies have but to open their eyes to meet the kisses of the sun. The soul has but to uncover its face and keep the life uncovered and open toward God, and it is filled with all His fullness. And this we may do by putting Him first in all our aims and plans.

THE MORAL POWERS.—Here in the deeper nature lie the richer things. Here are the affections, sensibility, conscience, and will; here is where God is to gather His main revenue; here is where the things grow which honor and please God—even the mint gardens here have imperishable fragrance.

Trust and love grow here—the one positive, the other negative. Trust is the little child with arms folded and asleep upon its mother's bosom. Love is the little one wide awake with arms clasped about her neck. Trust rests upon the bosom of God, while love clings to Him with undying grasp. We honor a man when we trust him fully, and the soul honors God when it surrenders all to Him, when it comes with its interests, its destiny, its all, and nestling in the divine arms says, "O, God, I know not whither I am going, but I know thee, and that is enough!" Let some poor sin-tossed soul trust Him that way today, and there will be joy among the angels.

THE LOVE POWER.—This is the great unknown and immeasurable force which inheres in God's nature, and by its mighty dynamic power is ever moving God Himself. It moved Him toward us in our state of ruin; He was so moved by love that "he gave his only Son for our redemption." It was this love that moved Him to create our race. His mighty fatherly affection called for children in His own likeness, hence He made man like Himself, and the blessings that crown and crowd us daily are but the outflow and overflow of His love.

And it is this love, "shed abroad in our hearts," that moves us toward God. This is the divine dy-

namo within that moves us heavenward and causes us to honor God by trying to think, in some
sense, as He thinks, and love as He loves, and do
as He does.

Love is a divine electricity. It is too subtle to
be understood, we know it by its thrill. It is a
Horeb flame which burns but does not consume.
It is this love fire in the heart of your little child
that gives you joy. God put that fire in the little
soul when He made it; and its flame has warmed
your heart in many a desolate hour. You see the
light in the little eyes and feel the impulse in the
pressure of the little arms about your neck; your
whole nature goes out to it, and you almost worship it. "Call not that man wretched who has a
child left to love." This love-power is the power
of your child to make you happy.

The same is true of God's child. I say it reverently; we have the power to make glad the heart
of our heavenly Father. He is no unfeeling force,
but He is a God in moral sensibility. He is "our
Father," with all a father's feeling, and He longs
for our love. This is all He asks, all that His
great heart desires. "Love me with all thy
heart, soul, mind, and strength." This is all He
wants. Shall we prostitute this love power, turning its flame downward, and spend its force on
things that perish? Shall we rob God of all that
He asks of us? Shall we waste this only power
that can bring joy to the heart of our Father in
heaven, by turning it down upon the dirt and rub-
bish of this world? Nay! "I will render unto God
the things that are his."

We have seen that our real possessions are within, composed of the powers that shall never perish. Can we survey these powers—the power of thought, memory, imagination, and the moral power of love, and trust—then placing the hand upon the heart and looking up to God, can we say, with this Pharisee, "I give tithes of all that I possess?" God make us able to do this!

CHAPTER XXIV.

THE HUMAN AND THE DIVINE ADAM.

Text: "The first man Adam was made a living soul; the last Adam was made a quickening spirit."—1 Cor. 15:45.

Here we have the head of the race, and the head of the church; we stand related to both—ruined by the sin of one and redeemed by the sacrifice of the other. Between the two lies the great field of volition, and we come to the royal right of choice. It is between the going down in Adam and the resurrection in Christ that our *will* is consulted.

We stood in purity in Adam, but it was not of our choice, we were created so. But when we rise and stand saved in Christ it is by our own volition and choice; hence, out of man's first misfortune comes his highest prerogative, that of choosing a destiny for himself.

THE FIRST ADAM.—He is farther from us than any other that ever lived, and the distance dims the view. He is so far away that the picture is indistinct; he is less discussed than any other that was so prominent in history, he seems almost beyond history. Like the sun, rising on a clear horizon and suddenly passing behind a cloud, his sun rose upon a horizon of glory such as none other has ever seen, but passèd quickly into the eclipse of sin. We shall try to use this text as a field-glass to draw him nearer, while we try to look into his character who is the father of us all.

HE WAS CIRCUMSTANCED AS NO OTHER EVER WAS.—He was not born, he had no childhood, he knew nothing of the long and labored conflict in coming to maturity and into possession of himself, he was made in the meridian of a perfect manhood, he awoke to consciousness amid the splendors of the divine glory, and in the strength of a nature like his God. There was no blur on his mental sight or paralysis on his powers, he read nature as we read familiar lines, and gave to the animals names that expressed their several natures. With perfect mental sight and no paralysis on his powers, he loved his God. He was the first and the last human being who ever loved God with powers unaffected by sin. His was a peculiar love, a love to itself and none other like it.

HE FELT HIS SIN AS NONE OTHER COULD.—We cannot feel sin as Adam felt his. He had known only sinless perfection, while we were "conceived and born in sin," and never knew perfection. God puts His stamp upon everything. Everything in the universe has a nature peculiar to itself and different from all other. This stamp of *identity* is so verily a part of the nature that nothing can erase or change it.

You may expend a million upon a hog, and you cannot raise it above its hog-hood. Combine all elevating influences upon a dog, and he will still be a dog. Found a university for donkeys, if you will, and carry them to graduation, and you have a braying alumni after all. So in the vegetable world; cultivate the fox-glove and the nightshade to perfection, and there is death in them still. So in the mineral; you can polish the pebble but you cannot give it the diamond's flash. Beat the dull iron until the judgment, and you cannot give it the glitter of gold. Why this? The answer is, God's stamp of IDENTITY. The babe is born with a perverse nature as verily as with hands, feet and brain, and that perverse nature develops with its development, until God shall change that nature and make it a "new creature." And until this is done that evil nature leads the little hands and feet into mischief.

Adam never knew depravity, while we have known no other nature, and we know things by contrast. It is the force that intensifies every feeling. Sudden transitions from extreme to extreme produce a shock; as when a speaker suddenly drops from the sublime to the ridiculous, or when we receive sad news in the midst of mirth.

None ever felt the shock of sin as Adam felt it. He passed in a single hour from fellowship with God into the shadows of sin and death. Jesus suffered as never man suffered in bearing our sins, but Adam suffered as never man suffered from the shock of his own sin, hence he was the type of Christ in his suffering for sin.

THERE WAS NO PRECEDENT OF PARDON.—We cannot appreciate his feeling when he found himself a sinner and separated from God. We have precedents of pardon, we know of sinners of deepest dye, who have been pardoned, we have the constant and urgent offers of pardon preached and sung into the soul, but Adam stood in his sins without a single precedent of pardon; that sin could be pardoned had never crossed his mind.

The angels had sinned and their sin had been visited with vengeance. What then could he hope for? God could blot him out and originate a new race, and that without frightening a bird or withering a flower.

Think of preaching to a soul until it is awakened, until it cries for mercy in its despair, and then have no hope to offer; to whom you can tell of no one that was ever pardoned, and no plan or promise of pardon. Think of this, and you will know something of Adam's feeling in his sin.

HE WAS THE MAKER OF DEATH.—He sowed the seed of death and reaped the first and awful harvest in his own home and family. Death never came in a more fearful form; it was fearful because it was the first. They were not accustomed as we are, to death; it was to him and his a thing unknown; they had never looked upon a pallid cheek or pulseless form, and the sting is double since the one son has died at the hands of the other. They looked upon the one a corpse, the other a murderer.

I have seen a painting of these first mourners. The bloody and lifeless form of Abel lay upon the ground, the father kneeling by it, and the mother kneeling by his side with one arm about the neck of her husband, and her dishevelled hair falling over her form. The two were gazing down upon their murdered son with a strange, half-dazed and wondering, heart-broken look that bespoke such sorrow as could not be put into words. We are well used to death; the hearse is as familiar to us as the pleasure carriage, the cemetery as well known as the city. Not so with that family—they had never seen a grave, nor was there a human bone in all the vast bosom of earth.

HE OPENED THE DOOR OF DEATH.— Death is the dark and silent vestibule of eternity, but its door had never been opened. But Adam opened that door and his own Abel was the first to enter and tread its solemn precincts, the first to disturb its dust and leave a footprint in the hitherto untraveled way. But when once that door swung back upon its icy hinges it was open for all time. Vainly have men tried to close it— medicines, enchantments, prayers, tears, and even Christian Science avail nothing.

I have seen the father place an extra fastening upon the yard-gate, and the mother as she watched to keep it shut, that the "wee ones" might not pass it and suffer harm, but this gate of death, hung with icicles that never dissolve, and clouds that never rift or vanish, we cannot shut; we may try and cry in vain, the dear ones pass through and are gone from our arms and our sight.

THE LAST ADAM.—He is nearer to us and more closely identified than the first Adam. He passed infancy and childhood, and all the phases and experiences of life, and "was touched with the feeling of our infirmities." He stands over in opposition with the first Adam, as the fountain of life as against the powers of death—"the pseucha against the pneuma, the physical life against the spiritual life. Adam took life at its highest and purest and wrecked it; Christ took life at its lowest, and in ruins, and restored it beyond its original glory.

Out of the gloom came the glory! It was out of the cloud that settled upon Eden that came the refreshing from the heart of God. It is the child fallen sick that draws out tender ministries and loving solaces from the parent. It was man's misfortune and misery that drew forth the promise, "The seed of the woman shall bruise the serpent's head." It was man's misfortune that brought God closer to him, brought him to man's form and condition, and into all the relations of life. God came near enough to dwell in our homes, and teach in our streets, and stand by our sick-beds, and weep at our graves. The darkness of our misfortune is the background that brings out the glory of God in the highest.

THERE IS SAFETY IN CHRIST.—Infinitely better is our restored than our original condition. How much stronger as we stand in Christ. Mark the contrast—the head of the race and the Head of the church. Both had a battle with the adversary, Adam fought in a garden, Christ in a wilderness. Adam had all that he could ask, with only one interdiction. Satan struck him on that and he fell. This is the power we would have if we stood as Adam stood. We should fall hopelessly and that at the first attack.

Christ met the enemy under every possible disadvantage. With hunger and physical exhaustion, He met the attack which was malignant and repeated. Failing at one point, the enemy approached from another only to be stunned, routed, and driven from the field. This is our power as we stand in Christ. All the divine power is placed at our command. "My grace" all of it, "is sufficient." "Ask largely." That power by which Jesus conquered in the wilderness is at our command. Standing in Christ we can command it all. I speak it reverently, but this is what the divine word tells us.

Then I ask, Has not the misfortune of the fall worked for good? Are we not infinitely safer in Christ than if we were in original purity, and the soul resting on a single stake, and holding that stake ourselves.

THE LAST ADAM A QUICKENING SPIRIT. —Jesus Christ came to a dead world—a world "dead in trespasses and in sin." The planet was a cemetery of souls when the Son of God entered its precincts, but He came "that it might have life." "In him was life." He was a quickening spirit, He could send prophet, seer, patriarch and apostle; He could send hope and promise and light, but He could not send life, He must needs come and bring that. He was the true light, and the light was the life of men. He came that "they might have life, and have it more abundantly." Men began to be quickened and to rise from the dead as His life began to permeate humanity.

Whole nations have arisen, they are rising now, men in all lands are beginning to live this resurrection life. How wonderful the new life unfolding under His power today! The peoples of the Orient and the islands of the sea are arising from superstition and pagan darkness to the light and life of the children of God.

CHRIST OPENED THE GATE OF LIFE.—As the first Adam opened the death gate, so the last Adam has opened the gate of life, and this lifegate is closer to us than the gate of death. Time will bring us to the gate of death, but the gate of life is brought to us NOW. We may enter through it today. "Today is the day of salvation." "Strive to enter in at the strait gate." The gate of death we must enter. "It is appointed unto man once to die." We have no choice, but we enter the gate of life by our own choice. This royal right of choice is what makes us like our God. If we do but choose to enter in at the strait gate, then we have no fear of the gate of death. We will find it only a "shadow," and we may shout as we pass through it, "Thanks be to God who giveth us the victory through our Lord Jesus Christ," but refuse to enter in at the strait gate, and the gate of death will be a reality, horrible and eternal.

THE GRAND THOUGHT.—With all the shadows and darkness that hang about death, there is light all around. The first man who walked its vale, walked it as a conqueror. The first foot-fall along the silent way was the tread of triumph.

"And the blood of Abel yet speaketh." Abel was first and Christ shall be the last,—conquerors in front and rear. Christ will bring up the rear after His victorious hosts, and will review the old battle ground and see that none are left, before the final fires.

Then shall the death-gate close to open no more forever. "There shall be no more death." Think of this! Forever free from the fear of sin and death. How you fear for your little ones lest they fall sick and die! How you fear when they are grown larger, lest they fall into sin and are lost! But to have them with you at last, and know that the gates of sin and death are forever closed, safe in soul and body, and safe forever—that is the security we have in Christ. Weary, sorrowing, dispirited child of the first Adam, take courage! The promise is to "you and your children." Safety and rest that are ETERNAL!

CHAPTER XXV.

RELIGION PERMEATING LIFE.

"And as they were eating, Jesus took bread, and blessed it, and gave it to the disciples, and said, Take, eat; this is my body."—Matt. 26:26.

(A SACRAMENTAL TALK.)

AS THEY WERE EATING.—Men seek a place for religion outside the common walk and work of life, as if religion needed a place, an occasion, or a great ado. All it needs is to be permitted to pervade and inspire the whole life; it does not demand a place apart for itself, it is a divine breath, and only needs to breathe on and through our daily life.

We do not make a place in the clouds and the earth, for the electricity, it comes in and dwells in all those unless there is some repulsion or non-conductor to prevent. Religion does just this. It is the electricity of God, the elixir of divine life, coming in to fill every life wherein there is no sin or guile or resisting element.

CHRIST'S MOST IMPERISHABLE MEMORIAL IS INSTITUTED "AS THEY WERE EATING."—He connects it with the most commonplace thing in life, thus teaching us that we are not to hunt places or occasions for our religion, but make it the salt and seasoning of the entire life.

The salt and leaven are the invisible elements permeating and making the loaf what it should be, and what it cannot be without them, yet you cannot tell where in the loaf they are located. They are all through it, they have no definite place, and yet are the life and luxury of the loaf.

Such is the kingdom of God in the heart and life, not clamoring for a place or an hour, but satisfied to pervade and season the life, to beautify it and make it what God intends it to be. You ask, "Where is such and such a man's religion?" I answer, "It is like the leaven in the lump," it is nowhere very loudly or ostentatiously, but all through his life very beautifully.

When a man's religion runs all into one idea it is like the salt or leaven when it all runs to one spot in the loaf. Too much salt, when you strike it, is exceedingly unpleasant. Too much leaven in one idea makes the hobbyist, and to meet such an one is like striking the salt all in one place in the loaf. Jesus would have His grace richly diffused through our whole nature and being, making us beautiful with the "Beauty of the Lord our God."

We may have the highest communion amid the humblest work. He refutes the notion that we cannot commune with Him until we are abstracted from life's duties and isolated from men. We are to look for the grandest disclosures "as we are eating," conversing, toiling or suffering; either pressing life's duties or passing its experiences.

RELIGION IS TO BE LIVED RATHER THAN DISCUSSED.—Men give themselves to business

so absolutely that they do not think of inviting the
Lord into the store or the shop during business
hours. The sign over the factory doorway reads:
"Positively no admittance," or "No admittance
except on business." The Holy Spirit comes to
many hearts only to find the sign up, "No admittance except on business." And the Lord has to
have very special business with some of us if He
gets a hearing in business hours. Brethren, pull
down the signs from over every place, and hour,
and circumstance in life. Let God come in and
beautify life in all its common walk and work,
then will life itself become sacramental. That is
the way that "Enoch walked with God." He did
not have to climb the delectable hills and get away
from the world and men; he did not have to go to
God, but God came to him. All we have to do is to
keep the heart and life open toward God. We do
not hunt a place to put the sunshine; we wish it
to go everywhere, we make doors, and cut windows, and set transoms to let the light in.

Suppose we quit hunting a place or hour for our
religion, and just open the doors and windows of
the soul, and swing back the transoms and let it
come in and shine through the whole life, business
and all.

RECEIVE THE SACRAMENT AS A LITTLE
CHILD.—Our benefit from this sacrament is not
determined by our understanding it. It is easy to
raise questions as to how it conveys to us the divine life. Your little one at the breakfast table
may ask, "How the morning meal is made to be-

come life-force, and bone, and blood, and muscle."
Your inability to answer the little one does not
make the facts any the less true. The mysteries
of that breakfast table are as deep as the mysteries here; there is gospel enough on a country dinner table to refute all the infidel writings of history. A score of articles, more or less, with different excellencies, each distinctively different,
and all adjusted to the taste and enjoyment of
those at the table, and all from the same earth,
either directly or indirectly. To say that there is
not a divine intelligence back of it all is to proclaim one's self, in Scripture language, "a fool."

WHY IS THE LITTLE ONE AT THE TA-
BLE?—It is not there to raise hygienic or scientific questions, but simply because it is hungry—it
comes from a felt want in its own nature. The
desire is very real and it does not like to be put
off; it wants to be at the first table, and thinks the
time long when it has to wait. It eats and is satisfied and nourished, and yet knows nothing of the
nature of the process.

Even the "wee one" that cannot walk is propped
up in its armchair and fed and benefited just as
much as the grown-up ones. The babe is a very
unworthy member of the circle; never did anything to merit a place at the table; indeed, never
did anything, unless it was to kick and squall and
keep others awake. It has been a perpetual tax
ever since it came into the world, but we don't let
baby stay away and starve, for all this. No, indeed! If there is one in that home that is espec-

ially cared for, it is the babe. Its very helplessness constitutes its claim.

Thus are we to come to this sacrament. Not
because we are very wise and understand its mystery, and the vicarious death that it represents,
but we are to come "as a little child," because we
are hungry, and because the soul is longing and
thirsting after God.

Some of you perhaps have never come to the
table of the Lord; you have felt you were not
worthy, and, like the babe, have been only a tax
on divine beneficence all your life. Suppose you
have, what are we all but a perpetual tax on our
Heavenly Father? Yet He loves us and has special regard for His "little ones."

HEAVEN HAS A MULTITUDE OF ARM-
CHAIR SAINTS.—The church on earth also has
a multitude of the arm-chair fraternity. The
church—like a Methodist parsonage—needs about
as many arm chairs as any other kind. But our
Father does not love us any the less because we
have to be propped up, and even tied in the chair,
to keep us from wriggling out and falling from
grace. It is not whether we are wise and worthy,
but are we hungry for the "Living bread?" This
is the qualification, and the only one we need, in
coming to the table of our Lord.

IT IS LIFE-GIVING.—This sacrament is not a
piece of super-symbolism, nothing transcendental
about it, but while it is symbolic it is at the same
time real. It is not to be looked upon and ponder-
ed in some mystic sense, but the injunction is,

"Take eat," "drink ye all of this." Neither the real nor symbolic is to be ignored in this sacrament.

Men sometimes get so wise, so direct, so matter-of-fact, as to ignore the symbolism of the church. They say, "There is nothing very essential in baptism," "The Lord's supper is not a necessity," and some conclude they can get on without it. They tell us, "If the heart is right, that is all that is necessary," but the heart cannot be right while we habitually ignore the appointments and commands of God. He has commanded us to observe these things, and no heart can be right that disregards them.

THIS SACRAMENT IS UNIFYING.—"Drink ye all of this." The Master's design had not been met had one of the number failed to partake. His wish today will not be met if one of His children shall fail to come to His table. There is parental solicitude when one of the children is absent from the family board. The vacant chair raises the inquiry, "Is the dear one ill?" Absence from this table indicates spiritual decline and begets solicitude in heaven. It is at the table that the family all meet. Duty may call them in different directions in the toil of the day, but they come together at the family board. This table of the Lord is the one place where His children meet and unite on one common level. However widely their work and sphere of life may differ, they are one at this table. Though we may not work together on other matters, we are one family here. and "his banner over us is love."

THIS SACRAMENT HAS A VOICE.—How wonderful the relation between two hearts that are in love! We do not think so much of how we feel toward the one we love, but we think of how that one feels toward us. It is this that governs our feeling. How sacred the memento, the letter, the keepsake, that tells of a true love.

Many people are much concerned about how they feel toward God. They are ever at work at their feelings, work more at their feelings than at their duty. If every part of our religious nature were as well nagged and tugged at as the feelings we would be kept well awake.

I am most concerned to know how God feels toward me. His feeling toward me is infinitely more momentous than mine toward Him. My feeling may fluctuate, He does not change. Let me know how He feels toward me. You tell me of His wisdom and wondrous power, I believe all this, I see the works, I hear the voices—"the heavens declare His glory." I hear all this, but tell me how He feels towards me, a poor helpless sinner. Has He said anything about me, Hear the voice of this "body, and this blood." "He loved me and gave himself for me."

Ah, brother, men may deceive you, your own feelings may deceive you, but there is no deception in this dying testimony of the Son of God, sealed with the blood of His own heart. "God loves us with an everlasting love." Other loves may weaken and die, and there is no chill like the chill of an expiring love, but when all others have ceased to love me, Jesus will love me still.

THIS SACRAMENT CONFIRMS THE RES-
URRECTION.—The life work of Christ was to
bring the human into one with the divine, and
that life was a connected life—no lapses, no mistakes, no disjointures. All His acts were relation-
al; the deeds of His life are as a golden chain,
quarried at first from the depths of infinite love,
forged in the fires of vicarious suffering, and
drawn by the hand of self-abnegation through human destiny and made eternally fast to the throne
of God, and this last and final act, this instituted
sacrament, connects not only with His death, but
with His final coming. It points to the judgment
as well as to the cross, it is to "show forth His
death." That is true, but for how long? "Until
His coming again."

His work was two-fold. It was as verily for the
body as for the soul. He bears our sicknesses as
well as our sins, He inserts Himself into the woes
and wants of the body as well as into the soul.
This sacrament holds Him forth as redeemer of
soul and body, and does it through emblems of
His own body and life. It keeps the resurrection
body clearly in view. If He had intended for the
soul to live without the resurrection body, then
He would have used wine without the bread, He
would simply have represented the life without
the body. But it was Himself for myself, His
body for my body, His soul for my soul.

Careful to save us from the fogs of mysticism
by keeping the resurrection body in sight, hence,
when we receive this bread we receive Christ's

own pledge that these very bodies, receiving it, shall live forever and be fed and nourished by Him whom it represents.

As we "feed on him here by faith," so shall we feed at His hands hereafter, "for the Lamb which is in the midst of the throne shall feed us, and shall lead us to fountains of living waters."

CHAPTER XXVI.

DIVINE HUMAN PARTNERSHIP.

"We are laborers together with God."—1 Cor. 3:9.

This text announces a "Labor Union" of God with man. This earth is like a ball which is played back and forth between two, it plays between the human and the divine. While man works upon it, God works in and through it, thus co-working with God, man produces that on which he lives, gets physical development and some lessons to prepare him for the higher realities of the other and endless life, while the church is the training-school, educating us for those higher realities.

THIS PARTNERSHIP WAS PLANNED IN CREATION.—God could have made the world all that we have made it. He could have flecked it with fields and dotted it with cities. It were as easy for Him to place the marble in the palace wall as to bury it fathoms deep in the quarry, and to spread the meadow with its velvet finish as to create the jungle out of which the meadow is evolved. But He created with the view of partnership and co-working with us. He made the crude elements, and then made one in His own likeness to polish them; hence it was left for man to change the wilderness into the classic grounds where cities rise and villas nestle.

God could have made us—like the first pair—in full maturity and without the processes through which we pass in coming up to man and woman-hood, but character is involved, and that must be of our own making. God could give us a nature, but could not give us character. This was the absent element in Adam; he was pure, but that purity was not of his own choice; God made him pure, while he had no volition in the matter.

WE ARE UNDER GRACE.—We are safer, standing under grace in Christ than Adam was standing in his own native purity. Grace always begins at the bottom—I am glad this is so. Had grace begun higher it might have passed over me and left me out. Grace begins with infancy—at the lowest point—and it begins with volition, continues with volition and ends with volition; volition is the keynote of salvation, In the words of the Master, it is unto everyone, "be it unto thee even as thou wilt." When we have pressed on and up, and toiled and suffered, until we have come to full character in Christ, that character has in it the spinal column of volition. As the storms bend, but strengthen, the giant oak, the life-storms make the bone and sinew of Christian character. The soul combats and conquers the opposing forces in coming to full character, and therefore is better prepared to "hold fast that whereunto it has attained."

THIS GIVES CHANCE TO MAKE OUR-SELVES.—We often hear of "self-made men," as if there were any other kind of men. Every man is self-made; his fortune may be an inheritance, and his reputation an accident, but his self-hood is of his own making. Some have ready-made facilities, while others have to make their facilities, and then make themselves. One has the University, while another has the pine-knots and the chimney-corner for his study, but both alike must labor to come to scholarship. So in Christian life, one may have facilities far beyond another, but each must make character for himself. You are but a specimen of your own work; every man is just what he has made himself under grace.

Some men fear the day of judgment. This is strange when every man determines his own destiny. The day of judgment will not affect your destiny in the least, you fix your own destiny, and God simply places His seal on what you have done—nothing more. This day is fraught with things more dreadful than the day of judgment, and is more to be dreaded.

GOD'S PURPOSE IN THE PARTNERSHIP. —There is nothing of the mercenary in His purpose. Men seek partnerships for profit. Among the many advertisements which I have seen, I have never seen one calling for a "bankrupt." You want a partner with capital, influence, business ability, something to your advantage in the compact, but it is the wonder of grace that God seeks association with creatures without capital—a race of moral bankrupts, "without God and without hope in the world."

His aim is not speculation, there is nothing to be made off a race of bankrupts. God is not in the partnership for what He can make off us, but for what He can make out of us, what He can make us to become. "He was rich, yet for our sakes he became poor, that we, through his poverty, might be rich." He has invested His love, His labor, and His life, that He may bring us from bankruptcy to boundless wealth.

The old notion that "God's chief end is to glorify himself," is a reflection on the divine character; it makes Him the impersonation of infinite selfishness; just such a God as some men would be, if we could raise them to god-hood. If you will say that "man's chief end is to glorify himself," you will come nearer the truth. All the risk is upon God's part in this partnership. We need not hesitate, we risk nothing, because we have nothing to risk. Stay out of this labor-union with God, and we go to destruction at best.

THE REQUISITION FOR MONOPOLY MEMBERSHIP.—None can be members of a great monopoly save the money kings. The moneyless toiler can have no part, but Christ gives the poorest a part in the great work of rescuing the race. The Bible was written by men, the gospel is preached by men, the songs composed by men; only one thing in which we can have no part, and that is in the atonement.

When "his hour had come," He said to the three favored disciples, "Tarry ye here while I go and pray yonder." There was a circle into which they could not enter. "He must, and did, "tread the winepress alone." Outside of this sacred circle we have part and partnership in all that God does.

GOD FURNISHES ALL THE CAPITAL-STOCK.—We are co-workers with Him, but we are not join stockholders. He provides the soil, seed, sunshine, and rain, then takes us into the work with Him to plow, plant, sow, and reap, and "gather into barns." We are but handling our Lord's material, while we have invested nothing and have nothing to invest.

So in the realm of grace. God puts in the capital-stock, "without me ye can do nothing." I have no countenance for this idea that man has a certain amount of purity and power by which he may lift himself to moral eminence and excellence. As well talk of lifting himself by his own boot-straps. In either case the downward gravitation is greater than the upward force.

Just as we get vegetable life out of the earth by the power of the sun, so we get spiritual life out of the incarnation, by the power of the Holy Ghost. Our resources are all in Christ. The incarnation is God come to us in such manner that we may apprehend and appropriate Him. Out of the riches of the atonement we grow the graces, as the fruits and flowers out of the earth. Every virtue we have is a levy upon the investment He has made for us.

To illustrate: In my fancy I heard a tiny baby-apple talking to itself. It was a wee thing, just born into the world and resting in its bloom, had not yet put off its long, white baby clothes. I heard it say, "Here I am, away out on the tip of this limb, and perfectly helpless. I cannot run, walk, or fly, and I need so many things; I need strength from the earth, light from the sun, nourishment from the rains, and yet, all I can do is just to cling to this stem." And that was all it did, but the tree furnished everything—life from the earth, strength from the sun, nourishment from the rains; everything it needed. And that little apple grew, ripened, got large, and mellow, and rosy; a temptation to every boy that passed that orchard.

So we have only to "abide in Christ." And drawing all our resources from Him, we grow and ripen, bringing forth sweet hope, and rich faith, and mellow peace, and all the fruits of the Spirit.

GOD DOES ONLY WHAT WE CANNOT DO. —He gives seed and soil, then waits for us to plow and plant, and He will leave the seed to rot, and the sower to perish before He will do our part. He will do nothing for us that we can do for ourselves. There are things essential to us, and yet to us impossible. These constitute His part in the partnership. He does the impossible things, He is the God of the extreme hours, "a present help in time of need."

God aims for the church to save the world; His blood is upon it, His Spirit leading it, His gospel the weapon in its hand, and His command impelling it. "Go ye into all the world and preach my gospel to every creature." And He will no sooner carry the gospel independently of the church than He will plow and plant independently of us. If we fail the heathens perish, and their blood will

He require of us, hence we see that unless we try to save the heathen we ourselves cannot be saved. It is a solemn thing to belong to God's church and be in partnership with Him, it is just as easy to go down to hell in the church as out of it.

HOW WE GET OWNERSHIP.—While we have nothing to put into the compact, yet our labor invested produces a real possession. Only self-investment can produce ownership. Give a youth great wealth when he comes to his majority, and he has title to a fortune, but does not own it, and soon perhaps someone else owns him and the fortune too. He did not own it because he had made no self-investment in it—had not invested his brain, thought, and muscle, sufficiently to make it his own.

God intended us for ownership, hence He made the world in the rough that we might transform it by our labor, and so get ownership; and out of the wilderness we have now what we call "our lands, our farms, our cities." And what made them ours? Simply the energy, industry, and selfhood which we invested in them.

You knew the old farm on which you grew up, every old stump, slipgap, and crooked rail in the fence where you crawled through until you wore the place slick. You plowed that old farm until you plowed yourself into it, and got an ownership that will never perish; you call it now "your old home."

So we get ownership in souls, as you did in the old farm, by expending labor, energy, and suffering, to bring them to higher and nobler character, and there is no joy like it. Observe your flowers on a hot summer evening, wilted and drooping, the heliotropes fainting, the fuchias sick, the geraniums adroop. You bring the cool water, and under the sprinkling they revive and lift up their heads, and you feel a peculiar pleasure. But to go out into the great sweltering world where souls are sick, and faint, and dying, to go into the places of poverty and carry "the water of life," and see those souls revive under your ministry—there is no joy like this—not watering flowers, but watering souls. This is coming to ownership, this is getting rich with riches that can never perish. St. Paul understood it when he said of Philippi, "Ye are my glory, my joy, my crown." This is true wealth. There is no real property after all, but spirit property; all material ownership ends with time, our real and lasting possessions will be the betterment that we get upon our own souls and the souls of others. This wealth will endure.

THE ONE WORK OF THE CHURCH.—That one work is to SAVE SOULS. God did not establish the church simply to take care of herself, He will take care of her, while she tries to save the world. He expects the church to reach men in all conditions, the lowest as well as the highest. There is no soul so debased, and no place so disreputable, as to be out of the range of our commission. It is to "every creature." We hear a man say, "We must guard the church." If the church will do her work, God will guard her while she does it.

Suppose the sun should take a notion to take care of himself, and should say, "I am a fine old sun and cannot take risks of contamination; I cannot afford to go into the dells and bogs among the slimy serpents and noxious vapors, and poisonous fungi; I cannot afford to shine into the huts and hovels, and places of squalor, and disease; I am going to stay out on the high places where the air is pure."

But God didn't set the sun in the heavens for any such self-service. It is the low places that most need His light and warmth; it is the dwelling of misery that has hardly any other blessing, that most rejoices to "let the blessed sunshine in." It is the poorest and most abandoned who most need the ministries of the church. We are to open the way for the "Sun of Righteousness" into the jails, the penitentiaries, work-houses, and chain-gangs; we are to reach the lowest and most hopeless. "The mission of the Master is to save that which was lost."

I've seen men with whom I was familiar, as they came out of battle, so covered unto blackness with powder, and perspiration, and dust, that I did not recognize them, but they were also covered with the glory of triumph. What if the church at the last day shall stand weather-beaten and scarred and powder-begrimed, and her war-harness wellworn? What of that, if she has only done her work, and won her victory? Oh, that the church may forget herself in her God-appointed mission to save humanity!

OUTSIDE THIS PARTNERSHIP THE CHURCH IS POWERLESS.—Find the church which has stood for years as a place of Sunday-resort and without a conversion in all that time, and you find a church which has dissolved partnership with God, and is doing business for itself, satisfied if it has the preacher it wants, the music it wants, and the tone it wants. Such a church has not much interest in the unsaved at home or in the heathen abroad.

There are vast buildings, representing hundreds of members, and millions of money, and run at a cost of thousands a year, yet withal, no souls brought to Christ, and we call them "churches," whereas, they are simply magnificent dead-houses, majestic mausoleums, wherein the spiritually dead are sleeping.

FINALLY.—Try your telephone when the connection is not perfect, and you have a faint and far-off jargon. You call, "Central, please give me a better connection". Now you hear distinctly, and recognize the voice. What our Methodism needs is a better connection with the source of her power, a clearer utterance from God. Oh, that the Holy Spirit—the central Agent—may give to our Zion a closer and clearer connection, that she may feel the thrill and recognize the voice and orders from her divine Commander!

The sine qua non is not more money, more churches more higher education. All good and desirable, but the need of the hour is fewer dead churches and more life in those that are not dead.

Give us the full tide of the divine life in the thirty thousand churches in our Methodism and we will soon capture this southland for Christ.

There stood a vast merchant mill, built at great cost, with massive walls and splendid machinery, all complete, and yet motionless. Nothing broken or misplaced, but all in perfect order. On going down to the basement it was found that the fires had gone out.

How many churches with perfect equipage, splendid architecture, wealth in the pew, eloquence in the pulpit, and yet doing nothing. And why? The FIRES HAVE GONE OUT! It is largely a matter of fire with the Zion of God. Brethren, let us seek first to have the fires rekindled on the altars of our church, then will she begin to move again with the giant's tread, and souls shall be born to God!

CHAPTER XXVII.

CHRIST AND HUMANITY TRANSPOSED.

"For I was hungered, and ye gave me meat; I was thirsty, and ye gave me drink; I was a stranger, and ye took me in; naked, and ye clothed me; I was sick, and ye visited me; I was in prison, and ye came unto me."—Matt. 25:35, 36.

These words will be addressed to the blood-washed at the final Judgment. And could they change places with their Judge, they might reply to Him in the same language, "We were hunger-ed, and ye gave us meat; we were thirsty, and ye gave us drink; we were strangers, and ye took us in."

THIS TEXT REHEARSES CHRIST'S MINIS-TRY TO US.—There is in the text a touch of that divine humility that belongs to Him who came to wash the feet of a fallen race. Christ represents Himself as having received these ministries, whereas we first received them at His hands. "I was a stranger." This is the inspired history of our race; the moral moorings of the world were severed; we were let loose from God, and were drifting on the dead-sea of sin, that deceptive sea with placid, but deadly, waters, and shores lined with dead-sea fruits. Our planet had strayed from the flock of loyal worlds, no longer in com-pany with the "ninety and nine," but alone, a wanderer in the wilderness, "without God and without hope," lost and drifting upon the coasts of despair, seeking, as a stranger ever seeks, with a sense of uncertainty, for some distant light or hospitable door at which to find deliverance.

For ages the world sought refuge amid the phantoms of superstition, and the so-called halls of science, and the altars of idolatry, but in vain. She found not where to lay her head, until one "Came from Edom, with dyed garments from Bozrah," calling, "Come unto me and I will give you rest." A broad and blood-sealed hospitality, a house of refuge open upon the plan of free grace, where the worn and wasted stranger-world was taken in. He died for the sins of the whole world, "He tasted death for every man." The sweetest memory that wakes the world's gratitude is, "I was a stranger, and ye took me in."

NAKED AND YE CLOTHED ME.—In his fall from God, man awoke to the consciousness of his nakedness, physical and spiritual, soul and body. And though he devised a covering for the body, there was no covering for his immortal nature, but it remained unclothed and exposed to divine wrath. But Christ not only received the unclothed stranger world into the Covenant hospital, but also clothed it with garments of salvation. He wrapped the race in the Crimson robe of Redemption as the gentle mother would wrap her babe from the winter's breath, and spread the atonement as a covering over it as broad as the unfurled skies, so that we were no longer "unclothed, but clothed upon with our house which was from heaven." And this scarlet raiment, like Israel's vesture, which waxed not old through the wear and tear of the decades, has not failed in a single shred, nor lost a shade of original beauty. It endureth forever, because its warp and woof are alike of pure divine love, and "love never faileth."

I WAS HUNGRY, AND YE GAVE MEAT.— He who fed the hungry multitudes by His power, gave His own flesh to be the life of the world. He came to meet the moral starvation of the race, and announced when He came, "I am the true bread which came down from heaven, which if a man eat he shall never hunger." He has "prepared a table for us in the presence of our enemies," in the midst of devils, and wicked men, and unfriendly surroundings; the table is always spread and there is room at the feast.

"Thirsty, and ye gave me drink." The gratified hunger and satiated thirst are synonymous. He spoke with a woman of the world, and by her to the world, saying "Whosoever shall drink of the water that I shall give him shall never thirst. My flesh is meat indeed, and my blood is drink indeed," and the symbols stand perpetually before us in the bread and wine of the sacrament, and while these remain with us, the man who dies of spiritual hunger starves in the midst of divine plenty, and only because "he will not have life."

I WAS SICK AND IN PRISON, AND YE CAME UNTO ME.—A dark, dank prison is a dreadful place, and though we fail to appreciate the sun-light, and are sometimes even annoyed with its rays, yet if just one single sunbeam kindly creeps through a crevice into the prisoner's cell it carries a thrill of joy to his heart, and if a friend can only visit us and bring a little sunshine into the place, how it cheers us and makes the place seem more tolerable. I speak from experience. And now the reader wonders how I came to be in prison? Well, that is a personal matter.

"We were in prison, and Christ came unto us." We were prisoners in the dark dungeon of sin when Jesus Christ came to us, and His coming was the flashing of the immortal sunlight into the wretched confinement in which we lay "without God, and without hope." He came as "the light of the world." It is no wonder that angels shouted when that light broke its way through the darkness at mid-night and fell upon the fields where "the shepherds watched their flocks." Redeemed humanity will talk through eternity, of that visit of the Son of God to the world in prison, and though He did not stay very long, yet the old prison has been much more tolerable since He came. The world has been brighter since Christ passed through it, and the fragrance from "the rose of Sharon" is ever reviving the weary race, and the Star of Bethlehem comes to "stand over where God's child is," and gives him light in every dark hour; indeed, all the joys we have come from this blessed fact, that "Christ came into us." If it were not for this, how little would life mean!

"If all our hopes and all our fears
  Were prisoned in life's narrow bounds;
And the traveler through this vale of tears
  Could see no better world beyond;
Ah, what could check the rising sigh?
  What earthly thing could pleasure give?
  Ah, who could venture then to die,
  Or who could then endure to live?"

If at last it be our privilege to hear the words
of the text as a salutation from the Master, and
as we look back over the completed life-journey,
shall we not realize what He has done for us as
never before? And shall it not give added volume to the shout of final victory? "Unto him
who hath loved us, and washed us from our sins
in his own blood, unto him be glory, and honor,
and majesty, and dominion, and power, forever
and ever."

HERE WE SEE OUR DUTY TO OTHERS.—
Christ's ministry to us expresses what ours should
be to our fellow-men. He hath loved us after this
manner, and expressed His love in this way, and
thus are we to love our race and express our
love to "strangers" to the way of life. How many
are yet strangers, both in our own and in foreign
lands. And to us it is given "to take them in."

It is no very hard matter to entertain strangers
when the means are furnished to our hands. With
us it is an easy thing to keep a gospel entertainment because the Son of God supplies the feast.
What rich provisions we have, "A fountain filled
with blood," in which a world may wash and be

clean, the ever-present Comforter "leading us into all truth," and the infallible word, as a lamp to our feet, and a promise firm as the rock of ages for every returning footstep, and a supply of grace which only God can measure. May we not well go out and tell the straggling strangers of the world's highways and hedges "that all things are now ready?"

Every child of God has a commission to call and welcome strangers into the household of God. And this is blessed work. What a privilege to feed a beggar, or to give bread to the hungry child that asks at your door. There is a subdued happiness of soul in this which we cannot, and do not wish to express, but there is a deeper joy when we can lead a sinner to Christ, and let him feast upon the living bread. There is no joy this side of heaven like it. Did you ever feel the joy of bringing a soul to Christ? If not, may you have that joy soon. It is a foretaste of heavenly felicities.

And with a very little of the Lord's money we may send a card of admission to some soul, in foreign lands, to the gospel feast, one whom we will never see on earth, but who will with eternal gratitude recognize us in heaven. The money spent for an hour's entertainment at the opera would send the truth and prepare the way for some deathless soul through the gates of grace, and into the Eternal City. God gives us our means, but bids us beware how we use them. "Lay up your treasure in heaven."

MULTITUDES HUNGER WHILE WE HAVE
THE BREAD OF LIFE.—The man whose home
is by the riverside knows very little of the thirst
of the child of the desert. We, who are "planted
by the rivers of water," are liable to forget those
who thirst for what we enjoy. We occupy the
great center, so far as the privilege and gracious
means are concerned, but a little way from us,
in the country places, their privileges are far less,
a sermon once a month, and sometimes not so
much as a prayer meeting, and in many places
not so much as a Sunday school. Go still farther
and privileges diminish, and when we pass the
bounds of Christendom we come to the heathen
millions who are perishing for the want of the
gospel.

It is a fearful hunger of the soul that leads the
mother to give her children, an offering to a
heathen god, that she may obtain peace and rest.
A missionary in India held a mass-meeting with
the children, and in the midst of the joyful occasion there came a mother to him in tears, who
said, "Why did you not come sooner, then my
little boy could have been here too, but you did not
come until I had taken him into the jungle and
sacrificed him." How fearful to be without Christ,
and without hope in the world. When the grave
has closed above all that was dear to us, and we
feel that soul-hunger which only God can satisfy,
what would it be to be without His precious word?
Sympathy and kindness might soothe, but could
never satisfy. Such is the case with millions who

are without the gospel today. Then to send them the gospel, is to feed the hungry in the truest sense. Do all possible to send the good news of "Jesus and the resurrection" to the darkened homes and aching hearts of the heathen world.

You visit the poor and afflicted who are near by, and you can give sympathy and kindness, if you have not other gifts. And the "Cup of cold water shall not be without its reward," and your money, when given to send the gospel abroad will flash the light of life into the places where multitudes "sit in the region and shadow of death." It is thus converted into the "living water and bread from heaven" to feed and refresh the starving. It is frequently said, "We must win the fearful war now raging." So we must win this war for Christ, we are His warriors, the world His battle-field, and life is the campaign. Our opportunities are two-fold: our labors at home, and our money sent abroad; our dollars and dimes are our missionaries sent to do what we cannot oversee in person. They are our servants for Jesus' sake and it is no uncertain investment. We may invest in a college, and it may collapse, or in a bank, and it may fail, but there is no failure when we invest for Christ and humanity.

A man of wealth gave $25,000 to build a church in New York, in a part of the city where the people were too poor to build for themselves. The church soon became a power for good. After this the gentleman lost all his fortune. A friend, with an eye to the world, said to him, "If you now had

the money you put into that church it would help
you in your misfortune." He replied, "That is the
only money I ever saved, if it had not been in the
church it would have gone with the other." That
investment could not fail, It will come back upon
him in the eternities, "an exceeding and eternal
weight of glory." Brethren, "Lay up for your-
selves treasures in heaven."

CHAPTER XXVIII.

THE SPIRIT OF THE WORLD.

"And be not conformed to this world, but be ye transformed by the renewing of your mind, that ye may prove what is that good, and acceptable, and perfect, will of God."—Rom. 12:2.

WHAT IS MEANT BY THE WORLD?—Nothing is perhaps more difficult to define; it is not material or personal, not a thing of geography, agriculture or commerce, nor all those together. Faber says, "It is a name for a certain system of maxims, modes, and fashions. It is not matter altogether, nor is it entirely Spirit: not man alone, nor Satan only, nor is it exactly sin."

It is an inspiration, an infection, a life, a taste, a witchery, an impersonal, but quite a recognizable thing. Its chief and distinguishing feature is its AVERSION TO GOD. It is wholly incompatible with the divine life and nature, it is an atmosphere without God.

It is difficult to tell its bounds. You cannot bound an inspiration. You cannot draw a sharp line and say, "Things on this side the line are worldly, and things on that side are not. You can draw definite lines on the various sins, but the world is not sin, it is the soil out of which sin grows, the air that sin breathes, the light by which sin does its work, and the element in which it lives. The fish can live only in the water, and sin can live only while it breathes the atmosphere of the world. Only let the spirit of the world be displaced by the coming in of the divine spirit, and sin will fly from that community. A spiritual atmosphere is as deadly to sin as arsenic air to the insect tribes.

IT IS GENTEEL.—The spirit of the world seldom discovers itself by coarseness; it is almost invariably genteel; it may be ignorant, or poor, but it strives to conform to the modes of the world, and to keep up. Its efforts are often ludicrous; it will say things it doesn't mean, and do things which its better nature doesn't approve. It will utter compliments, when the hollow falsehood hardly covers the disgust. There is an artificial quality upon the spirit of the world, like the galvanism on crude metal; it glitters on the surface while it conceals the brass and the canker beneath.

IT INTRODUCES ITSELF.—Unlike the spirit of our Christianity, it takes an effort to bring that into anything. Some people never get their religion into practical life. Men say "Business is business, and religion is religion," that the two are not necessarily related. If the Siamese twins were related, then religion and business are related. A religion that does not enter your business cannot enter your character, nor will it stand at the final day.

IT IS UBIQUITOUS.—It comes into business, society, church, home-life, and indeed into all departments of life. It is on hand in the sad as well as in the sunny season; it makes no exceptions.

It is at the wedding, at the ball, in the sick-room, at the funeral; in the pulpit, and in the pew; it determines the cost and the length of the burial procession, and modifies the grief at the grave.

This spirit comes in everywhere. Close the doors and windows, and like the air, it finds its way in; it can be excluded only by the coming in of the divine Spirit. How glorious when God does come in and drive it out for a time; we never forget those seasons, we call them "revivals." Times when God comes close to us, times when strong men are converted, when bitter enemies become friends and make peace with each other, times which linger in memory and about which we talk in after years.

If we could only shut it out forever. This impersonal thing we call "the world," this thing which cannot be damned because it is not a person. Oh, if it could only be blown away! If all in life, in home, in church, in business, were simple, sincere, and true, free from hollow shams, and frauds, and insincerities; what a heaven this earth would be! The very locks would drop from the doors, suspicion would die in every heart, and distrust cease to rob men of their rest.

It would be a millennium if this spirit of the world were only exorcised forever. This will be an element in the fruition of heaven—the absence —the blessed and eternal absence of the spirit of the world.

IT IS TYRANNICAL.—The ages have been cursed with their respective tyrants, and the world is bleeding today as never before, from the same curse of tyranny, but each tyrant has been confined to his own age, and generally to his own land, but this spirit of the world has cursed all ages and all lands.

It assumes high authority and issues most preposterous edicts, and its most silly mandates must be met to the letter. Young and old must cater to its caprice. When it pipes all mankind must dance. Whether it is to disfigure the person by senseless and grotesque dress or manner, to make speech ludicrous by affected lisps, broadened "A's," or far-fetched accents; to hazard health, or even life, by such dress as makes the modest wince and the undertaker smiles; to ignore common sense, and murder conscience. All such commands must be obeyed without question.

THE TYRANNY IS ABSOLUTE.—It knows no mercy and no bounds; it is infernally heartless. The sinner may break the commands of God and then find mercy, but whoso breaks the command of this tyrant is cast out without mercy. Who dares to come to the world's marriage feast without the wedding garment?

However pure the pedigree and perfect the life; the person must be worth so much money, no matter how he got it—must dress and talk and act as the world does, or be excluded from the "charmed circle." Crossing the sea some years ago, there was on board a couple of Opera Troupes, coming from France to Brazil, to dedicate a two million dollar theatre building in Rio, Brazil.

Among them was said to be the most illustrious woman known to the stage at that time. While on the voyage those French people gave what they called, "a dress ball." I had never witnessed anything of the kind, and trust I may never witness such a thing again. To me, it appeared much more like an "undress ball" than a "dress ball."

It is a slavery that is pitiable. The slaves of the south and the slaves of Brazil have been free for a generation, but the slaves to this spirit of the world are in bondage still, and their secret groanings are often deep and sad. Its audacity has no limit. Like the devil, who had the effrontery to ask the Son of God to "fall down and worship him," this spirit of the world will blush at nothing. It comes brazenly and makes its demands without apology. You may be under most sacred vows to "renounce the vain pomp and glory of the world,' you may be an officer in the church, and wish your influence to be a moral force in the community, but what of that? The world comes in and boldly invites you to a place in its circle, to its clubs, and its carnivals, where God is ignored and His name unmentioned unless it be a little modest profanity.

This spirit has the effrontery to come, sometimes, in the person of some so-called "hightoned body", who has membership in somebody's church and call for your children, to take them from your home altar and teach them the "light fantastic step," and train them to be devotees to the spirit of the world. Such advances are an insult to a

man or woman of God. It simply says, "We regard you weak enough to surrender conviction,
conscience, and peace of soul, rather than take
issue with the world."

ITS CHIEF SIN IS OMISSION.—It is not so
positively bad, not high-handed and defiant of
law; it is not that which sheds blood, and wallows
in shameless pollution and crime. There are three
chiefs among the enemies of God; "the world, the
flesh and the devil." Note, the world is the first
mentioned. The flesh and the devil are instiga-
tors and perpetrators of actual outbreak and
crime. The "world" is the genteel devil, the well
dressed devil, the aesthetic and much admired
devil among the three. Not coarse, not repulsive,
but simply negative toward God. It gives him
the go-by. He is to it as though he were not. It
does not love God, doesn't think of God. It takes
up life and leaves no place for him; its danger
is subtle, and its doom fearful—"the wicked shall
be turned into hell, with all the nations that forget God."

GOD IS DISTASTEFUL TO IT.—Nothing is
more out of taste and offensive in a worldly circle. What right has God to be intruded upon a
cultured company when they are discussing politics, literature, or the latest fad? What right
has a preacher, in this day of advanced thought
and higher criticism, to stand in his pulpit and,
like a blatant ignoramus, begin to preach about
a hell, or a personal devil, or future retribution
and all that silly stuff just to frighten the folks?

True enough, the Master warned of a hell and a devil, and future retribution, but He did not have the wise and scholarly of this age as His auditors. He preached to the "common people," the sea-side crowds and mountain multitudes. The doxies, isms, and ologies, were not developed then; they knew nothing of hypnotism, Christian Science, theosophy and the occult in general. Even the disciples were so crude and verdant as to believe there was such a thing as the sea of Galilee, with real fish in it, and Peter even thought he had a home and a mother-in-law. They hadn't found out that all this was delusion, that the sea, and the fish, and the mother-in-law were mere "forms of thought," and there was "no such thing as matter" in existence. O, the ignorance of that people and that day!

Be this as it may we shall still hug the old delusions, and continue to believe in real material men and women, and houses and lands. We shall still hold to the teaching of Him who walked the waves and hushed the winds. We shall preach what He preached, and teach what He taught, until He return and revises His teachings. Christ must revise His own "everlasting gospel" before we are ready to listen to the late and lofty non-hell and non-devil doctrine, which is so full of comfort to the servants of the world.

BE NOT CONFORMED TO SUCH A SPIRIT. —"But be ye transformed." How? "By the renewing of your mind", by an inward change of the immortal naturre." Nothing less will meet the case; shame may cover sin, but cannot cure it; education may prune and lop it, but cannot grub it up by the roots. Clip the wings of the bird and it will cease to fly, but will flutter and make the effort; cut the claws and break the teeth of the lion, and he will cease to tear and destroy, but the lion nature remains, and he would tear and kill if he could.

There is too much clipping of the wings, and cutting of the claws of sin. When sin only has its wings clipped or its claws cut—like Samson's hair—they soon grow out again. Hence many who join the church soon backslide, from the simple fact that they do not have far to slide. Conversion gives us dominion, sets us free, not only free from sin, but free from the tyranny of the world. God's free man has liberty of that higher kind, by which He overcomes the world. He says to the world, "I have nobler use for all my powers, I have higher pleasures than you can give; my thoughts, time, energies, all move on a higher plane. You can entice, threaten, ostracise, as you may, but none less than the living God can rule over my spirit and command the homage of my immortal nature." Conversion puts us in warlike relation to this spirit of the world, and it takes the spirit of the stake, and the den, to face the world and say, "I am no longer thy servant."

CONVERSION ADJUSTS US TO THE WORLD.—Being adjusted, and being conformed, are very different conditions. Religion so adjusts us that while we are in the world we are not of the world. We may be in the world, and still have all the time a heavenly trend.

The river has its windings, its rough places, and its cataracts, but its course is ever towards the sea. So with life, it has its turnings, its rough scenes, and its cataracts, yet it may hold its heaven-ward course. The Christian can no more escape the world's current than the river can escape its channel. And there is often a grandeur in the wild dashings of a godly life. The river is not expected to leave its channel and climb the mountain side. God doesn't require us to turn the world and force it to go our way. This is the folly of fanaticism, which always ends in confusion.

THAT YE MAY PROVE WHAT IS THAT GOOD, AND PERFECT WILL OF GOD.—Here we have His will concerning us, that we may be free from sin, free from the tyranny of the world, free from all fear; "If the Son shall make you free you shall be free indeed."

That ye may prove—that ye may experience—His "good and perfect will." Religion is a thing of experience, as practical as agriculture, mechanics, or the professions, and like these, it can be known only by the experience.

There sat a company of grave philosophers discussing a strange old harp of antique style. One said, "It is David's harp, and capable of wondrous melodies." Another said, "This cannot be, as the wood bears evidence that it did not come down from so distant a date." Another said, "It is an unmusical old relic, and not worthy to be called a harp." The controversy continued, until a gray-bearded old harper came in. In place of answering them, he quietly drew a stool up to the instrument, and sitting down, he swept his hand over the strings, awoke the long slumbering melodies, and rang out the rich music of the hymn, as they sat silent and entranced. They tried to prove it incapable of music, but failed to test it, but the moment the old harper touched it, it became its own argument, and hushed all controversy.

Christianity is not controversy, not an argument, but an experience, a glorious harp-touch, that fills and thrills the soul with music divine. Touch it by faith, and it becomes its own argument and hushes all controversy.

THE INFIDEL ANSWERED.—An infidel lecturer closed his lecture—as they often do—with a challenge to "anyone who wished to reply to him." An old lady, dressed in antique style, and carrying a basket and an umbrella, and bearing the marks of poverty and age, stepped upon the platform, and putting down her basket and umbrella, she said, "I paid threepence to come in here to hear something better than Jesus Christ, and I have not heard it. Now let me tell you what religion has done for me. Then tell me something better, else I am cheated of my threepence. I have been a widow thirty years. I was left with ten children. I trusted in the Lord and He helped me, and comforted me, and enabled me to bring up my children, and they are all grown and respected. You don't know the troubles of a poor lone woman, left with a family of dependent children. I have gone to the Lord sometimes when I was very low—hardly anything to eat— and once when sick, and at the point to die, and knew not what would become of my little ones, but the Lord raised me up. Religion is no fancy, it is an experience. Such has it been to me."

The poor lecturer, chagrined and mortified, tried to reply, but the old lady said, "After God has done so much for me, I could not sit and hear you talk so about Him, without telling what He has done for me." The audience, deeply moved by the old lady's talk, shed tears and shouted, Amen! Amen! And the lecturer left the hall in utter discomfort. This is logic, this is experience, this is power. Will you prove His "good and acceptable and perfect will today?"

CHAPTER XXIX.

THE PIVOT OF DESTINY.

"What shall I do with Jesus, who is called Christ?"—Matt. 27:22.

As the winds drive ships upon the rocks, circumstances drive men upon responsibilities and wreck them. By a train of fortuities Pilate has drifted in between Christ and Cæsar. He must break with the one or the other; his official interest will not allow him to break with Cæsar, nor will his conscience permit him to break with Christ. In all his career, Pilate was never in such relation; he was not confronting Herod, or Cæsar, or any other magnate, but he was face to face with the Son of God, and with the whole question of destiny on his hands, and unable to decide between his conscience and his worldly interests. His conscience said, "Espouse the cause of the Nazarene," his lust of power and love of regal favor said, "Heed the demand of the mad multitude."

THUS CHRIST COMES BEFORE EVERY SOUL.—We wonder at the providence in Pilate's case, and fail to see the same providence which brings every soul to the same juncture. Christ before Pilate is the expression of God's *providence*. Christ on the cross is the expression of His *love*. The chain of providences which brought Him before Pilate will bring Him in like manner before every individual.

246

God's providence concerning Pilate was never met until he had confronted and disposed of Christ. So His chief providences touching you and me will culminate when we decide what we will do with Christ—when we settle the question by accepting or rejecting Him.

PROVIDENCE CONNECTS US THUS WITH NO OTHER.—No other character stands as the end of divine government and human destiny as does Jesus Christ. A thousand great minds have shed their light, and made their impress upon the ages, and we may, or may not, know them. No chain of providences compels us to confront them. A man may, or may not, know Solon and his statutes, Plato and his philosophy, or Mohammed and his fraudulent revelations. These men have no bearing upon a man's welfare or destiny. Not so with Jesus Christ. Like the gulf-stream driving its course through the ocean, God's providence forces its way through circumstances, and happenings until Christ is brought before every man's conscience. As the fish and the tempest were confederate together to capture the recreant Prophet when flying from duty, so divine providence and the Holy Spirit are at work together to bring Christ before your heart and conscience, and they will perform their work.

A man may fly from the church, and from religious society, as Jonah fled to Tarshish; he may seek to sink his convictions in a sea of worldly pleasure, or try to forget them in his wild rush for wealth, but in vain. God's Spirit will find the sinner and awake him, as the soldiers awoke Jonah in his sinful sleep. There are a thousand responsibilities that may never come before us, but as surely as He stood before Pilate, that surely will He stand before you, and I press the question, "What will you do with Jesus, who is called Christ?"

PILATE WAS FORCED TO ACT.—Never did unfortunate man struggle harder to evade responsibility. He pronounced Christ "innocent," he "sent him to Herod," he proposed "to scourge Him and let Him go," but all to no purpose. Other responsibilities he might evade, but when he in whom all the eternal designs are centered stands before Him, there is no evasion.

Nothing is more common than shifting responsibility. A man goes into a combine; that combine, or trust, monopolizes some commodity and forces the poor to pay to extortion or suffer. He says, "This is wrong, but I cannot help it; it is the work of the combine." But God will show that man, at the day of judgment, just how innocent he was. There is something you could do for the good of your community, but you leave that to another; some duty in your home, but you leave that to your companion; a child is wayward and needs the strong hand of the father to correct it, but you put on your hat and go down town and leave that to the mother, "who understands the dear child better." Ah, there is a lovely liberality in men in disposing of their responsibilities. But Pilate's responsibility none can evade, "What shall I do with Christ?" No excuse will answer here. Providence and the Holy Spirit compel a decision.

SOME ADOPT A COURSE OF INDIFFER-ENCE.—Many persons have no interest, care, or concern on this question. This is the state of multitudes at the present time. Christ does not come into their thought, He is to them as if He were not. You know people whom you neither love nor hate, you simply do not have them in your thought unless you hear them mentioned. This is indifference. Such is Christ to multitudes; they neither love nor hate Him, nor so much as think of Him, save when the preacher brings Him to their mind.

Such a life is perpetual offence. If anything will offend and injure you in your moral feeling it is indifference. For a man to pay no attention to your presence, or your words, is a supreme offence. When you deliver God's message from the pulpit, to have one grow listless, and another go to sleep, and still another bowing assent to what you say by unconscious nods, shows an indifference that is synonymous with insult; and yet the Son of God stands, and waits, and calls, and endures this perpetual and spirit-freezing indifference; and this indifference is intensified in its effect when we consider the issues at stake. Heaven and hell hang upon it, and still men are indifferent.

WE MAY GIVE CHRIST A SECOND PLACE. —Thousands do this, not willing to place Him first, nor just willing to give Him up entirely.

Like a wild and dissipated son who is half ashamed of his old father, and yet afraid to quite give the old man the go-by, knowing that he holds the estate, and would come to his help if he came into trouble. Hence he gives his father a sort of second place, with as little prominence as possible. So it is with many toward the Master, ashamed to make Him first in life, and first in all things; ashamed to let their worldly associates know that "Christ is all to them," and at the same time afraid to renounce Him entirely, lest they come to grief and none other could help.

A man in time of war is drafted into the army, but a noble brother volunteers to take his place, leaves business, braves dangers and death in his brother's place, then returns to find that brother indifferent toward him, and even careless of his comfort. What of such a man? A monster of ingratitude.

Jesus Christ, our elder brother, has gone a warfare for us—volunteered, suffered, died in our stead. He forfeited all, "he became poor that we through his poverty might be rich." He then returns from the field where He conquered all for us, and now only asks for our love. "Son give me thine heart." But men have prospered under the blessings of redemption, and are now too much engaged with worldly things to give any heed to Him, "who loved them and gave himself for them."

They say, "I will serve self and the world to ultimate satisfaction, then if aught is left I will give that to God;" "I will squeeze life, as a lemon, until I have gotten the juice, then give the hull to God." If there be left aught of time, or strength, or affection, I will give these to Christ. This will I do with Christ—give Him a second place.

YOU MAY REJECT HIM ENTIRELY.—This is what Pilate did at last, and he did it by refusing to espouse His cause. True enough he washed his hands in the waters of innocency and declared, "I find no fault in him," but the rejection was the same.

Thousands now laud the life and teachings of Christ, but fail to become His disciples. Pilate could not shift his responsibility; you cannot shift yours; you may as well try to escape "the pale horse and his rider" as try to evade this issue.

And this decision is the turning point in destiny. It was so with Pilate. When he let Christ go, God let him go. He passed the pivot of destiny when he surrendered the Son of God to His enemies, rather than surrender himself to the Son of God. Doom and destiny lie at this point. To become willing for Christ to have His way with the soul, is to reach the highest conquest. "The kingdom of heaven suffereth violence, and the violent take it by force." The violence of holy desperation, that violence that dashes the last Dagon from the throne of the soul and exalts Christ as its sovereign ruler.

But to decide against Christ is to fall into destruction. Pilate turns Christ away and falls adrift, his power wanes, his position is lost, his prospects fade, then follow banishment and desperation, and suicide ends the awful drama.

Sinner, when you pass Pilate's point, the current of destiny will turn. When the hand of providence lets you go, and redeeming love gets out of the way, then the descent to ruin is fearful in its rapidity. How quickly some men go to destruction! Some soul may pass that point this hour, and at this service. God help you to realize the awfulness of the hour.

BUT WE MAY MAKE CHRIST OUR GOD.— We may give Him first place and "crown him Lord of all." Pilate might have espoused His cause, though it would have been at a cost. The hatred of the chief priests would have led them to any measures for His destruction. They shouted, "If you release him you are not Cæsar's friend." And Pilate was not willing to pay the price, not willing to be counted other than the friend of Cæsar.

It costs now, as it did then, to espouse Christ and His cause. If you accept Christ you are not the friend of the world, you array yourself against all the powers of evil and stand in warlike attitude to all that is unholy, but at the same time you bring all the powers of truth and holiness round to your side. When you accept Christ there is not a saint on earth, nor an angel in heaven but that is confederate with you, and shoulder to shoulder with you in the battle for God and the right. And if you are only "faithful to the end" it will take eternity to tell what your influence has done.

A certain Senator was in love with a beautiful and wealthy young lady, who belonged to a family in the highest and most fashionable circle. He and her friends, without her knowledge, arranged for a fashionable ball in her honor. The Senator called to ask the privilege of "attending her to the ball." She said, "Senator, I shall not attend the ball." Surprised and almost stunned, he responded, "Miss, can you give me one good reason why you will not attend?" "Yes," said she, "I could give you several reasons, and I will give you one. I have a class of young ladies in the Sunday school, and I would not give up my influence with that class for all the balls that could be arranged." The Senator sat a moment, as if under a strange spell. Then said he, "Miss B———, if every Christian was like you, then more men, like me, would be Christians." I give this incident for the benefit of such young persons as may be trying to carry their religion and the world, side by side, in the life experience. "Ye cannot serve God and mammon," you must let one or the other go; give up the world or give up Christ.

CHAPTER XXX.

SINS OF OMISSION.

Text: "Therefore to him that knoweth to do good, and doeth it not, to him it is sin."—Jas. 4:17.

The soul has a double hazard—positive and negative. The negative is the greater. Omission destroys more than commission. Wretchedness, here and hereafter is not so much from what men do as from what they fail to do. We deal now with this more fatal and less noticed side of our responsibility, and call you to remember that we are as much responsible for that which we fail to do as we are for that which we actually do. The devil is a tactician, and makes a sort of decoy of the common vices and actual sins of life, and he sends them out to engage our attention and draw the pulpit fire. And while the pulpit is pouring its broadsides into them, the main army is around on the omission side destroying its millions without let or hindrance.

THE MAN WITHOUT ACTUAL SINS NEEDS PARDON.—If one could be found without actual sins, his sins of omission would sink him to destruction. Had you never broken a commandment, and should the whole troop of vices testify to the fact, all swearing to your innocence, it would be small compliment, a poor eulogy, to have all the cut-throats and jail-birds swear in my favor.

Besides, the natural state must be changed. Ill

growth is from soul conditions. It is the marsh that produces the fungi and the swamp; sin is the outgrowth from the depraved and corrupt heart. "Out of the heart proceed evil thoughts," etc. The word of God, the Spirit of God, and the inner consciousness, all testify "Ye must be born again."

We should count our sins, not by what we have done, but by what we have omitted. Count them as God counts them. Perhaps every day of life has added to the omissions, while the rolling years have increased them almost without number. These sins of omission lie back in the dim past half forgotten, and could they materialize they would stand up as a mighty army; they are only waiting until the final judgment. Who can look back over his unforgiven sins of omission and bear the sight?

THEY ARE MOST SUBTLE.—Actual sin has in it an element of alarm. The libertine hurries from the scene of his debauch, the murderer flies from the sight of his pale victim, actual sins are a clumsy pack, and cannot break in without giving alarm. The young sinner commits his first sinful act with fear and a flutter of the heart, it is like a boulder of hell's fire cast into his conscience, it is only in the advanced stages that actual sin loses its alarm. It is when the moral nature has mortified and is rotting, and the conscience is dead.

But sins of omission carry no alarm, they produce no fear. Even the rattle-snake will give warning before it strikes, but sins of omission are worse than the deadly serpent, they move on muffled feet with a velvet footfall, and do their work as noiselessly as the passing of a spirit, so noiseless that we forget their presence. We may neglect duty so long that we may finally forget that we are neglecting it.

Nature has a certain chivalry and warns before she destroys. The volcano rumbles before it erupts, a strange stillness precedes the storm, a singular roaring warns of the cyclone, the singing of the rattles before the serpent's death-stroke—these all give their alarms, but sins of omission destroy without warning. Vampire-like they fan and soothe the soul while sucking its life-blood. God's word and the Holy Spirit are the only monitors. They cry, "Awake thou that sleepest and arise from the dead, and Christ shall give thee light." "How shall we escape if we neglect?"

THEY ARE REPRODUCTIVE.—Sin in all its forms has wonderful power of reproduction. Like the cockle-burr, the tares, and the briers, these vegetable children of sin come of their own accord, and it requires a constant battle to prevent their coming; but in no form is sin more prolific than in the form of omission. It was omission that doomed Dives and the five virgins, and made most of the wrecks recorded in Holy Writ. Negative though it be, it grows and outgrows almost all things else.

You may neglect duty to God, to your child, or yourself, until you will absolutely forget the neglect, but the product of that neglect is growing all the time. A little child was with an older brother when planting apple seed, and with his tiny hand he dropped some seed into the ground. Years passed, he grew into manhood, became a minister, and returning to his childhood home, found the seeds he had planted, when almost an infant, had grown into fruitful trees. And there, in an autumn evening, he gathered the golden fruit.

This is life. We stand in life's evening, under the shadow of what our life has produced, and we will eat of its fruit in eternity. Neglect duty and devotion in youth, and gather hardness and hopelessness in old age. Fail to correct that perversity in your child, and that perversity will grow with its growth, engulf its character, and in mature life that child will be a disgrace to you, and despised of others. Then will your early neglect fling its shadows over your spirit, when in grayhairs you sit 'neath the evil tree of your own planting.

THEY ARE DEATHLESS.—Some seeds rot in the ground and never germinate, but the sins of omission never die. Every such sin has in it indestructible seed-germs, like the nut-grass of the south, which nothing can kill, and which will germinate and grow after years of exposure. What is back of much of physical suffering and premature decay? Only neglect of the laws of health. What is back of much of the poverty and want of old age? Only the neglect of opportunity and economy in younger life. And what will be back of the hopeless cry of multitudes of the unsaved at the final judgment? Only the neglect of the golden opportunities of this probation-life. Unsaved one, beware! Oh, beware!

SINS COMING TO JUDGMENT.—"Some men's sins are open before-hand, going before to judgment, and some men's follow after." The murderer's, the libertine's, and the tyrant's sins, precede them to judgment and await their coming, but with most men their sins follow after them.

The majority of us are kept from the crimes, and have no fear of the judgment on that score, but are we ready to meet the sins of omission and neglect? Duties to myself, to my family, or my country; failing to lift my voice, my prayers, my influence, my vote against wickedness and wrong; declining to take ground, lest I become unpopular and provoke criticism. We may go to the judgment little thinking what may follow.

But every sin in the long list of omission—unless washed out by the blood of Christ—will produce its results and follow on to confront us at the final reckoning. How shall we meet this multitude? No wonder a dying Archbishop prayed, "Lord, forgive my sins, and especially my sins of omission."

Here is the need of a day of judgment. You ask, "What need of a judgment day if men are judged and sent to their doom when they die? Here is the answer: "Their works do follow them." The crop that comes from a life of sin is not ripe when the sinner dies, it grows on and multiplies with time, and is not fully mature until the end comes.

Standing at the judgment, I see something as a cloud in the distance, ill-defined but advancing; it grows darker as it approaches, and its awful shadow falls over my spirit. Now I realize it is the "cloud of witnesses," the army of my sins of omission with all their awful results. I cry, Lord! Lord! but in vain, it is the mountain of my own making now sinking me to destruction. "Whatsoever a man soweth that shall he also reap." Are we ready to meet the harvest of our omission and neglect?

THEY ARE THE MOST HOPELESS.—Sins, like diseases, are divided into two classes—curable and incurable. This may have the ring of heresy, but it is true. There are incurable sins, and they all lie on the omission side—the silent, subtle, negative, and unnoticed kind. For every actual sin there is possibility of pardon. Christ stands between the actual sinner and the judgment, "to take away his sins," but the sins of omission are the seductive serpents, charming the soul onward until it passes the waiting Christ. God Himself cannot save the man who neglects to repent, and pray, and exercise faith.

Sins of omission operate like malaria, doing their deadly work while we sleep. In the church or out of it, neglect of duty means death. We once saw two soldiers to whom morphine had been given in large quantity by mistake, and they had lain down to their final sleep. The means used to save them were severe; their comrades forced them to

260 The Simple Gospel

walk, threw cold water on them, whipped and chaffed them, and by this cruel kindness saved them from death.

Do we not need to be aroused? Are we free from the fatal morphine of neglect? Is our genteel, orthodox, neglectful sleep a safe sleep? Are there no omission sin-shadows following us to overwhelm us at the final hour?

ONE NEED OF THE TIMES.—And this is conviction for the sins of omission. The church needs this. We ministers fire our gospel shots into the ball-room, the theatre, and the euchre-club, and this is but cutting the branches and leaving the tap-root. There is something back of all this, there is a prayerless home back of it, a home in which God has no altar, and in which He is neglected, if not ignored. Go to those places and find out how many left the home-altar after the evening prayer to attend them.

Some years since eleven hundred went down in a burning theatre, in the city of Chicago. How many of them went from home altars to that awful holocaust? Not one in one hundred. People who pray much do not hunger for those places; they have "meat to eat the world knows not of."

Let parents be aroused and brought to duty in their homes; let the time come when the Bible is read daily and prayer offered in every household; let the children coming to manhood and woman-hood be reared in this way, and we shall have a revolution on the question of worldly amusements and worldliness in the church. The remedy must be established in the HOME.

CHAPTER XXXI.

INFANT BAPTISM.

Text: "Suffer the little children to come unto me, and forbid them not; for of such is the kingdom of God."— Mark 10:14.

Infant baptism is held by the Methodist Church as a scriptural requirement, and therefore a solemn duty, hence we wish to ask, and then answer, two practical questions: Why do we hold and practice infant baptism? and, What benefits accrue from it?

A godly mother may bring her child to Christ in baptism, and at the same time be unable to give an objector satisfactory reasons for so doing. Hence we raise these two questions, that we may assist such a one in stating clearly why she has her babe baptized, and what benefits she expects it to receive from the ordinance.

Origen, Tertullian, Irenæus and Justin Martyr, all testify to the custom of baptizing infants in the early history of the church, and their testimony dates back to within less than 200 years of Christ, and from that to the present time the Greek Church, the Roman Church and all Protestant churches (save the immersionists) have practiced infant baptism.

THE GROUND OF THIS ORDINANCE.—The ground of it is the UNITY of the church. The church is a unit, it has been ONE in all ages, the

Patriarchal, the Mosaic and the Christian. Three
in one, like its Great Head, a trinity in unity. The
apostle calls it a "family," the whole family in
heaven and in earth,—divided, yet unbroken; both
worlds in the family circle and that circle never
to be broken. When one comes into the church
he comes in FOREVER; nothing but sin can exclude that one. Death does not exclude us. To
die is only to take a certificate and move the
membership up higher.

The early church and the church now, being
one, we ask what was the door to the early
church? God said in His covenant, "I will be your
God, and ye shall be my people." And the people
said, Amen! and sealed the covenant with circumcision. Circumcision then was the door to the
church, and this door was open alike to infants
and adults. Abraham was circumcised at the
same time with his son, and God fixed the time
for this rite in very early infancy, even at the "age
of eight days."

Why He did not command them to wait until
the child was old enough to know and understand the meaning of the rite is a question I
leave to those who wish now to "wait until their
children are old enough to know what baptism
means."

A CHANGE IN THE SIGN ONLY.—Circum-
cision being the sign of the covenant, or door of
the church, and baptism now coming in lieu of
circumcision, it becomes the door of the church in
the present age. There is simply a change in the

sign, but no change in the thing signified. He consents to be our God, when we, in baptism, covenant for ourselves and our children "to renounce the devil and all his works."

Then if the church is a unit, and baptism is in place of circumcision, and infants were circumcised as well as adults, how dare I forbid my infant child that baptism which brings it into covenant relation with God? Abraham did not question, but obeyed, and I should tremble to come between an infant and that Savior who rebuked His disciples and warned them that "They get not in the way of one of his little ones."

THEY ARE MEMBERS OF HIS KINGDOM. —If infants were members of the church in the family of Abraham, and are also members of God's final kingdom on high—if they were in the church at first, and are to be in it at last—then who has any authority to shut them out at any point between the first and the final church triumphant? As we follow the stream of church history in its unbroken course, from Abraham through the ages and on to the church triumphant, we ask who has the commission, and at what point is he instructed to land "the old ship of Zion," and put off the "little children."

THEY ARE INCORPORATE WITH CHRIST. —Jesus Christ came into humanity, not into certain phases or parts of humanity, but into HUMANITY, infant as well as adult, hence the infant is a part of Himself. Hear Him, "Whosoever shall receive one such little child in my name, receiveth me." Is He not then in the child? Strange that the "little ones" are members of the church at first, and at last, and so identified with Christ that in receiving the little child we receive him, and yet they are not proper subjects for membership in the church at this period in her history. Thank God, the doors of our church, like the arms of the Savior, and the gates of the Celestial City, are ever open to receive the children! And may the time never come when she shall close her doors against one little lamb that has a blood-bought right to a place in the fold!

THE APOSTLES BAPTIZED INFANTS.—It was their custom to baptize the believer and his household; that is, children, servants and all that constituted that household. But it has been said, "There were no children in those households." Let us consider this statement.

We have the jailor and his house, Stephanas and his house, Lydia and her house, Cornelius and his house, and Crispus and his house. Here we have five households. Now it must be shown that there was not an infant in any one of these five households before it can be proven that the apostles did not baptize infants. This cannot be done. But if this could be shown, then, we ask, why are these five cases recorded? Are they not specimen copies of apostolic work, recorded for our instruction? Do they not show that in every case where the head of the house was baptized the household was baptized also? Not a single exception in the entire history.

Then if these five cases are specimen copies, representing the apostolic custom, it must be shown that either these are false copies, or there was not an infant in anyone of all the families converted under the ministry of the apostles, and such an effort would be an absurdity. We are forced to take one or the other horn of this dilemma, or accept the "TRUTH, the whole truth and nothing but the truth," that the custom of the apostles was to baptize infants.

THE NATURAL RELATION CALLS FOR IT. —Your child is a part of yourself, it is your offspring, "bone of your bone, and flesh of your flesh," and both nature and grace bind you to supply its wants until it can supply itself. You are bound to care for it, body and soul, and it would be unnaural and monstrous to refuse, hence it is as much your duty to believe for it and bring it to the open channels of grace, as it is to feed and clothe it. Christ opens the channel of grace to the infant in baptism, and it is wrong and unnatural if the parent should shut that channel which Christ has opened, and thus debar it the benefit and blessing God designed it should have.

Again, if your child be part of yourself, you are not wholly given to God until your child is baptized. Why could none of the regenerated heads of families be baptized without their households? Simply because their children and families were one with themselves. They were answerable for them, hence they go not into the churches without their little ones, but dedicate all for whom they were responsible. But you ask, "What good can it do the child when it doesn't understand it?" Then we ask, What good will food do the child when it doesn't understand it, Men talk learnedly of their understanding the economy of salvation, while the infant and the idiot get all the benefits as fully as they with all their understanding.

THE BENEFITS WHICH ACCRUE.—First, the child receives its name in a dignified and impressive ordinance, and in connection with the name of the Father, the Son and the Holy Ghost. And without this there is nothing that seals the name to the child. Ask one who was never baptized, "What is your name," Answer, "My name is Joseph." How do you know that is your name? Answer, "They began to call me that at first, and have always called me by that name, and have never called me by any other name." Ask one baptized in infancy, "What is your name?" Answer, "My name is James." "How do you know that is your name?" Answer, "I know it because that was the name given to me in holy baptism, and sealed to me by an ordinance of the church, in the name of the 'Father, Son and Holy Ghost.' " And when grown up and at the head of a family that one can say, "I got my name, like I got my wife, in a most honored and sacred rite of the church of God."

ITS FIRST IMPRESSION IS FOR GOD.— There is immense importance in the first impres-

sions; they are deepest and most lasting. A noted
skeptic said, "Give me the first five years of a
child's life and I will make it an infidel." Let the
babe be given to God in holy baptism, and when
intelligence buds let the first thing it learns be
that IT BELONGS TO GOD, that it has been giv-
en to Him in the most sacred manner, that God's
claim upon it is first of all. Teach it thus from its
cradle and you have God's impress upon it and
God's claim established before the world and Satan have chance to take possession of the little
heart.

This ordinance is a safeguard to the child.
When we are conscious of the existence of evil
influences we feel safer when we have used the
best efforts to fortify against them, and while we
do not believe that there are regenerating powers
in this ordinance, yet there is a blessing and a
shielding influence coming to the child through
baptism. It is God's ordinance, and it becomes,
in a sense, a spiritual protection to the little ad-
venturer just entering upon life.

When a mother feels that her child has its very
name linked with the name of God, and that it is
covered by covenant relation to Him, and wearing
the badge of loyalty to Him, she realizes that it is
protected from evil influences as it could not be
without these things. Her child has advantages
not given to the child that is debarred these privileges.

IT OBLIGATES THE PARENTS.—The blessing of this ordinance is not less to the parent

than to the child. The obligation taken by the parent brings that parent nearer to God. Nothing can bring one to feel one's need of divine help more sensibly than to realize one is now responsible for another immortal spirit, and has to answer for another soul, as well as for one's own. Many a careless and indifferent parent has been brought back to God by the power of the vow taken in bringing his child to God in holy baptism. "A little child shall lead them." Dear parents, it is a mighty bond to bind you to duty and to God! The father of Hannibal, though a heathen, took his son to the altar of the gods, and swore for him eternal enmity to Rome. And daily he would say to him, "My child, you are sworn to smite Rome." It became a principle in his life, and he did smite Rome as Rome was never smitten. Swear your child, at the Christian altar, to eternal enmity to sin, teach it to him daily, make it a principle in his life, and that child will be as mighty against sin as Hannibal against Rome.

CHAPTER XXXII.

CHILD TRAINING.

"Train up a child in the way he should go: and when he is old, he will not depart from it."

Every relation and position in life has its moral bearing and effect. The moral effect of a man's wealth does not end at the tax-books, but goes into all that affects his destiny.

Children are not given to us as mere agents to perpetuate our race and name. They are a "heritage of the Lord," and as the handling of property develops the practical, so the possession of children develops us in the higher moral and affectional nature. While we educate them, they educate us in a higher sense; they lead out soul powers that nothing else will or can; they make us sympathetic, unselfish, and sacrificing; they are the teachers sent from God, to impart to us the higher education, and the home without these prattling preceptors is incomplete.

A mansion where lives a pair in quiet splendor, with everything painfully prim; no tiny boot or bonnet, or broken top on the floor; no stain of little fingers on the window panes; no child in that home—a paradise with no bird-songs. A something is needed to give the cold, dead splendor warmth and beauty; that something is a half-dozen happy, hearty, rollicking children; that would put life and soul into that home of icy splendor.

THE OBJECT TO BE TRAINED.—A little commonplace creature, such as we see on the streets, and hold in our arms, and yet when we think of the relation we stand appalled. My child. What is it? A bird that I must train to sing for a season and then let go from its cage to the dust? a flower, to bloom for once and be no more? an oak, to develop in strength and yield at last to time and tempest? a something to be, then die and be forgotten, Nay! Nay! But a young immortal, a little breathing eternity, and I responsible for its soul, body, and spirit. Here is a new field; not agriculture, nor horticulture, but soul-culture—the highest science in God's universe.

The little one comes into your home, a tiny, pulpy, pulsing, cooing, half-conscious form of flesh and blood, and this little cuddling immortal is committed to your charge. Study its capabilities, and your responsibility is augmented. Here is consciousness. How strange if your flowers could know of your care and feel your touch. The little child knows your every touch and tone; its sensitive nature vibrates to your frown, or smile, or intonation of voice. Here also is the power to love and hate, with memory from which nothing can be erased.

Thus, when impressing the child-mind, I am writing what can never be rubbed out, chiseling upon a tablet that eternity's cycles can never efface. Cut your name on the sturdy beech and it may be read by the coming generation, but the unpression made on the child-mind will be legible at the bar of God. In the awful light of the judgment we shall read our own hand-writing on the souls of our children. The scar, the blur, the stain you made on the immortal spirit will be legible there.

TRAINING THEM UP.—This word "training" comes from the Hebrew language and means to dedicate, initiate. The young immortal is on the verge of human experience, at the gateway of life, of which it knows nothing; it is entering upon a way beset with dangers, and its destiny dependent on the direction given. Hence the instruction; "initiate" them rightly, and let them be started in the right direction.

It would be only a monster, morally, who would direct his child in a way across which was a great chasm into which it would fall to its destruction. Yet this is just what the parents are doing, who are rearing up children while they themselves are living in sin. No parents can lead their child in the way of life except they are walking therein. Your child will go as you go, believe as you believe, and live as you live. Hence this text implies a godly life on the part of parents.

FIRST GET CONTROL OF THE WILL.—Control before teaching. This is the first thing with all intelligence, from the lowest to the highest. The scholar in school must be controlled before it can be taught; even the horse or dog cannot be taught anything until brought under subjection to the will of the teacher.

Let the child learn, for its first lesson, that the parent's will is its law. In learning submission to the will of the parent it gets the great lesson of submission to the will of God, because the parent is God to the child until its is old enough to know the true God. Away with the notion that "I must explain, and give reasons to the child as to why it should obey my command." It should obey because the parent commands, and the child that never learns submission to parental authority will array itself against the laws of the land and the laws of God when it is older. It is the children without home-control that fill your police courts, and your prisons, and supply the victims of the gallows and electric chair.

Let this training begin early, even before the child can walk. You cultivate your corn or your flowers while they are young and tender. That deformed and crooked oak that defaces the beauty of the forest might have been straightened in its twighood. So the child, if perverse or awry in disposition, should be straightened while very young and pliable. The scars and the blight upon thousands of homes might have been averted, had the wayward boy been controlled in his early budding. When Professor Webster, who killed Dr. Parkman, stood under the gallows he said, "This is due to a perversity in my nature which might have been eliminated in my early childhood."

Much correction will not be found necessary. There is a power in loving firmness that commands the heart, and when the rod *must* be used, let it be done in loving sorrow, let the child feel that your pain is deeper than what it suffers.

HAVE DISCIPLINE IN THE HOME.— There are general laws of health which apply to all alike, and we may have general rules in the family for the good of all, but when it comes to "training," correcting the habits, and eliminating the perversities, we can work by no general rule. Men cut wheat by machinery because every wheat-stalk is like every other one, but they prune grape vines one at a time, and adapt the pruning to the special case. If every child were like every other child, then we could train by rule, a sort of machine work, but each child is a grape-vine to itself and requires a treatment to itself.

The means used must be gentle and delicate in proportion to the nature of the child, the severity necessary for one would wilt another as the sensitive plant wilts under the touch of violence. You lead a pet lamb with a ribbon string, but it takes a rope to lead a mule. And we have to deal with children in proportion to the per cent of lamb or mule in their nature.

TRUTHFULNESS AND PROPER ASSOCIA-TION.—Let the child be taught an unswerving adherence to the truth. Without this you cannot build a character. With an unquestioned obedience to rightful authority, and an uncompromising adherence to the truth, you have the foundation for a right and solid character.

Then be careful of their association. Know where they are and with whom. The power of association is next to nature, and will absolutely change and remake the character. The young nature becomes largely what its associates are.

The farmer, with fine hogs or cattle, knows their range, whether that range is good for them, and whether they will thrive on it. The refined society lady, who has conscientious views in regard to her prize poodle or imported pug, which in the providence of God she has adopted, and on which she benevolently bestows her time and thought and caresses, is very careful of the association of that pug. It does not go where there are diseases or danger.

We ought, at least, to be as careful with our children as the farmer with his hogs and cattle, or the pious lady with her pug. We ought to know their range, and whether the mind and heart are in jeopardy.

HAVE YOUR CHILDREN HEAR THE GOSPEL.—"The gospel is the power of God unto salvation." God has chosen to convert men by the "foolishness of preaching," not by foolish preaching. It is His plan and appointment, with His own seal upon it; the only thing in the economy of God that is peremptory. A man may superintend a Sunday-school or let it alone, he may act as steward in the church or let it alone, but when God calls him to preach the gospel he has no option—he is, as St. Paul expresses it, "Christ's prisoner, Christ's slave."

And while He makes it obligatory upon us to preach, He also makes it obligatory upon you, and your children, to hear the gospel as we preach it. To see the children going from Sunday-school as the parents are going to church, is a sad picture. All honor to the Sunday school, but God never intended it to do the work of the pulpit, and that work it can never do.

There is a spiritual influence and power that come over the heart as you sit silent under the gospel message, which will affect your child as it sits by your side in the pew as nothing else will affect it. Let your child habitually fail to hear the preaching of the gospel, and it fails of the only means on which God has placed special emphasis for its salvation. Dear parents, you will be held to account in the final judgment for allowing your children to grow up without hearing the gospel. I beg you think of your responsibility and meet your duty!

TALK WISELY TO THEM ON RELIGIOUS MATTERS.—There is a "zeal which is not according to knowledge." The parent should talk to the child at the proper time and in the proper manner, but not too much. Some good people talk like Pollock's priest prayed—"by the quantity." Nothing begets indifference so soon as too much talk. Religion cannot be dinned into the child mind by constant talk; you can live it in, and live it in with more success. Our conversation should be "seasoned with salt," but not too much salt. We should talk to our children on religious matters at proper times, and to a proper extent, but holy living is mightier than holy talk.

ABOVE ALL GOVERN YOURSELF.—Never undertake to admonish or correct your child when you are vexed or out of patience. Wait! Wait until you are in complete command of yourself, if you have to wait until the next day. And if you have to correct the child by corporal punishment, pray with it first; let it feel that your heart is involved and not your temper, then the correction will have right effect.

Make your children your companions; take them into your confidence, and love them so that they will prefer your society to any other. The moral power of love is beyond all other save the divine power.

Finally, "Train up the child in the way it should go." What does this mean? Not in the way of mere morality, gentility, good manners and respect for religion, but in consecration to God. See and *know* that your child is soundly converted to God, taught in holy things and leading a spiritual life, Keep them in this way while you have them under your control, and influence them in the same way while you live, and when they are old they will not depart from it.

You can then leave this world in your advanced age with full confidence that your children will follow you and greet you in the "better and sinless life."

CHAPTER XXXIII.

HUNGER FOR THE HEAVENLY.

"But now they desire a better country, that is, an heavenly; wherefore God is not ashamed to be called their God."—Heb. 11:16.

THE SPHERE OF THE TEXT.—It is intensely interior; it penetrates to the secret place of the desires. Here is where God lays His judgment lines concerning us; down at the bottom like the electric cable down on the ocean's bed.

Men know nothing of our desires unless we express them, they may inwardly burn and consume while none know of the fires; but the invisible smoke of those subterranean burnings is ever ascending, either as incense or insult, to that God who "Knoweth our thoughts afar off."

The cravings of the moral nature come out from the very roots of that natrue. Everything must have food "convenient for it." We cannot feed lambs on raw flesh, nor eaglets on grass. The tiger wants flesh wet with warm blood; the crow calls for the carrion, and the dove for the grain scattered in the field. Tell me what a man desires—what is food for his soul—and I will tell you what manner of man he is.

The pure in heart seek to know and cultivate that which is pure. Some people have their moral olfactories sharp-set for everything that is unsavory and subject to criticism. If there is a weak spot in the church, or a flaw in the moral make-up of a fellowman, they find it with unerring certainty. The practical piety of some people consists principally in smelling for things. Confine a vulture in a king's conservatory and he will die of hunger; he has no taste for the royal fruits, but give him range over a deserted battle field and he gorges to fullness.

WHERE THE JUDGMENT SCALES WILL SIT.—Down in the subsoil of the soul, down amid the moral appetites and at the very roots of the inner being, the balances will hang which shall determine destiny.

Take the clear water from the surface of an old well, dip it deftly and do not disturb its depths, and how clear and seemingly pure! but go to the bottom, down beneath the crystal surface and stir up the sediment of long accumulation, and you find all manner of mud and rottenness, full of the elements of death.

If God would only dip the surface water, note the surface of life which is lived out before the world, that which is seen and lauded of men, then would it be an easy matter to pass the judgment hour, and most men would be saved.

But God will go to the bottom and stir up the sediment; He will find the old and unrepented habits, and hatreds. and lusts—many of them perhaps long forgotten— which lie rotting far beneath the surface of life. It is a disgusting sight when an old, neglected well is cleaned out; and the scene will be fearful when the secrets of all hearts are made known, when the judgment well-ropes shall lift the sickening sediment of all human hearts to the surface.

It was because the faithful souls named in the text were pure and high in their desires, that "God was not ashamed to be called their God." Oh, for a clearing out of heart-wells, that there may be no sediment of which God will be ashamed in the final day! "Cleanse thou the thoughts of our hearts by the inspiration of thy Spirit."

THE DESIRES OF THE UNGODLY.—The desires of the man of the world do not run in a heavenly direction; the ungodly do not desire a "more heavenly country" but only a larger part of the country they now have. If they could increase their modest possessions to a few millions they fancy their desires would be fully met. They would not have a heritage one whit more heavenly; they rather like the earthliness of it, if it were only a little more enduring. The world is not going to perish for want of appetite, or desire, it has a most voracious appetite, but it is of that earthly sort that craves the "things that are seen."

And when those desires become vitiated they are then insatiable. Drunkenness, with which our land has been so long and sorely cursed, is but the leprosy of an appetite which has become vitiated; it puts its victims out of society as truly as did the leprosy of Palestine; it takes him away from society, home, church, and everything high and noble, and makes him a hopeless outcast.

If the present awful world war will but clear

the world of this curse, then will it be a blessing in blood, and the nation should be on its knees, giving thanks for the prospect of deliverance.

THE FASHIONS OF THE WORLD.—The desire to conform to the styles of the world, with its hollow conventionalities, its silly exactions, and its nonsensical follies; that it is which leads the rich into that hollow and heartless region beyond all that is simple and sincere, beyond all that is socially warm and real, and where the more generous and real heart nature is paralyzed and frozen.

This desire also keeps the poor unhappy and mortified in spirit because they cannot pay the passage out into that soulless territory. This desire is only an appetite, a little less coarse, but hardly less fatal, than that which destroys the inebriate.

THE DESIRE FOR MONEY.—The avarice appetite is another horse-leech in the soul ever crying, "Give! Give!" To fall under this desire is to become less than human. Its eating only intensifies its hunger. The billions of dollars expended in this world-war could not satisfy one soul with this leprosy of avarice. Oriental leprosy eats out the bones, but the avarice leprosy eats out the conscience.

The poor may cry for bread, but it has no ear responsive to that cry; widowhood and orphanage may writhe under its merciless surgery, but—Shylock like—it claims and cuts its pound of flesh from nearest the heart.

THE DESIRE FOR POWER.—This desire when fully in control is now proving itself the most hellish of all the vitiated appetites. One man, one human being, has gone so far under the desire for world-rulership, as to declare, "There is but one will, and that is my will; there is but one law, and that is my law." And under this insanity he has sent three millions of his own countrymen into eternity, killing the men, and worse than murdering the women, and murdering and maiming little children for life, and leaving only desolation and silence in lands which were filled with happy homes and vocal with the songs of progress and contentment.

NOW LET US LOOK AT THE OPPOSITE DE-SIRES.—"But they desire a better country, that is an heavenly." Abraham had no complaint to make of Canaan, it was a goodly land and suited him, only he did not care to own it, only so much as a place to bury his dead.

Here is a distinctive mark of the child of God,—CONTENTMENT. Recognizing himself as a sojourner, he is satisfied with things as they are in the order of God's providence. A restless dissatisfied disposition is marked evidence that we are not close to God. The near vicinity to God is a restful state. Persons who are ever chafing under their environment, and ever in a fret, can never have a bright and cheery experience. But those satisfied with their lot are the ones who have power with God and influence with men. Our usefulness depends more on our contentment than on our condition. We have seen this illustrated in the ministry—a preacher dissatisfied with his appointment, and ever complaining, and we never knew one such who was a success in his calling.

RELIGION IMPLIES SATISFACTION.— When our chief interests lie above and beyond the world, when we truly "desire the heavenly" we are not hard to satisfy. When the pilgrim regards this world, not as home, but as a land through which he is passing on his way home, then is he cheerful by day and restful by night.

We may, as tourists, be well satisfied with a country through which we are passing and sightseeing, while we should have no desire to live in it.

We might try a trip across the Great Sahara just for the novelty, but we should not be willing to locate and try to live in its sandy wastes.

When I came first to the South, it was a snowy day, and passing the poor ridges between Chattanooga and Atlanta, I felt a bit gloomy. But then I did not have to stop, and when I reached the cheery city of Atlanta I thought it was of little consequence what sort of country I had to come through to reach such a city.

So we are sure that any kind of country is good enough to travel through, when going to such a land and such a city, and such society, and above all, to such a SAVIOR as we shall meet at the terminus of the life pilgrimage.

The early gold-hunters thought an ox-cart conveyance and a bed on the ground good enough when going to the gold fields; and the rich man's pavement, and the gathered crumbs afforded rest and rations for the helpless Lazarus when on his way to "Abraham's bosom."

THE SUNSHINE AND SHADOWS OF LIFE. —Every year of time has its March winds, its storms, and its dark days, but after all it has more bright days than it has days of gloom. The average life has more sunshine than shadow, and in the rough places of life as we go jolting at a fearful rate, we often have the cheering thought, "I do not have to pass this place again," it is only for once. How glad we are that some storms can never recur, some bitter days can never come back and make us suffer the second time.

Another help in life's hard places is the thought, others have gone through it before us, we do not have to pioneer life's way, the track is well beaten. We have had to swim a few rivers in life, and we were always careful to note the tracks left by others, and to go in and come out where they did.

Thus, in the deep and dangerous places in life, where the waters are muddy and mad, we can follow the beaten track. If no one had ever suffered or been unfortunate, how we would tremble at the thought of those things! If no one had ever died we would shudder at the thought of death.

THE EMIGRANT.—When one has determined to emigrate to a far off country, that determination will cause him to change all his plans, and he largely loses interest in the land in which he has lived. His thoughts and aims are all toward the country to which he is going, he winds up his affairs, dissolves all partnerships, pays off all debts, and forms no alliance that would hinder his departure. And no one need think of being a heavenly immigrant who fails to have things straight when he departs. He must leave the world with a clear record. One may have a position in society when his private record would not bear the light. There are many moving in the commercial and social world who would blush to see their private life written out—like Babylon's king—in letters of fire on the wall.

The heavenly society is so high and pure that nothing that is impure can enter there. Then if you propose to go over, and up, and live with your loved ones in that land of purity, the sooner you sell out and settle up and get ready the better.

GOD IS NEVER ASHAMED OF PURITY.— However weak, ignorant, or poor, God will recognize the "pure in heart." The text speaks of such as "desire the better, and heavenly country," and says, "Wherefore God is not ashamed to be called their God." The life of which God is not ashamed is a grand life to live, and its determination—like the beauty of a cloudless sunset— will be its grandest feature.

But if a man so live as to have shame in his own inner consciousness, his friends ashamed, and when he is dead, the preacher ashamed to touch his traits at his funeral, and the audience afraid that he will allude to them, how shall such a one stand before God?

"Set your affection on things above, and not on things on the earth." Transfer your desires from the earthly to the heavenly. Let us seek that blessedness which is promised to the "pure in heart," then shall our God not be ashamed of us in the judgment hour, but we shall then hear the words of eternal welcome, "Enter thou into the joys of thy Lord."

CHAPTER XXXIV.

HOW TO BE SAVED.

"Sirs, what must I do to be saved? And they said, Believe on the Lord Jesus Christ, and thou shalt be saved."—Acts 16:30, 31.

This is the greatest question ever propounded. If the building be burning or ship sinking, the first thought is not of the valuables, but of life. With death and the judgment just ahead, the first rational aim is not for success and accumulation, but for salvation. How shall I be saved?

RESOLVE TO BE SAVED.—Do not resolve to be saved if I can and do something else at the same time, but resolve to be saved if I never do anything else. Great ends are not achieved by fortuity and mighty purposes are not reached by accident. Men first resolve, then count the cost, then concentrate their forces and drive for that end. Bolivar resolved to be the liberator of the South; Washington purposed to lead the colonies to liberty; Louis Napoleon resolved to hold the reins of the French Republic. Men are saved on this same principle—"First resolve, then invest life and all in the resolution."

MUST BE UNCONDITIONAL.—Dealing with men we may dictate terms; not so when dealing with God. He is the absolute party in the contract, and it remains for us to come to His terms.

Men think to come to God with conditions, bargaining to do so much for Him provided He do so much for them, as if He needed or could be benefited by their service.

Think of a geranium peeping up in spring-time and proposing a bargain with the sun. It says, "Smile on me and make me grow and bloom and become beautiful, and fragrant, and attractive, and proud of myself, then I will look up and honor you with an undying gratitude." How much would the sun make by such a contract? How much can a geranium add to the glory of the sun? God realizes just that much by our proposed contracts. Just what the sun gains by a bargain with the geranium, or a Jamestown-weed, with all the odor of its native depravity.

THERE MUST BE CONVICTION OF SIN.— A man must have a profound sense of the sinfulness of sin, a reformation, a quitting to swear, a washing out from debauch, a joining the church to please his wife. All this may improve a man's decency, but will make him no better or purer inside. It requires the deep ploughing of conviction, the tearing up and tearing out of the roots of the evil nature.

The after religious life is in proportion to the depth of conviction when a man turns to God. It is the deep sub-soiling of repentance that prepares the heart for luxuriant growth in the things of God.

How strong must that conviction be? It must always be strong enough to drive the sinner to Christ. Conviction varies in intensity; sometimes it is a gentle and gradual awakening, again it is a sudden and awful revealment, driving the soul almost to despair. You cannot fix a degree and say, "That is the point at which I must turn," We do not ask how severe the attack must be before sending for the physician. We know the disease. Sin is a moral disease, incurable and deadly. Then if you know that you are a sinner, that you have the dreaded disease, then call at once for the "Great Physician,"—"the only name given under heaven whereby we may be saved."

MEN MURDER THEIR CONVICTIONS.—They love sin and are unwilling to give it up, hence they stifle conviction when God graciously sends it. It is a great grace to feel a sense of sin, and yet this feeling is often murdered, a species of murder for which there is no pardon. It may be that some are present, who are trying to throttle and destroy their convictions. Better murder wife or precious child. God might perchance forgive, and the blood of Christ might wash out the stain, but murder your convictions and the blood-stain can never be washed out. When you have murdered conviction you have killed the only influence that can bring you to Christ. Save your convictions! If they are bleeding and half dead, staunch the blood and nurse them back to life! This is your only hope.

But one says, "I have not made up my mind." God's mind is made up, graciously made up, and that at the cost of His own blood; but men cannot make up their minds to let God save them.

We had a sinner friend at the point to die; he was asking for just a little time to give himself to God." I saw him a few weeks later, after he had recovered. He was then debating the matter and saying, "As soon as I can make up my mind." His mind was made up when he lay at death's door. Malignant disease helps a man to make up his mind.

Suppose I am on a ship in mid-ocean and that ship is about to sink. The life-boat is lowered and I am about to step into it, when I am caught from behind and told, "This is a life and death matter, better take time to consider and make up your mind." I will turn and knock the lunatic down, get free from his grasp, and leap for my life and consider afterwards. "Escape for thy life" while opportunity is at hand!

QUIT ALL KNOWN SIN.—This is the only thing you can do with sin. You cannot control it, polish or taper down on it. The only thing you can do with it is to quit it. You cannot repress it, its very nature is lawlessness. You cannot restrict avarice and satisfy it with the legal rate per cent. Intemperance cannot be repressed to moderation. Chain a bulldog, and you limit his liberty but intensify his ferocity. Sins of all forms are but hell's bulldogs, and the fetters of repression do but inflame their hellish nature. Had Samson quit the deceitful Delilah at the first betrayal he would have saved his eyes, his honor, and his life. Dalliance with sin is like playing with serpents, and only fools play with serpents.

SEEK PARDON FOR PAST SINS.—Salvation is more than the quitting of sin and facing about for a better life. It is not enough that the outlaw or felon be willing to turn about and do better. His past sins are upon him and will damn him, go which way he may, unless he gets pardon. The whole commonwealth is against the outlaw, it is the state against the criminal. There is either the Governor's pardon or a gallows between him and liberty.

When the sinner turns to God, he has all the sins of his lifetime to settle. Not a commonwealth, but the moral universe is against him. Then the first thing is the mercy seat. Fly to Christ and trust in the merit of His blood to wash away your sins. There is no substitute, no evasion. It is forgiveness through faith in Christ, or damnation because of your sins.

SIN IS INDESTRUCTIBLE.—Bury the sinner in the best style, and earth and time will corrode his casket and consume his bones, but his unforgiven sins will endure and will meet him at the judgment. We may forget our sins, but forgotten sins are not forgiven sins. Only one thing in this universe can destroy sin, and that is the blood of Christ. "His blood cleanseth from all sin."

THEN HONOR THE BLOOD.—Here, and here alone, is safety. When we hear one talk of his morality, "what he has done," and what he "intends to do" we have little confidence. But when we hear another say, "I am sheltering under the blood," we think that one knows the secret of safety. On the fatal night when the first born were slain, the Hebrew was safe, not because he had paid his tithes and said his evening prayer, but because the blood was over his doorway.

We had a friend of fine character, and a successful physician. We received him into the church. He ran well for a time, then indulged in the social glass to intoxication. We admonished him and sought to lead him to the source of help, but he thought he could stand in his own strength. He said, "I am a man, I can refrain from drink, it was the company that influenced me." Again, and again he fell. Finally he asked me to "walk with him." We crossed the field, and under the shade of a tree he fell upon the ground and cried out in despair. "I am ruined, I am ruined, I cannot keep from drink." I kneeled beside him and said, "Doctor, I have more hope of you than ever before." He passed through a great struggle of soul, but cast himself in his helplessness under the blood and was saved.

DEPEND AT ALL TIMES UPON DIVINE HELP.—With past sins forgiven and sheltered under the blood, then seek constant help from God. Saved on earth you still have much need of help before you are safe in heaven. The new life begins by divine power and can continue only by divine power.

There is abundance in this earth to feed all that is earthy in men. Plenty to feed their pride, and fatten their avarice, and gratify the basilar nature. The appetites and lusts of men grow and fatten and get so big and strong that they turn upon them and devour them. Men are being eaten up every day. The animal gets so huge, and strong, and unmanageable that man surrenders and is devoured. The mortuary report says, "Died of brain trouble, heart failure, or some latin ailment." All of which, when translated into naked truth, means eaten up by appetite, or consumed by lust.

There is nothing in this broad and beautiful world that can feed the soul—the immortal man. Only that "living bread" which came down from heaven can satisfy the deathless craving.

REPENT AND COME TO CHRIST NOW.— No man intends or expects to be lost. All expect to come to God at some time. The apostle says: "The times of this ignorance God winked at," God overlooked, "but now he commandeth all men everywhere to repent." You have the light of the gospel, and every day you live without repenting is a day of sin. In this light it is a sin not to repent; then, if you know this, and still remain unrepentant and sinning, God will not overlook it in you as He did in the heathen who had not the light. Then what does your life mean? It means, that I am telling God deliberately that I know that I am sinning, but when I have satisfied myself with sin I will then come to Him and tell him, "I am sorry for all this sin." How long dear sinner, do you suppose God will bear with this kind of presumption on your part?

When Titus besieged Jerusalem and overran Palestine, there was one fortress which refused to surrender to the Roman conqueror. The Roman commander sent a flag of truce to demand its surrender. The commander of the garrison met the officer on the beach and proposed to consider the terms. The Roman officer drew his sword, turning its point downward he drew a circle around the other officer, and stepping back he said, "I defy you to step outside that circle until you have surrendered unconditionally."

As the ambassador of God, I now take His word, this Bible, this sword of the spirit, and draw a circle round you, just as you sit, and in the name of the Great Emperor of heaven and earth, I demand your surrender unconditionally to Him. You have no right to leave this church—nay, you have no right to move from your seat until you repent. With the full light of the gospel, every moment you live without repenting is a moment in sin; every hour, and every day, is an hour and a day in sin. Now! Now! Now! "He commandeth all men everywhere to repent." Leave this church without repenting and you leave at your own eternal hazard.

CHAPTER XXXV.

NECESSITY OF CONVERSION.

Text: "Marvel not that I said unto thee, Ye must be born again."—John 3:7.

Nicodemus was dazed and astonished beyond measure when the Master told him that "he must be converted." What? Have I not been long in the church, a preacher, and a ruler in the synagogue, and yet not saved? But Jesus repeated the statement, "Marvel not that I said unto thee, Ye must be born again."

John Wesley was a churchman, minister, and missionary, and he was as much surprised when Spangenberg asked him "if he was saved," as Nicodemus was at the Master's statement. Charles Wesley was as much surprised to find he was unsaved as was his brother John. A man may be in the church, a minister, presiding elder, or Bishop, and yet be unsaved.

To anyone relying on anything but a conscious conversion, this text is one of the most alarming utterances of holy writ. We bring it before you today, praying that it may awaken the unsaved—whether in the church or out of it—to their need of a conscious conversion and pardon of sin.

THE NATURE OF THE SOUL DEMANDS A CHANGE.—The lion of the African wild, or the tiger of the jungle of India, with all their native ferocity, may never come in contact with man, and therefore remain harmless. But not so with the human soul. The soul itself is a "power of an endless life." It was the act of a single soul that wrecked our race and cost the blood and death of the Son of God. A single tyrant may subvert a kingdom and cause its very skirts to drip with blood. This we have recently seen illustrated, when one man caused the world-war and the sacrifice of twelve millions of men. The standing armies of the world are but the police protection against souls in revolt.

Should God leave one soul out of harmony with Himself, such are its powers that it would endanger the harmony of the universe. The peace and safety of the divine government demand that every soul shall be in harmony with God.

There is more at stake in your conversion than merely your own welfare, more demanding it than your own eternal interest. God's government and economy unite with the Son of God in the declaration, "Ye must be born again."

EVERY SOUL IS DESTINED TO MEET ITS GOD.—Let the soul begin its being when and where it may, and its course and history be what they may, it is destined to meet its God. The powers of the soul are such, and its relation to God is such, as demand they shall meet and harmonize. Harmony with God, else destruction, is the eternal decree that rests upon every soul. God has done all that it was possible for Him to do to bring about this harmony with the souls of men. He has given His only Son and that Son has given the blood of His heart, to make this harmony possible, and therefore, the soul that refuses this stupendous sacrifice of God shall be driven from His presence into everlasting destruction.

Brethren, be indifferent and uncertain toward any other interest. Indifferent, if you will, toward the proprieties, styles, manners, and to all other matters, but I adjure you, be not careless or uncertain in regard to your conversion. "Except a man be born again, he cannot see the kingdom of God." Have you this conscious peace with God, through our Lord Jesus Christ?

THERE IS NO SUBSTITUTE FOR CONVERSION.—You can as easily substitute something else for life as for conversion, yet nothing is more common than the effort to make this substitution. A large per cent of the heresy and agnosticism with which the church is cursed begins with this effort.

Development is first among the substitutes. The notion that the heart is not totally depraved, that there remains a germ or particle of purity that may be fostered and developed into right character. Here the old serpent is coiled under the very cornerstone of the Christian system. Here is where infidelity and Christianity cross swords. If there is a something in man that may be developed into right condition before God, then he does not need conversion. If he is not wholly lost he does not need a Savior. This development idea is as false and fatal as it is subtle.

THE TEST OF DEVELOPMENT.—Try development in any department of nature. And truth is the same in all departments, and its lines are parallel and never cross. What can development do in nature? Gash a tree, and leave it to development. Will development heal the hurt? Nay, it only grows the gash wider and the scar larger with the passing of the years. Gash the arm of a child, and what is the process for healing it? Development will only grow the gash wider and more ghastly.

But there is a nursing process which sets up from within. Development must stop and wait until the breach is repaired. The growth of the child is checked for the time, while the mysterious invisible workers—known as "the lives," set to work to repair the damage. The "lives" that are building in other parts of the body are turned toward this break and they unite in filling it up and healing it over, and when this is done the development or growth begins and proceeds as before.

Then, if development can do nothing for the wounded child, how can it do anything for the human heart, which is not only gashed and wounded, but is actually "dead in trespasses and in sin?" The heart—like the wounded arm—must be healed from within, there must come a new power into it, which imparts a new life and quickens it from within. And unless this is done, "Except a man be born again, he cannot see the kingdom of God."

EDUCATION IS ANOTHER SUBSTITUTE.
—The cry is now, "Educate, educate." And this is
essential and proper, but education will not do as
a substitute for conversion, any more than development. You cannot educate sin out of the
heart. Education will do much, it will even polish sin, but it will not grub it up by the roots.

Clip the wings of a bird, and it will quit flying
for a time, but it will flutter and would fly if it
could. Cut the claws and break the teeth of the
lion, and you check his powers of destruction, but
he still has the lionish nature, and would tear and
destroy if he could.

Here is one secret of the lack of power in the
church today. There has been too much demand
for the ecclesiastic chiropodist; too much paring
and polishing of the nails of sin, making it a little
more decent, while it remains sin after all. And
sin with its wings clipped and its claws cut is only
disabled for a time, and a short time at that.
Samson's locks grew again before the Philistines
were aware of it. Lopped-off sin will flourish
again in a very brief time, hence the reason for so
much backsliding—they do not have very far to
slide.

We have seen the living as they were decorat-
ing the graves of their dead in the cemetery and
we thought, "You can cover their dust with beauty and fragrance, but God must come and speak to
them before they can live again." The grave pictures the home. We may educate, refine, polish,
and make the outward life as fair as the flowers

on the graves, but Christ must come and speak with resurrection power before our dear ones can live in the true and immortal sense. The dead are in our homes as well as in our cemeteries. We live and walk with the dead. "Bone of our bone and flesh of our flesh."

WHEN CONVERTED WE KNOW IT.—The first evidence is a *consciousness* of the fact. This is the first evidence of anything in human experience, it is the highest evidence, too high for the reasoning powers. Consciousness itself is a mystery, but a fact. And there come to the consciousness facts which we can know in no other way. Facts come to our consciousness, and we know they are true, and that is all. We can neither reason on them nor explain them, so when one is converted it comes to the consciousness, and is known as a fact, the most momentous and glorious fact of life.

We know that we are alive by this same evidence of consciousness. The apostle said he could know when he was saved. "Being justified by faith we have peace with God." That peace was the evidence of his being justified. Peace is the result of harmony. I know when I am in health, because every part of the physical being is in harmony with every other part, and also in harmony with the air, and the elements from which I live. Health is physical peace, and known to the consciousness. The converted soul is at peace with God and in harmony with itself. It is the soul in high health, and pulsing and bounding with the life of God.

CONVERSION MAY NOT BE INSTANTANEOUS.—Conversion is not invariably, but it is most commonly, instantaneous. St. Paul, St. Peter, the Wesleys, Spurgeon, and the majority who have made history in the church, were instantaneous conversions. They could tell the time, place, and circumstances. A change so radical, so mighty, so glorious, is apt to come to the consciousness with marked certainty and clearness. And yet this is not always the case. There are those who come gradually to a knowledge of their conversion. It is not so important as to *how* we come to know we are saved—whether instantly or gradually—only so we know the *fact.*

You may have had a lingering illness, and come nigh to death, but a change came, and slowly and very gradually you recovered, and today you are in perfect health, yet you cannot tell the day or the hour when you got well. You were dying of sin and Christ healed you, and you became conscious of it, and yet you cannot tell the exact time it was done. But you can say, with one of old, "Whereas I was blind, I now see." Another one may be like the dead maiden who felt the Savior's touch and came instantly to life.

Have you the consciousness that you are saved? No matter how it came. Do you know the blessed fact, and is "The Spirit itself bearing witness with your spirit that you are a child of God?" If His Spirit and your own consciousness witness to the fact, then all is well.

OTHER EVIDENCES FOLLOW.—C h i e f among them is an earnest desire to see others saved. Every truly saved person wishes to help to save others. One may be in the church, and even in the pulpit, and living a correct moral life, and yet have little concern for the salvation of others, but if the heart is full of the divine life there will be unrest, solicitude, and effort to bring others to Christ. The church is active in proportion to the divine life within it. Increase of numbers may not mean an increase of power, and sometimes the church gets spiritually weaker as it gets numerically stronger.

All difficulties vanish when the church is "filled with the fullness of God" and the power that always attends that fullness. May that fullness of power come upon our Zion at this unprecedented time of her need of such power—power to drive the "Centennial Movement" to a glorious success, and turn the heart of humanity back to God.

CHAPTER XXXVI.

LIFE OUT OF DEATH.
(A GOSPEL TALK.)

"Verily, verily, I say unto you, except a corn of wheat fall into the ground and die it abideth alone; but if it die, it bringeth forth much fruit."—John 12:24.

We have seen a small instrument in which was set a tiny glass, so small that it was difficult to bring the eye to bear upon it, yet through it we obtained a perfect view of a broad landscape with a splendid waterfall.

Here we have a grain of wheat so small as to elude the keen eye of the bird as it follows the sower, but it gives a full view of the two great principles—life and death—in their perpetual procession.

LIFE OUT OF DEATH.—This is nature's universal law. "Except a corn of wheat fall into the ground and die it abideth alone." It must come under the dominion of death before it can multiply its own life. Every wheat-grain must pass the death valley in order to come to a fruitful life. There is no quickening except it die. The perfect grain left in the garner for a thousand years would abide alone, but if it fall into the ground and die, then there comes an Easter morning and a resurrection hour to the tiny sleeper. It is no longer alone, but it rises to a new and fruitful life, "thirty, sixty, an hundred fold." The giant oak— lordly, sturdy, enduring—which has measured arms with a thousand storms, had its origin out of death. A tiny acorn fell into the ground and died—like Rachel—that it might give life to a greater than itself. The wheat-grain life, and the giant oak-life—greatest and least in their kingdoms—are born out of the same principle and stand alike upon the dust of death.

SUCH IS SPIRITUAL LIFE.—While death does not contain the life principle it is an inexorable law that death shall precede life. The sinner has all the possibilities and capacities for spiritual life. He is as verily immortal as the saint, and we have no countenance for the heresy that teaches otherwise; but like the wheat grain in the garner, he "abides alone." He is lifeless and fruitless in the things of God, and will so remain until he dies to self and the world.

The grain when it yields its own self-hood and crumbles to dust, God gives a new and fruitful life. So the soul when it surrenders the world, and the old self-life, God then gives a new life—the man becomes "a new creature."

And the contrast is not so great between the little nut-brown grain which fell into the ground, and the golden stalk swaying gracefully in the breeze, as between the sinner who was a walking power of darkness and good for nothing but to break the hearts of other people, and the child of God, clothed in beauty of character, and honoring God in all his ways.

LIFE FEEDS ON DEATH.—The young life not only begins with the dying of the old grain, but it feeds from the dust of that old grain. We feed and fatten the famished field with the products of death, we feed the infant corn on bone-dust, as you feed babies with milk. Give the barren field enough of this death-dust and it laughs with a rich harvest.

Thus the soul is nourished by the continual dying of the old nature. Happy is he who can say with the apostles, "I die daily." As the earth nature dies the new life grows stronger. Such is the divine husbandry that God uses the bone-dust of our dead ambitions to enrich our spiritual life. He sometimes grinds up the very bones of our pet idols and favorite projects and pours their dust about the roots of our character to make it grow and flourish. Find the man growing luxuriantly toward God, and you will find his beauty of life rising from the death of his old self and old loves. Every evil, or earthly thing, that dies in us only makes us stronger in our higher nature.

I have seen rocks enough on the face of an old sterile field, that had they been pulverized and spread over it, would have made it abundantly productive and rich in its yield. And some of us have forces enough in our hard and selfish natures to make us rich in holy things if God's forces and fires were brought to bear upon us. Kill the pride, selfishness, and worldliness in the church, and throw their remains about the roots of her faith and her devotion, and she will become "bright as the sun, fair as the moon, and terrible as any army with banners.'

THE PRINCIPLE IS UNIVERSAL.—It lies at the basis of our civilization and liberty. Our forefathers had to contend with death in all its forms; savage men, dreadful beasts, deadly serpents, and fatal fevers. And our republic is built upon their bones.

The church rests upon the same principle—life out of death. The tragedy of the cross is at its base, there is blood at the bottom. Christ is the divine wheat-grain that must "fall into the ground and die." This *element* of suffering and death constitutes the power of Christ over man, Take these out and He is weak and powerless as another man. This is the magnetism of the cross, which thrills and breaks the hearts of men, and draws all men to Him. Christ, one hour dead, had more believers than in all His laboring life. The multitude that mocked while He suffered, returned to the city "smiting upon their breasts."

THIS PRINCIPLE IS THE LAW OF MISSIONARY SUCCESS.—The man or woman who dies for humanity has more power dead than living. They die into the moral feeling of humanity, and thus get a hold upon it like Him who "Loved us and gave himself for us." Every dark land that comes to the light, comes on that principle. Some one dies that others may live. Every mission field has its martyr. The Dark Continent is coming to the light, but not until Livingston's heart was taken from his body and buried under the molar-tree in African soil. Birmah too is rising, but it is out of the blood of Judson and oth-

ers who toiled with him. Brazil is rising up, but
its ascent is out of the dust of Koger and Matti-
son. China will come to the knowledge of the
truth, but it will be through the martyrdom of
thousands who professed faith in Christ. Christ
said, "I came not to bring peace, but a sword."

The present world-war will, we trust, bring the
nations nearer together and result in the final destruction of autocracy, but if the nations rise it
will be from more human blood than has been
shed for centuries.

THIS PRINCIPLE IS RESURRECTION LAW.
—Out of Christ's death the forces have arisen
which are revolutionizing the world and saving
the millions. It is the life out of His death that
causes the earth, blighted and blasted by sin, to
blossom as the rose. By virtue of that death we are
to come forth from the grave. "Because he lives,
we shall live also."

Soul-blight and body-blight are the works of the
devil. Decrepitude, palsies, blind eyes, deaf ears,
dwarfhood and ponderous corporeities: these
are the blurs and blotches, the finger-marks of an
infernal hand upon a once faultless humanity. But
"Christ will destroy the works of the devil," He
will remove the wrinkles, clear the dim eyes,
round out the withered hands, and make elastic the
unsteady step, while the form shall be fired with
the vivacity of fadeless youth. His missions will
not be complete until "earth and sea have given up
their dead," and humanity is again every whit
whole

We have specimen copies of His work. When struggling with the mysteries of arithmetic in your boyhood, when you came to a new department you found the rule, and a worked-out example; you read the rule and then worked by the example. In the mystery of the resurrection we have the rule and the example. Here is the solution to every question. Science asks, "What about amputated and withered limbs? Will they be gathered from the four winds?" Here is the rule: "Bone to its bone, and flesh to its member." And here is the worked-out example: "A man with a withered hand—flesh gone and particles wasted. Jesus bids him stretch the dead thing forth." And it is restored. How? Like some other man's arm? Not so, but whole like the other.

Again, witness that Gethsemane midnight scene by the torch-light. "The servant of the high-priest," half dead with fear and minus an ear, while the blood is flowing to his feet. Jesus touches the ear and it is healed. Here are two examples—one of long standing, the other fresh and still bleeding, while both alike are healed.

THE SECOND QUESTION.—Will these identical bodies be raised up at the last day? What is the rule? "This corruptible must put on incorruption, and this mortal must put on immortality." And here are the examples: The ruler's daughter, dead an hour; Lazarus four days dead, and the saints which arose, dead for years. All were raised in veritable individuality and readily recognized.

Time or condition have no meaning here. Long standing infirmities, wounds fresh and bleeding, the dead of an hour, the dead of four days, and the dead of years, all are alike subject to His power. No matter how deep, or long standing, the scars on soul or body, He who came to "destroy the works of the devil" will remove it all, and humanity shall be made whole in the absolute.

THE FRUITS OF HIS DEATH.—The universe is one connected and harmonious whole. Other worlds may share in the joys of our redemption. The tree of life may fling its shadows upon other planets than ours. We do not know. But who can tell of this earth's fruitage from His death? What a harvest from the divine-human grain which "fell into the ground and died" the ignominious death of crucifixion. What fruit from that tree whose roots strike down through the sacred sepulchre, and whose healing shadow falls over every land. Millions are now on the heavenward march, while the armies of the holy dead are bivouacked beneath the sod, and only waiting the morning reveille of the resurrection.

Again, the noble charities that dot the earth, like the footprints of the angel of mercy among men—hospitals, homes, asylums, places of refuge and rest for destitute and despairing humanity; these are the fruits of His death, and they spring and grow where the gospel goes, and nowhere else.

THIS FRUITAGE IS INCREASING.—Barriers are down, obstacles are removed, ports are open, and the way is fast preparing for Christ's coming to every "nation, tongue and people." The dark continent is divided among nations who know the Lord; China and Japan are no longer sealed and isolated, the Latin lands are throwing off the oppression of a Christless ecclesiasticism and coming into the liberty of the sons of God.

The mighty river, long locked in wintry ice, when the warm impulse of spring-time comes and swells and bursts its icy bosom, floats that ice-gorge out to sea, its channel left unobstructed.

So the warm breath of the gospel, with its holy impulses, is bursting the age-crusted ice beds of superstition, breaking up heathenism from its great deep, and clearing the channel of the ages. And now, at this marvelous time in history the nations of the earth are in council for the federation and final salvation of the world.

THE ULTIMATE FRUIT GATHERING.—To this we hasten. To the hour when "Christ shall see of the travail of his soul and be satisfied." You may have little interest in the church and the success of the gospel, but you have vital interest in that final "harvest home."

There is a precious grain fallen into the ground somewhere that holds your heart. A "wee" tiny infant it may be, but by the law of the text it has "brought forth much fruit" since it fell into the ground. It has changed your being and your life. We are never the same after these shadows fall upon our pathway. After these sorrows, we are less earthly and more spiritual. Oh, the richness that comes into our lives from the dust of our dead! Sometimes we feel as if we could reach out the hand and almost touch the atmosphere of that other and sinless life.

The hour hastens, when earth shall be full of open and empty graves. Arimathea's empty sepulchre is the prelude and prophecy of the universal emptiness of earth and sea, for both alike shall "give up their dead." The flowers which now deck your altar bring thought of the final coming and glorious triumph of the risen Christ.

Riding with a friend on a funeral occasion, we came into the well-kept and beautiful cemetery. An April shower had just passed over. The crystal drops clung quivering upon the grass and new-blown flowers. It was a scene of freshness, beauty and life, and my friend and I simultaneously remarked, "How beautiful!" The thought came, "How appropriate to plant and cultivate the flowers, and keep them blooming by the pathway where, erelong, the Mighty Conquerer shall walk in resurrection power." It was a moment never to be forgotten. The flowers had a language unheard before; as lifting their heads—still wet with the baptism from the skies—they proclaimed: "We are decking the pathway for him who 'Cometh from Edom, with dyed garments from Bozrah, mighty to save.'" We were lifted up in spirit, and, for the moment, could almost hear the resurrection shout of triumph!

Toil-worn and weary marchers in life's way, take courage. You shall be present and share with Him in that final triumph!

CHAPTER XXXVII.

ANSWER TO PRAYER.

"For everyone that asketh receiveth."—Matt. 7:8. "No good thing will he withhold from them that walk upright-ly."—Psa. 84:11.

PRAYER IS CONSISTENT WITH NATURAL LAW.—God teaches no inconsistencies. He has taught us to pray, therefore prayer is consistent with His economy. The wiseacres now tell us that, "If God should answer our prayers for any definite thing, He would have to change the laws of nature," and as we cannot expect Him to change the laws of nature, therefore we cannot expect Him to answer our prayers."

In the old-time log school-house of the early day, when the birch was liberally used to stimu-late the sluggish idea, the school was governed by laws which were called "rules of school." Those laws were written out and tacked up in full view, and by these laws, to miss a certain number of words, or to do certain things, brought out the inevitable birch.

But what did the urchins care for those rules, had there not been a stern intelligence back of them in the person of the school-master? Let him leave the school ground and every fellow did as he pleased.

Thus the power of nature's laws lie back in na-ture's God. Leave Him out and nature's laws have no more power than the rules of school when the master is away. Every element in nature—like every child in school—is under law, under control of the Omnipotent School-master. The old field pedagogue could change places with every class and change every pupil in every class without changing his rules. So God changes the elements in nature without changing the laws of nature. You see this every day, cool today, warm tomorrow; clear today, cloudy and raining tomorrow; clear in the morning storming at night. We say, "There is a change in the weather," but we do not say, "the laws of nature are changed." Then what is it? It is the master changing his pupils without changing his rules; it is the Sovereign Creator changing the elements according to His will without changing the laws of His government.

THEREFORE—If He can so adjust the elements as to give rain today and sunshine tomorrow, a freeze today and a thaw tomorrow, then in answer to my prayer He can so adjust the elements and marshal the clouds as to bring rain upon my parched field, or so temper the atmosphere as to cool the fever that is consuming my child, and send the breeze, like an angel, through the window to fan the little burning brow; and all this without miracle or change of any law.

Think of a father so fencing himself off from his children as to make it impossible for him to reach them in a moment of pain or peril. I love to think of my God as He stands back of all those forces, as an infinite intelligence—and not as a blind unfeeling force—knowing what to do and what is best to be done, and at the same to know that He is "my father."

The parent on the evening pleasure drive will allow the tiny boy to get his hands on the lines at a safe place and drive where there is no danger, though he keeps his strong hand over the little hands upon the reins. So God, in running this universe, sometimes allows His child to put his hands on the reins and drive. He let Joshua drive, He let Elijah drive, and He will allow the veriest tot lifting its hands in prayer, to put those hands on the reins which control all things.

IT IS A LAW IN OUR NATURE TO PRAY.— So far from being against law for a man to pray, it is a law of his being. This prayer-law is down in the very bedrock of his nature. In a moment of peril he will instinctively cry out in prayer to God. A dying infidel cried, "Oh God, if there be a God, have mercy upon my soul, if I have a soul." The fifth story of a burning hotel with escape cut off, or the cabin of a ship on fire in mid-ocean, is a place where all pray. Whether saint or agnostic, vile or virtuous, all pray. When peril probes deep enough it finds the prayer law—one of the deepest laws in man's nature—it will teach him to pray.

In 1852, before we had steam on the ocean, a ship was becalmed off the coast of Mackinac, in the Pacific. Fresh water was exhausted, and seventy had famished and died for want of water. The Captain called the company to prayer at 10:00 in the morning. The prayer room was well filled. He called again at 2:00 P. M., and the place was crowded. Again he called at 5:00 P. M., and every soul on that ship was present that could leave his post. And that was one time and place where men prayed, under a sense of helplessness, knowing they were lost without God's help. While they cried to God a brisk wind set up and the vessel began to move. This continued until the next day when they went into port and were saved. We say prayers often, but seldom do we pray. We fail to send up the cry, and to feel that we are lost unless God hear and help us.

OUR BLESSINGS ARE TWO-FOLD.—They are temporal and spiritual, and God promises both in answer to prayer, but on different conditions. He promises temporal things *conditionally*, and spiritual things *without condition*. The first text does not refer to temporal things. It is in the sermon on the mount, and the Master has passed that part of His sermon teaching us to trust for temporal things by the "fowls and the lilies." He is now in the higher realm, speaking of the Holy Spirit, and says, "Everyone that asketh receiveth." St. Luke says, "If ye know how to give good things unto your children, how much more shall God give the Holy Spirit to them that ask him." All our blessings come from God, but they come over two different lines. We get both news and groceries from New York, but one comes by freight and the other by electricity. One comes lumbering over the earth, the other comes like a spirit through the air.

NOTE THE TWO LINES.—Our material blessings all come over the "natural-law line." This is the freight line. It brings our wheat, corn, fruits, and every material thing. All comes from God but comes over this line. All physical nature is in harness and works in the natural-law gearing, and cannot work otherwise. Like produces its like, and cause is invariably followed by effect. Nature never changes her train time. No varying in arrival and departure of trains. God gave the schedule to Noah as he stepped forth from the ark, and it has never varied. The A. C. L. and other systems may change, but no change here. "While the earth remaineth, seed time and harvest, and cold and heat, and summer and winter, and day and night, shall not cease." That old Ararat schedule is the schedule today.

WHAT IS PHYSICAL NATURE?—It is simply God's adjustment of Himself to our physical being. He has fixed certain laws or processes for us and does not change them, and cannot without damage to us. The sun rises and sets, the seasons come and go, and the whole movement is harmonious and punctual to time. Our very habits and processes of life are but our response to the movements of nature. We have our spring, summer, autumn, and winter habits and recreations. Indeed, there could be no development of character without this system. If the sun were uncertain in his time, or the seasons unreliable in their march, there could be no such thing as habit or regularity in life.

This never-varying process of nature is the habit of God. I speak it reverently. "With him there is no variableness or shadow of turning." He sets the example, He shows us His integrity, day by day. We may loiter and get behind, but He is on time with every opening morning, and every quiet nightfall. "Day unto day uttereth speech, and night unto night showeth knowledge." God's faithfulness is sounded in the silence of every passing hour, and told in the quiet of each watch in the night. It is thus that God teaches the faithfulness of right habits and helps us to live in them. There is a gospel in every opening morning and in every dying day. The ticking of the pocket watch and the tolling of the tower-bell are but notes of His gospel.

HE DOES NOT ALWAYS GIVE TEMPORAL THINGS.—Sometimes we get what we pray for, and sometimes we do not. Hezekiah prayed for longer life, and God added fourteen years to his life. David prayed for the life of his sick child but it died. You and I have prayed as earnestly for things we didn't get, as for others which were granted to us. Should your little child cry for the beautiful fox-glove flower you would refuse it, not because you do not love it, but because you love it too well to risk it with a flower that has a deadly poison drop in its heart. We sometimes pray for things that would be hurtful, perhaps fatal, if granted. You give your child what is good for it and refuse all else. God deals the same way with His children.

You conceal the phosphorus, the strichnia, and deadly weapons, and keep them out of reach of the little ones who do not know their danger. God hides many things from us and puts them out of our reach; holds them under combination locks whose numbers we can never learn. Lock up, murmur, whine, cry and scream as we may, still He lovingly denies us.

GOD DEALS DIFFERENTLY WITH DIFFERENT CHILDREN.—You cannot deal the same with each of the half-dozen in your own family. Neither can our heavenly Father deal alike with us. Some men can have and handle great wealth without moral damage, while others are destroyed by it. One man has authority and uses it wisely and well, another becomes a tyrant and a fool. One man may serve God best when in perfect health, while He has to half kill another before he will think of serving Him. God knows us best and what is best for us. He knows our temperament and nervous structure, and just how much fire and how much hell-fire there is in every man's nature, and He deals with us accordingly. And to say, "He will give every temporal thing we ask," is the same as to say, "He is not wise enough to know what is best for us, or else he is not good enough to care whether he gives us an egg or a scorpion."

BUT HE GIVES EVERY SPIRITUAL BLESSING WE ASK.—This He does because it is always safe. There is no risk in giving what always makes us better. Hence, "everyone that asketh receiveth." We always get what we ask over this line; there is no poison here.

It is a special grace that gives the desire for spiritual things. It does not require special grace to create the desire for worldly things. The earthly loves and lusts—like the weeds—grow naturally. It doesn't require Sunday schools, sermons, and songs to keep these things flourishing. We have never heard of parents having trouble to get their children to love money, and pleasure, and worldliness. Like the web-footed fowl that takes to the water as soon as it leaves the nest, we are born morally web-footed, and ready for the swim of pleasure in earliest childhood.

SPIRITUAL DESIRE GUARANTEES THE ANSWER.—God will give us no desire that He will not gratify. You would not kindle a desire in the mind of your child for a beautiful toy, and then coldly tell it that "you had nothing for it." Such a parent would be a moral monster.

And the yearnings of soul, the uprisings of desire for a better life, are but the intimations of the desire and readiness of our heavenly Father to give us the blessings we need.

Physical hunger is but the announcement that earth and ocean stand ready to gratify it. The field, the garden, the wing-cut air, and the foam-crested sea, all respond to this physical hunger. And like Augustus Cæsar, we decree that "all the world shall be taxed" for our gratification. The squirrel from the bough, the quail from the field, the buffalo from the plain, and even the stupid

oyster is pulled out of bed while asleep, and all are
brought to the general sacrifice. Seneca said,
"One forest is sufficient for a hundred elephants,
while it takes the whole earth to satisfy one little
body in the form of a man."

What is thirst? It is just the pledge of water
to slake it. Rivers flow, fountains leap, and rains
fall, in response to this thirst. So every sense of
soul-hunger is proof of the readiness of the "living bread," and each feeling of soul-thirst is evidence of the presence of the "living water." But
there is a difference in the quantum and limitations of the two. Provision for the body is as
wide as the world and deep as the seas. Provision for the soul, deep as eternity and wide and
lasting as the life of God.

THE TWO LINES CONTRASTED.—Temporal
blessings come by natural law, spiritual blessings
by sovereign volition. Over these two lines God
sends the answer to our prayers. These principles were laid down at an early period. One of
them as they entered the ark, "My spirit shall not
always strive with man." That is SOVEREIGN
VOLITION. The other, as they came out of the
ark, "While the earth remaineth, seed time and
harvest, and cold and heat, and summer and winter and day and night, shall not cease." That is
NATURAL LAW. These laws stand, as massive
as marble columns, never to be broken. One beyond, the other this side, and the ark stands between them, as if God intended them to read the
two laws before entering upon their post-deluvian
history. There is a SHALL to the one and a

SHALL NOT to the other. Nature shall work on, but my Spirit shall not always strive.

NATURE IS OUR SLAVE.—Slight her this season and she will return to us the next. Nature will bring the food for your table, and the water to quench your thirst, though you curse her unto the going down of the sun. "But my Spirit shall not always strive." Nature may slave for you, but my Spirit is not your slave, but your Sovereign. Abuse the sunlight, and it will return in twelve hours; spurn the Holy Spirit, and He leaves you, it may be, never to return. He is not a blind force with which you may play fast and loose. Trifle, if you will, with the natural law line, but in the name of your eternal interest, do not trifle with Sovereign Volition. When you do you are trifling with the Omnipotent God who holds your destiny and will appoint your doom!

FINALLY.—I give you a fact, among the many facts, that I do not understand. We sometimes have our way over the natural law line when all material means are exhausted. A loved one is at the point to die, and medical skill has failed. You go alone to God in prayer, and get the assurance that the loved one will live. Again you go, in a like case, and are unable to make the prayer of faith, and the loved one dies. Now this is high ground. I do not understand it—but I have been in that higher court and so perhaps have you. Let me give an example of God's answer to prayer.

When a pastor in Louisville, Ky., I had an elderly Doctor in my charge—a man of sterling integrity, but peculiar. Entering my study, he said,

"Brother, God answers prayer, and I want to tell you how I know it. When I was a child of seven, my mother was a widow. There were six of us children, and we lived in the frontier part of Ohio. It was autumn and getting cool. One morning I discovered a sadness in my mother's face. She placed the little breakfast on the table, then drew on her bonnet and went down into the little field adjoining the house, which had but one room. I was more anxious about mother than about my breakfast, so I followed her. She went and kneeled under a tree and began to talk to the Lord. 'Lord, I come to thee, as the father of the fatherless, and the judge of the widow. I have just placed the last of my food before my fatherless children. I have no meat or meal, and the children are bare-foot, and it is growing cold.' She told the Lord all about her case. Then returning I thought she seemed more composed. But my child curiosity was fully aroused. I believed God would help my mother, but I wondered how He would do it. I lingered about the house; the morning seemed very long. But about noon a neighbor drove up, and coming in said, 'Sister L., I have just been to the mill (they sometimes had to go forty miles to mill), and thinking of you, I feared you might be out of meal, so I have brought some for you.' So he brought in the sack and poured it into the meal barrel which sat in the corner of the room, and it filled it nearly full. I thought, there is meal certain, now what about the meat and shoes? The neighbor went his way and the day wore on; the sun was declining toward the west when another neighbor drove up, and after inquiring after the health of the family, he said, 'Sister L., I have just killed hogs and am putting up my meat for the winter, and I thought perhaps you might need some, so I brought you some.' So he brought in a half a hog, and a big one at that, and laid it down by the meal barrel. I thought, there are the meal and the meat, but what about the shoes? The neighbor sat and talked and seemed happy (try something like this and see if you will not feel happy), and just as he was about to leave, he said, 'Sister L., how are the children off for shoes?' Mother had to tell him the truth, that we were without shoes. Said he, 'I am glad I asked, I have a lot of nice hides in tan, and I will take the measure of the children's feet, and will have shoes made and ready before it gets very cold.'

"So calling us all in, he had each one place a foot out on the puncheon floor, and marking between the heel and toe, cut a broom-straw the length of each, and rolling them up and placing them in the pocket of his coat, he said, 'The shoes will be ready in time,' and bade us good-bye.' "

Said the Doctor, "That has been nearly seventy years ago, but is fresh in my mind. I thought, there is the meal, the meat, and the shoes, all that mother told the Lord about this morning, and the sun is not quite down yet. I have gone in the strength of that meal and that meat for seventy years, and those shoes have shod the feet of my faith for the life-journey. When I am gone, you tell it, that GOD ANSWERS PRAYER."

CHAPTER XXXVIII.

CHRISTIAN LIFE ACTIVE AND PASSIVE.

Text: "Behold the fowls of the air   consider the lilies of the field."—Matt. 6:23-28.

With the majority of people in this world the food and raiment question enters largely into the daily thought. The aim of the Master in this lesson is to prevent an indolent presumption on the one hand and an over-anxiety on the other, to give us a restful equipoise between the two.

CHRISTIAN LIFE IS BOTH ACTVE AND PASSIVE.—Its active side is here set forth by the flitting families of the air, and its passive side by the motionless beauties of the earth. The fowls and the lilies portray that piety which is twofold in its character.

"Behold the fowls of the air." While we are taught that the birds, without barns, are fed, at the same time we are to note the manner in which they are fed. Activity is essential to life in all its forms. Stagnation means death. Life ceases when the life-forces cease their activity. Let the respiration and circulation stop and life is at an end.

Religion is a LIFE, and when the spiritual activities cease the spiritual life is ended, and as the stagnant pool generates the noxious things, so the dead church produces jealousies, bickerings, and other evil things.

323

Activity being so necessary to life, God puts us under the most energetic teachers. Not the fowls of the barnyard, which are made stupid and inactive by too much grain, but the "fowls of the air," the swift-winged denizens of the upper deep. Where is the Agassiz or the Audubon who ever found a lazy bird, or where the museum containing the remains of an indolent citizen of the air?

BIRD LIFE A LIVING LESSON.—Who ever heard of a bird dissipating through the small hours of the night until he slept too late next morning? The bird doesn't wake to yawn and rub its eyes, made red by midnight revelings. The birds do not have midnight euchre parties nor all-night germans. The bird goes to bed at the time God intended he should, and wakes in the early morning with a song, and sings to wake other people, and shaking the dew from his wings sails forth to seek the morning meal which providence has prepared for him.

Here is the lesson: The bird uses the best hours; while the air is cool with the crisp breath of the morning, and the sun has not wilted all nature by the touch of his hot hands, nor driven the insect armies to their retreat. The early hour is the successful hour for the laborer or the student.

THE INTENSE ENERGY OF THE BIRDS.— This is such that you are compelled to fortify against it. They will make the corn come up before it has time to sprout, and they will have a share in the garden seeds and play havoc with your grapes, and steal your cherries right before your eyes. Their very nature is energy; they never lag or mope. If on wing, it is with arrow speed; if on the ground, it is with rapid, nervous hop. For the consummate incarnation of energy, "Behold the fowls of the air."

THE LESSONS MISREAD.—No book is so much misread as the book of God's providence. Some people think that God will provide for them just as He does for the birds. And so He will, but they will have to get what He provides just as the birds do, by scratching for it late and early.

If the birds should wait for providence to bring their food to them they would wait until they starved and fell dead from their perch. Man must live by his labor and his energy, both in the temporal and spiritual spheres. I cannot live, as a Christian, with my spiritual faculties at rest. I may complain that "the church is too cold and doesn't warm my spirit," or "the preaching is too dry and doesn't feed me" And so I may wait to be warmed and fed, until I fall dead from my perch. Let me shake the dews of indifference from the wings of my stupid soul, and get down and go to work for God and humanity, then will I begin to feel new life and strength.

The world-field is white unto harvest, while millions murmur and do nothing. There are multitudes in the church, who would not be out of the church for anything, and yet doing nothing. The Master calls, "Go work today in my vineyard," "pray for laborers to be sent into his harvest-field." But harvest work is hard work; it means exposure to the heat of the sun, laceration by the briers and other infelicities, and many are unwilling to endure these things for Christ's sake. They are in the church, just over inside the gospel fence, sitting in the fence corners, shading. These gospel shaders are numbered by the thousand. If I could mobilize them all I would head an army greater than Xerxes led to Thermopylae.

Dear soul, if you have lost spiritual life, go to work, do something for someone else, and a reflex blessing will come upon you, and you will begin to gain strength. Like the lost companions in the Alpine snow, when one discovered that his fellow was growing stupid, which meant approaching death, he forgot himself and turned to work with his companion, chafing and rubbing him vigorously, and in this way saved his life and got a benefit himself. Oh, that God might wake the stupid multitudes in the church, as the birds that wake and sing in the opening morning!

CHEERFULNESS.—Our force is intensified by cheerfulness, and we get the lesson from the birds—"Cheery as a bird." They begin the day with a song, and, like little philosophers, they make the best of their misfortunes. Whether prosperous or adverse they sing just the same. You can tell by the length of the farmer's face whether his crop is a failure or a success, and you can tell when the merchant is losing, by his lugubrious look, but you cannot tell by the way the birds sing whether there is plenty of grain in the field or not. They will sing while the grain lasts, and when it is gone and there is nothing to feed them in winter's snow, they will then gather in the cedars and pick the bitter cedar-berries, and still sing. Even when caged in captivity they soon submit and begin to sing. And the bird that sings in its cage is wiser than the bird that beats its wings bloody in a vain effort to escape.

Let us get the lesson. Who has not some sort of "skeleton in the closet?"—something in life he would change if he could, but cannot. Then why shall I project my darkness upon the pathway of another? Shall I be ever parading my skeleton and rattling its bones to make other people's flesh creep? If I cannot break the bars of my cage and come out into freedom, then let me sit quietly within and sing in submission.

CHEERFULNESS IS A FORCE.—The gloomy man is never a success. He not only fails himself, but serves as a break to check the movement of others; his neighbors have him to carry. But the cheerful man is the locomotive in his community. Hear a man singing as he works, and you may know he is succeeding. Why? Because failure never sings. I can tell when I am going to get a good dinner by the way the cook sings.

The Psalmist knew the power of cheerfulness and joy. Hence he prays, "Restore unto me the joy of thy salvation, then shall I teach transgressors thy ways, and sinners shall be converted unto thee." It is when the church has joy that she has power to save men.

THEIR DISTANCE FROM GOD.—In the

home there is a circle within a circle. The children are the inner circle, then the pets, and the fowls, and the domestic animals. So there is a circle within a circle in the divine oversight. God's care reaches the farthest, and the smallest of His creatures; the sparrow, on the very outpost of creation; the most useless, worthless, and friendless of creatures, are under His care. We believe the Master referred to the English sparrow, for if there is a creature on earth without a friend it is that bird. "Are ye not better than many sparrows?" Are ye not in the inner circle? and closer to God than they? Then while He feeds them will He forget you? "Behold the fowls of the air," and be done with distrust. Do not doubt His gracious providence until the birds are all dead. So long as we can hear a cheery chirp, or catch the flitting of a tiny wing, so long let us have faith in our heavenly Father's care.

CONSIDER THE LILIES OF THE FIELD.— The bird-life and the lily-life are both from God, but unlike. While the one is active, the other is absolutely passive, and therefore is the better expression of character, of what one *is* rather than what he *does*.

The Master said, "Behold the fowls but *consider* the lilies." Put special thought here. The lily is only and wholly receptive; it puts forth no effort but simply abides in the elements which give it life, its roots receiving from the earth and its leaves from the air. The Master bids us note two things. First, their development, "How they grow." Second, their beauty, "Solomon in all his glory was not arrayed like one of these."

CHARACTER COMES FROM THE PASSIVE VIRTUES.—Back of the beauty of the lily there is a property of endurance. Mark you, it is not the lilies of the conservatory or the hot-house, but the "lilies of the *field*."

That means exposure. The heat of noon and chill of night, with all the beatling forces of the field; but under all, the lily stands passive, and comes to larger life and snowier whiteness; it comes to its glory through unfriendly elements.

Thus character has its fullest expression through its passivity. Christ is mightiest to us by what He endured. His omnipotence is an omnipotence of receptive suffering. He takes our sins and sufferings and sinks them in the divine life. Wondrous receptivity, that takes upon it the sins of the race! Wondrous power, that puts its lips to the serpent's wound and extracts the sin poison from humanity! "He bare our sins and carried our griefs; the iniquity of us all was laid on him."

This property is back of all moral beauty. None have deep religious life who have not learned to endure. Suffering is somehow essential to the religious sentiment. The soul must needs feel the palsy of disappointment, and the spear-thrust of antagonism, and the faintness of blighted ambition, before it will retreat into the bosom of its God and learn to draw its life from Him.

There is a sort of divine surgery in the economy of grace. When wounded by the world, and the hemorrhage is profuse and fearful, and the blood of self-confidence is exhausted, and the soul in its faintness falls back upon the bosom of its God, then is there a glorious transfusion of the Christ-blood and the Christ-life until the soul is made strong with a strength that is not its own. This is what the apostle meant when he said, "When I am weak then am I strong." Blessed weakness that fills the soul with the strength of God!

In what element, in your mother's character, was its beauty and power? Not in any positiveness, or noisy demonstration, but in her gentle and quiet endurance and sweet submission, and beautiful patience in suffering. What is more beautiful than suffering patience as it smiles up through its anguish? What more nearly divine than sorrow, when sitting by the coffin of its dead and looking up through its tears, and out of a broken heart to say, "Father, not my will, but thine be done."

HOW THEY GROW.—The lily grows by its very passivity. Resting in the life-giving element and keeping under the sunlight and helpful influences, it grows without effort and without knowing it.

In Christian growth we have but to abide in Him, and suffer no fiber of the affection to be loosed from God. Keep under the sunshine of grace and suffer no earth-foliage to shade us from His brightness. Drink in the life of Christ as the branch drinks in the life of the vine, and we shall grow without thinking of it, or even knowing it.

It is not good to be thinking of ourselves much anyway. Get into the life of God and do not think of yourself at all, then will you "Grow in grace and in knowledge of Christ."

All growth is mysterious but natural; all life is unknowable. How the beauty comes to the lily we cannot know. It is nature's mysterious chemistry, combining light and heat and dew and sunshine, and transmuting all into the purity of the perfect lily. It is mysterious but not strange, and we would think it strange if it were otherwise.

So there is a divine chemistry transmuting the elements of life into character; joy and sorrow, smiles and tears, sunshine and shadows, with the blights and the blessings. All are taken up and transmuted into the beauty of human character. Mysterious? Yes, but not strange. The lily is most lovely just after the storm, as the raindrops quiver on its petals, and it looks up through its tears to catch the kiss of the sunbeam through the rifted cloud. "Tribulation worketh patience." The soul is most subdued and saint-like as it comes up from the deep where "all the waves and billows have gone over it." What a way God has of transmuting the dark things of life—like the carbon—into perfection's jewels!

HAVE NO ANXIOUS THOUGHT.—The bird lives a day at a time, and seeks its meal with each opening morning, and when autumn tells it of winter's coming it seeks an opening in the oak and stores its acorns for its winter's food. Nor does it fail to sleep for fear its treasure may be stolen.

It may die and never need them. Catch the lesson. Put the acorns in the hole, use your energies and take care of your opportunities, but do not die from fear of losing what you have.

FINALLY.—There is a higher order of birds. We call them "migratory birds." Taught of God, they move by His direction. In opening spring they go to the far north. There they rear their young, and when the breath of autumn tells them it is time to migrate, they gather in a flock and rise and set sail for the sunny south.

Here we see the close of a God-directed life. The man who rears his family righteously, and life's late autumn has come, and his failing strength tells him it is near the time for migration, then, like the migratory birds, he adjusts everything for his departure, but unlike these birds, throws off the earthly tabernacle, drops the worn and weary body into its mother dust, while the immortal spirit, liberated and blood-washed, ascends above the air currents, above all worlds and all systems, and sets sail for the immortal hills and the City of God. Such is the close of a consecrated life.

With the energy of the bird-life let us labor to do God's will, while we abide in Christ as the lily rests passively in the sunlight. Thus shall we grow and bring forth the fruits of the Spirit, ripe faith, mellow peace, sweet hope, and all that makes perfect character. Let us hold the lessons from the birds and lilies, and may God impart to ⁓⁓ ⁓ʰⁿ energy of the one, and clothe us with the) ⁓ ⁓t⁊ of the other.

CHAPTER XXXIX.

OUR LIKENESS TO GOD.

"But I say unto you love your enemies, bless them that curse you, and do good to them that hate you, and pray for them which despitefully use you, and persecute you: that ye may be the children of your Father which is in heaven; for he maketh his sun to rise on the evil and on the good, and sendeth rain on the just and the unjust."—Matt. 5:44, 45.

WHAT ARE THE DIVINE FEATURES?— "He maketh his sun to rise on the evil and the good, and sendeth rain on the just and on the unjust." Here we see that God acts from what is within Himself, and not from the conduct of His creatures without. He meets out mercies to men as they need them, and not as they merit them. The blasphemer needs the common benefits of nature quite as much as the saint; he takes up as much room, absorbs as much sunshine, and is just as dependent on the regular rainfall as is the servant of God.

"He maketh his sun to rise." Here we have a hint of human helplessness. "HIS SUN." The sun is His and not ours, and yet every life is dependent upon that sun. We have no power over the sun, but God has that power, and He maketh the sun to shine upon the evil and good, otherwise death would soon end all.

It is as if the sun were unwilling, and that God's power was necessary to compel him to rise and bring daily benedictions to mankind. Could the sun be cognizant of the crime and corruption upon which he is perpetually looking, we would not wonder at his hesitancy. When we grow sick from the sights of a single day we can retire and shut it all out and forget it in sleep, but the sun is rising, perpetually rising upon it. As the world revolves its corruption comes in view. Black all around. "The world lieth in wickedness." Wickedness above it, wickedness below it, wickedness all around it, literally lying in wickedness—a mighty moral monster wallowing in sin and shame, and ever under the great burning eye of the sun. No wonder the sun should grow weary of the sight!

HE SENDS THE RAIN ON THE JUST AND THE UNJUST.—His power is beneath the ocean and behind the clouds, and He forces them to work together and water the thirsty ground, regardless of the character of those owning it. He fills the furrows and waters the ridges of the just and the unjust.

These blessings are neither drawn out nor restrained by the vices or virtues of men, they come from what is in God. It is the overflow of God's beneficence upon humanity. Then to be like God we must do good as He does, acting from what is within us, and not from the way men act toward us. We are to accumulate a vast reserve of love and beneficence within ourselves, then bestow these upon our fellowmen according to their need. We are not to be generous to a friend simply because he is a friend, neither ungenerous toward an enemy simply because he is an enemy, but get mighty moral reserves within ourselves, and then act from within—send blessings upon friend and foe.

"Love your enemy." Perchance he needs your moral help more than does your friend. He is, perchance, a worse man, and therefore in more danger of ruin and needs the sunshine of your kindness to save him from destruction. A small kindness, especially when unexpected, will often change a man's whole life. Many a one has gotten his first impulse for a better life from some unexpected kindness.

HOW IS GOD'S CHILD KNOWN,—The law of likeness is the same in nature and in grace. You may meet a young person whom you have never seen, but you know in a moment that it is a child of one you have known in other years. The likeness tells you this; the features, form, movement, manner, or voice. It would be strange indeed to find a child with none of these points of likeness to the parents. So when one is born of God and becomes a child of the Most High, he is expected to bear some of the features of the divine.

The first question in regard to the "new babe," "Does it favor the father or mother, or both?" "Has he or she some likeness to the Master?" Have they the marks and features of a child of God? It sometimes requires close inspection to find the points of likeness in the elder sons of God.

Time increases this likeness. This is true in nature. When the years are multiplied the likeness to the parents increases more and more. How often we hear the remark, "You are beginning to look so much like your father, or your mother." This increase of likeness is an unquestioned mark of the true child of God. And when they come into the "second childhood" there is a beauty that was not seen in the first childhood. Like the fruit in the orchard, which is not most beautiful in spring-time, neither in growing mid-summer, but in the autumn ripening. When it begins to take on the hues and tints of ripeness and begins to come loose from the twig, it is then that it is most beautiful and attractive. So with Christian character, it is when ripening and taking on the tints and colorings of immortality and getting ready to come loose from the world. Then it is most beautiful when it has the beauty of God upon it.

ALL DEPENDS UPON THIS LIKENESS.— Disharmony is ever the basis of unrest. To live in a home or locality out of harmony with one's taste is an abiding discomfort. To be associated with those whose spirit and manner are repugnant, is an intolerable affliction. Then if happiness depends upon harmony, how essential it is that we be like Him with whom we are to dwell forever. Christ is ultimately to "receive us unto himself," and if we are out of harmony with Him it will be a reception into supreme unrest; yea, into hell itself. This question of LIKENESS is a question of destiny. It determines the heaven or the hell of the future.

THAT LIKENESS MUST BE FORMED HERE.—Transformation of character is confined wholly to this life. All moral changes are crowded into the brief period which is measured by the rising and setting of the sun. The crimson of the atonement falls only upon the territory of time, it does not reach the white light of eternity. The soul must meet its God here in time, under the shelter of the blood, or meet Him uncovered in eternity. The Holy Spirit and the blood must do their saving work before the soul crosses the eternity line. "Today is the day of salvation."

Death affects only the physical, it can make no change in the moral nature. The human WILL determines every moral change. There can be no change where the will is not involved. The will is not involved in the article of death, therefore death can produce no moral change.

How careful we are when we sit for a photograph. And why? Because the picture will look for all time just as we look at that moment. How careful then should we be for that likeness which is to be eternal. What purity, what perfection are essential. Am I ready? Am I willing to cross over today and be forever just what I am at this hour? If the tree fall toward the south, or toward the north, in the place where the tree falleth there shall it be." There is no change beyond the death-line.

THERE IS NO SECOND PROBATION.—Death does not end all, but it does end all probation and possibility of salvation. There is a tim-

mountains, beyond which no vegetation can live.
All above it is barren and desolate. Death marks
the timber-line of the soul. Beyond this the saving blood does not reach. The last gospel call is
made, and its echo dies away as the soul crosses
that line.

A second probation would be of no avail. A
second failure is guaranteed in the first. If the
soul begin at first in infantile innocence and sus-
ceptibility to all good influences, with all the saving agencies that God can bring to bear upon it,
and by its own supreme perverseness it overrides
all these things and hardens and dies in bad character, goes into eternity enslaved by its own lusts;
to offer it a Christ and a gospel then would avail
nothing. Having had every advantage and yet
made ship-wreck, what hope for such a soul when
it must begin in hardness and in scars? With
everything against it; yea, its very self against it,
what could follow but a second wreck and a dupli-
cated hell?

THE VERY NATURE OF THE ATONE-
MENT IS AGAINST A SECOND PROBATION.
—Had there been another probation to come, God
would not have invested all to purchase the first.
When a second effort is contemplated there is always a reserve for that effort. If a reserve could
be found anywhere in the economy of redemption,
then might we conclude a second probation possible. But since God has given His only Son, and
that Son has given His life, neither Father nor

Son has aught more to give. God has done all He can do. The completeness, the very allness of the atonement tells us, beyond question, the worth of this present and only probation. Beyond it there is no other.

The future being changeless, it follows that the present will determine our destiny. What we are here we will be there. "Now are we the sons of God." Here the apostle argues from our present relation, and here he rests his argument on present sonship. Not on what we intend to be, not on a death-bed change, not on a second probation, but on the fact that we now have the *nature* and *character* that give eternal heirship. To hope for heaven without having sonship here is to hope for effect without a cause.

Many are hoping to be saved in some sort of a chance way, they know not how. Hoping at the last to be in the likeness of God, when they are now in the likeness of the world; sowing cockle to reap wheat, planting thorns to gather grapes. They forget the immutable law, "Whatsoever a man soweth, that shall he also reap."

But the apostle rests his case on the great principle that holds good in all worlds. He expects to have God's likeness in eternity, because he has it here in time.

WE MUST SETTLE THE RELATION.— Know that we are sons of God. The glory of that relation will be known in the future. "It doth not yet appear what we shall be." He argues from present relation. The future being changeless it follows that what we are here we will be there. Then having the consciousness and comfort of sonship, the glory of that sonship will appear in future. Certain flowers never bloom until the second season. It would be vain to cultivate them expecting fragrance and beauty the first year. So we cultivate the graces here in the first life, which are to unfold in all their beauty and glory in the next or second life.

The lowliest condition is often the prelude to the highest exaltation. The tiny rose-cutting is lowly and leafless, but it has the rose nature and is akin to the roses. "It doth not yet appear what it shall be." The worm, in the hush of the autumn days, weaves its wintry shroud, getting ready for its own burial. It is insignificant and almost repulsive, but it has the butterfly nature. "It doth not yet appear what it shall be." The eaglet, in its helpless ugliness, lies panting in the rude nest on the peak of the mountain crag. It has neither beauty, power, nor promise, but it has the eagle nature. It is the infant child of the king of the skies, "but it doth not yet appear what it shall be."

Later, I see the rose-cutting, a magnificent Marechal-Niel, full grown and fragrant. I see the worm, risen from its grave, a splendid butterfly floating among the flowers. The eaglet, waxed strong in wing, has left the nest and is soaring toward the sun or sporting with the storm.

The grave is the lowliest possible condition, but it is the prophecy and prelude to the highest exaltation We place the flowers, and sit musing at the tomb. Faith hears the words, "It is sown in weakness, it is raised in power; it is sown in dishonor, it is raised in glory." "It doth not yet appear what we shall be."

HE ARGUES FROM PRESENT CAPABILITY.—"We shall see him as he is." No man can see God in His true character—"see him as he is" —unless he has His likeness. That is true in this life. The outlaw and the atheist have no likeness to God, hence they do not see God in anything. They think of His name only as a swearing convenience, and use it only to emphasize their profanity. But the child of God can see his Father's hand in the things of every day life. And as we become more and more like God we see Him with more distinctness. We can see Him in the shadows as well as in the sunshine, in adversity as well as in prosperity. In our best moods we see Him most plainly; being like Him gives us the power to "see him as he is."

The culprit before the bar sees the judge only in his official character. He is not related to him in any way. The judge is there to vindicate the outraged law, and pronounce sentence upon that criminal. This done, that same stern judge descends from the judgment seat and enters his home, not as the judge, but as the father. His children run to meet him, and with arms about his neck, they have no thought of him as a judge, but they see him as their loving father, and rejoice in his love.

The culprit saw him as a judge, his children see him as a father. They "see him as he is." The wicked see God only in the awfulness of His judicial character. We who are "the sons of God" shall enter into the heavenly home-circle and "see him as he is." We shall see Him as our Father, loving us with "an everlasting love."

CHAPTER XL.

CHARACTERISTICS OF GOD'S LOVE.

"I have loved thee with an everlasting love."— Jer. 31:3.

Heat is the basis of life in the physical world; remove it and life will cease. Just as heat permeates and lies latent in the whole fabric of nature, so divine love permeates the entire realm of spiritual being. The divine love-fire imparts life to the spiritual universe. God is ever breathing into souls the "breath of life."

Heat modifies the state of material things. The river is warm and pleasant, a luxury to lave in its waters; again it is icy and its bosom hard as adamant. The earth is mellow and yielding, insomuch that an infant's feet will leave its imprint; and again it is frigid and hard as Gibraltar's rock.

So the divine love-force modifies our spiritual states. We freeze and thaw, melt and frost over, just in proportion to the love-heat in the soul. Some people are like a March day; they freeze and thaw and thaw and freeze a dozen times in a single day. The only preventive of this vacillating life is in keeping the soul full of the love of God. There is no possibility of a spiritual freeze where this exists.

OUR EXCUSES ARE INSUFFICIENT.— When we find ourselves in a state of religious congestion it will not do to attribute it to circumstances or misfortune. It is not always the clouds or the east winds that make the morning cold. Some of the coldest days in history were without a cloud in the sky or a breeze in the air—clear as crystal and still and cold as death. It is the absence of heat in the element that produces coldness.

Our religious cold states are not from misfortune, poor opportunity, or adverse east winds; they are the result of the going out of the divine love—the heavenly caloric. And like the coldest day with the clearest sky, our deadest religious states come ofttimes when our temporal condition and prospects are fairest.

THE SOUL HAS CONDUCTORS.—A cloud may gather over your home, surcharged with electric fire, but the well-adjusted rod, deep set in the earth and reaching its metal-tipped points upward, silently conducts that terrible fire downward into the earth, while the threatening cloud, robbed of its power, dissolves and floats away.

There are a thousand conductors round about us to draw off the heavenly fires and leave us as powerless as the clouds when robbed of its electric force, and these conductors are all deep set in the earth and drawing downward. There is a power in the "Things that are seen" to neutralize the religious life. And their work is done as silently as the cloud is robbed of its fire. When not thinking of danger we often come in touch with that which robs us of our power; an investment, a recreation, an indulgence in something incompatible with a holy life, and our power is gone.

HOW WE PERCEIVE THIS LOVE.—Heat is perceived through the medium of life. We feel the outward heat in proportion to the inward life. When the life-force is full we feel the slightest degree of heat, but when that life-force is low we feel the heat very feebly. You may cremate a dead man and burn his bones and he does not feel it.

We apprehend the divine love in proportion to the spiritual life within. When in high spiritual health we are keenly sensitive to the touch of that love; we feel it in every soul-nerve, and sometimes the reception is so full and glorious that we are thrown into ecstasies and filled with a "joy that is unspeakable."

The soul in its cold stages cannot be restored and revived by outward processes. You cannot warm a congested body through the hands and feet. Hot bricks and blankets and water bottles are of no avail until an inward stimulus reaches the heart and quickens the circulation and turns the blood back to the extremities, then the patient will tell you, "the room is getting warm."

You get no benefit from outward things in a religious chill. Gather all your good deeds and wrap them as a blanket about you; have whole jugfulls of good desires and warm intentions stacked round you, but there is no relief until you call for the Great Physician, who can reach the heart with a baptism of fire. Then will the life-blood flow through the whole being, while the earth will seem "full of his glory."

THE TEXT IS A STIMULUS.—Its contemplation should quicken the love-fires in us. "We must love him because he first loved us." And the evidence is beyond question, "He gave himself for us." Here is an argument to which there is no answer. Mythology tells us that "When the great chasm opened in the earth near Celanea, the king, Anchurus, was told by the oracle that, "The chasm would never close until he should throw that which was most precious to him into it." Whereupon the king threw himself into the chasm and it instantly closed.

God, in His great mercy, closed the chasm between Himself and us when He gave His most dearly beloved Son to be cast into it. A man may give much to a cause to which he has no devotion; he may give time, attention, or money, from sinister motives, but when he gives himself he passes all policy, destroys all doubt, and demonstrates his devotion. There is no question then.

When I go, in thought, and stand at the tomb in Arimathea and read the words, "He loved me and gave himself for me," all the arguments of the infidel world can never answer the silent argument from that sacred tomb.

THIS LOVE IS UNEXAMPLED.—God's love has no precedent. There was nothing before it, nothing like it, and we have nothing to measure it; we are dependent upon God for the suggestion. We had never conceived of such a thing as a tree, or a flower, if God had not first made them. But with them before us to spring suggestion, we are then able to think of other trees and flowers.

But God's love stands alone, unique and without precedent. No past, no present love like it, hence we have no way to reckon it. We try in vain, with all the tenderest, mightiest loves, parental, conjugal, filial. We tie them as we would tie cord to cord, and make the line as long as all human love can make it, and when we drop it into the ocean of His love, it is but the child's effort to sound the sea. Even the immortal spirits, who have gone through the cycles in the eternal life, have reported no soundings yet. It will be to us as measureless in the life to come as in this present state.

THIS LOVE IS PERSONAL.—God does not merely love us as a world, or as a race—all in general and no one in particular—but He loves us singly and separately. He loves me individually, with all my peculiarities, my weaknesses, faults and foibles—all that combines to make me just what I am. And He loves me just as I am, and to know there was never a time when He did not love me. How strange, that I had a place in His thought and in His heart before I had my being. But my consciousness of the fact had nothing to do with that fact then or now, more than to slight and abuse, and ofttimes to grieve that love.

In many cases it had been far better if the soul had never been conscious of that love; better to have been imbecile and irresponsible, rather than to have known only to abuse it. We know so little, nothing previous to creation, little in the present, less in the future, but when we are gathered into His society, then will He open to us "the treasures of wisdom and knowledge." He will tell us His thoughts and plans for us before we had our being. I shall learn more of myself in that sinless life, and in the bosom of God than I have in all the lessons of this twilight state. The light here is too dim. "We see darkly, but there shall we see and know as we are known."

THIS LOVE IS PERSISTENT.—Love has a strange persistency. It "endureth all things." Even in its lowest forms it has enduring power. Kicked, cuffed, and driven back, the faithful dog will slyly follow his master afar off. Bereaved in his master's death, the affectionate animal will not leave his grave, but lingers to perish and die, a martyr to his love for him. The wife will follow the husband to disgrace and death. The parent will pursue the child even unto the last fatal extreme.

But these lower and finite loves cannot portray the persistency of the love of God. We are the children of that love, hence it follows us. "Now are we the sons of God." Turned out of Eden in disgrace, this love has ever followed us; it has gone before us in clouds by day and fire by night, opened seas, destroyed enemies, made the rocks give us water and the skies rain bread. Ever getting closer, it came at last into our nature and form, and into our condition, took our sins and sorrows and bare them for us, went into the tomb to drive out its dread and rob it of its terrors, before we should come to pass through it. There is no place to which we have to go where this love has not gone.

LOVE IS THE ONLY THING GOD WANTS. —"Son give me thine heart." Love me "with all thy soul, mind, and strength." All else is worthless to Him without our love. He puts no price on anything else, and wants nothing else. Here is the divine desire, THE LONGING OF OUR FATHER'S HEART. He is not willing to do without our love. He not only follows and pleads, but even afflicts us to get our love. How often have we loved other things too well, and He had to remove them in order to get the love-place Himself.

Men are not so wrought with on any other matter. He may or may not follow a profession, he may or may not marry a wife, he may or may not cast his vote. There are no forces brought to bear upon him in these matters, but divine love has an organized system in constant effort to secure that love.

A revealed gospel, churches built, men called and sent of God to preach that gospel, the Holy Ghost striving to "lead us into all truth," and the Son of God pouring out the blood of His heart to wash away our sins.

Like the wild herd on the plains when under the chase, the strong escape while a few of the younger and less fleet are taken with the lasso and brought back. So the great human herd rush on to ruin, while a few of the love-chased race are captured and brought to Christ. The children, and such as have fallen under the shadow of bereavement or disappointment, are taken with the love lasso, while the impenitent rush onward regardless of the efforts to save them.

WHAT MANNER OF LOVE DO WE GIVE HIM?—Those of us who have yielded to the love-forces and have been pardoned for our sins. Sometimes we give Him the whole heart for a day or week, and it is like a day or a week in heaven. Then we forget Him for months, or remember Him only in a cold and heartless way. What remuneration does God get for all His pains, and labor, and blood?

And yet He is glad, and the angels are glad, and there is a jubilee in heaven when even one poor sin-slimed soul repents and consents to be saved. And that is the grandest moment in the history of that soul. Who can describe or express the joy of the soul new-born to God? Millions have tried it, but none have been able to reach the height and depth of that love that "passeth knowledge." St. Paul could not reach it even in inspired effort.

CONVERSION IS A LOVE-DELUGE.—We realize it much as the Patriarch realized the flood —the one is type of the other. There was first a sense of fear and then a work of preparation, a coming in and shutting of the door, a separation from the world. Then a breaking up of the fountains of the deep, and an opening of the windows of heaven, then a conscious ascent. The earth begins to disappear, valleys, hills, and, finally the highest mountains, pass from sight.

The outlook for the dove's keen eye is one vast and interminable waste of waters, and the ark but a speck on its bosom. Sink down where it may, is to sink in the floods.

Such is it to personally realize and experience God's love. There is first a fear—always fear enough to drive the soul to Christ—then a breaking up of the heart's great deep in repentance, a separation from sin, a shutting out of the world, a conscious rising towards God. Things of earth pass out of thought, and even the highest mountains—difficulties that towered above us and clouded the life—even these sink out of sight. Love prevails, and the soul, like the ark on the waters, is but a mere speck in the illimitable sea of love. Like the dove let loose from the ark, the soul, sink down where it may, can but sink down in love! God grant us today a dove's-eye view of that love, which is unexampled, personal, persistent, and "from everlasting to everlasting."

CHAPTER XLI.

FAITH AND THE HUMAN WILL.

"O woman, great is thy faith: be it unto thee even as thou wilt."—Matt. 15:28.

This woman comes and casts herself upon the will of Christ, and to her astonishment she is thrown back upon her own will. "Be it unto thee even as thou wilt." This is true of every soul in the matter of salvation. Not a soul in heaven or hell but is there by his or her own will.

ADJUSTMENT OF THE SAVING FORCES. —This adjustment must fit the nature of the creature to be saved. If a man be drowning, you simply throw him a rope, he adjusts it himself and is saved, but if a brute be drowning, you must reach it and adjust the rope.

The gospel to save man is adjusted to his nature. Man is intellect, sensibility, and will. The gospel is adjusted to his threefold nature. First, to his intellect. The inspired word makes its appeal, and if the evidence support the facts he is compelled to believe it. God does not ask a man whether he will believe the gospel or not. If the proofs are sufficient he is forced to believe and cannot help himself, unless he is a fool. We have to believe many things which we prefer not to believe. I may not wish to believe myself the victim of consumption, but if the hectic flush and hollow cough are in evidence, I am forced to believe it. The maiden may not wish to believe herself growing old, but if the crowfeet are about the eyes and the gray hairs mingle with her raven tresses, she is compelled to believe it. So the proofs of the gospel force conviction on the most ungodly men.

Likewise the Holy Spirit deals with the sensibility or the heart; it compels a man to *feel* that he is a sinner whether he is willing or not. God did not ask Felix, when Paul reasoned before him, whether he would be convicted or not. Felix trembled and could not help himself. So, at one time, with every sinner, he feels his guilt and cannot help it. The Word will do its work in the *intellect*, and the Holy Spirit will do its work in the *heart* whether we will or not. But when we come to the royal *will*, all saving agencies halt and wait. The word, the Spirit, the church, and God Himself stands there, while He says, "Behold, I stand at the door and knock; if any man will open the door (surrender his will), I will come in and sup with him and he with me." All things, and God Himself, waits on the human will.

A measure may pass both houses in our national legislature and then meet a veto at the hands of our chief executive. So the question of salvation may pass both houses, the intellect and the sensibility, and then meet a veto at the hands of the royal will. Men hear me now, who have been convinced in the intellect and convicted in the heart, and yet have vetoed the matter by their stubborn wills. What Christ said to this Cyro-Phoenician woman, He says to every soul in heaven, earth, or hell, "Be it unto thee even as thou wilt." As thou wilt for time and eternity.

THE FIELD OF FAITH IS INVISIBLE.—"O woman, great is thy faith." Faith is no more theological than it is agricultural, mechanical, or social; it is the foundation principle of every day life, it is that power by which we see future results of present action. A man believes a disaster is coming, he thinks, prepares, gets ready, and thus is saved from the calamity by faith—His faith saved him. This is saving faith, whether you apply it to save your reputation, to save your crop, or to save your soul. None of the five natural senses can reach the invisible. We need a sixth sense to reach that realm. Faith is that sixth sense.

There is no invisible world to the man who has no faith. There is no upper-room to his being, he is shut down to the basement of the material; nothing for him beyond the tug and toil of this life, his cradle and his grave are the extremes of his being, his beginning is puling helplessness, his end is feeding worms. Smallest and most pitiable of creatures is the man without faith.

FAITH AND REASON ARE IDENTICAL.— Infidelity ignores faith and deifies reason, as though the two were in conflict. They are one and the same. When the mind is at work with the material—the things that are seen—we call it reason, and when it is at work with the "things that are not seen," we call it faith. Faith is only reason in the higher field.

The success of science is the product of faith. Faith is at the foundation of all achievement. Columbus had faith in a western world before he discovered it. Morse believed in telegraphy before he invented it. Faith is back of every movement on the highway of science.

Men may deny the possibility of going to heaven by faith, but they go everywhere else that way, whether to New York, Novo Scotia, or the Klondyke. They determine to go, seek the conveyance, put themselves on the line, make the journey. Being saved is just that and nothing more.

FAITH MUST INHERE IN PERSONALITY. —Aside from personality faith means nothing, and aside from this all the virtues are meaningless; but faith, *impersonated,* becomes the mightiest force next to God Himself. Faith omnipotizes the soul until it stands up and prevails with God.

Nor is it dependent on human excellence. It requires neither the physical power of a Samson, nor the mental force of a Butler or a Burke. All it asks is a setting in a human soul, however obscure—whether a Publican with name unregistered, a thief suspended on a cross, or a heathen woman kneeling in the dust and pleading for her child. Faith carries its own power and is equally mighty wherever its battery is planted. It was faith, with its battery set in a human soul, that wrought the wonders of the 11th chapter of Hebrews; the recorded chivalry of the saints of God. And it is this mighty principle in the heart of this woman that is rising up to make its demands and have its way with the Son of God.

The chief field of faith is the supernatural, and its commerce is mostly with God. Sight halts at the horizon, faith looks beyond. The boatman needs only a pole to push his boat while near the shore, but to cross the channel he must lay down the pole while the oars are plied to pull him across the depths he cannot fathom. The snail, in time, may creep to the mountain crag, but it takes the eagle to measure the airy gulf between the peaks and know the quiet of the upper deep. Faith makes us familiar with the higher and the divine realms.

FAITH HAS SUBLIME DISREGARD OF OB-STACLES.—And that disregard was, perhaps, never grander than in the case of this woman. Never in a faith battle did the odds seem greater or the battle grow darker and more desperate as it advanced. Never was there a battle in which resistance was more steady and stubborn.

His *silence* was terrific. When the spirit is writhing and bleeding, how withering it is to be met with cold and speechless contempt. How a sensitive nature shrinks under it. Had He only spoken, even to deny her, it had been less severe. But there is no word, no look, no sign of sympathy—only a silent and icy indifference that seemed heartless as the grave—"He answered her not a word."

Here the disciples interpose. They, no doubt, were surprised to see their Master unmoved, and were perhaps sorry for the distressed mother, hence they intercede, "Send her away;" that is, grant her request and let her go. But their motive appears when they say, "For she crieth after us." She is an annoyance. How hard to get selfishness out of our very devotions. The little boy expressed it in closing his evening prayer, "Lord, give little Jimmy Bailey a knife, so he won't have to borrow mine every time." We wish the Lord would bless some people so that we could get them off our hands. This appeal has about the same effect as our prayers when offered from the same motive.

HERE A LIFE-LESSON.—How frequently are we discouraged in praying! We have a case that causes the heart to bleed and commends itself to the divine compassion. We cry to God for a child "grievously vexed with a devil"—a devil of unbelief, a devil of prodigality, a devil of indifference, worldliness or strong drink. We pray, and pray, the weary years go on and "He answers us not a word." The church joins its prayer with ours and yet no answer, and we get discouraged.

Here is this woman in the majesty of a faith that defies opposition; she prays and waits, and then commands what she will. Discouraged one, come and learn how to make your faith imperial, how to repress obstacles and have your way with God.

HERE IS A RACE PREJUDICE.—A mighty barrier always. The Jews regarded the Gentiles as beneath the divine notice. Jesus, as a Jew, is expected to expend His blessings upon them. A heathen woman can expect nothing from Him. This He confirms in His reply to the disciples when they ask Him to grant her request, "I am not sent but unto the lost sheep of the house of Israel."

How many break down right here. We can believe that God had special blessings for Moses, or Elijah, or the ancient worthies, but that He has special blessings for us we hesitate to believe. But note this woman. Her cries have failed, the disciples have failed, and the race prejudice rises as a mountain before her. Now what? Retreat? Never! Never! "Then came she and worshipped him." Faith always worships. There is a somewhat called faith, that worships on a commercial basis. "If God will I will, and if he won't I won't." If He will give me a good parsonage and a fat salary I will go cheerfully, and if not, I don't know whether I will go or not." It is a sort of bargain-making with the Lord, and He generally gets the small end of the bargain.

THE PAWN SHOP.—We make a sort of pawn-shop of the throne of grace, where we deposit our vows and pledges when we get into a close place and are compelled to have God's help. Then when we get out of the pinch we are ready to take back all this collateral. An inventory of a pawn-shop would be an interesting document. A little of everything, time-worn, dust-covered, and little worth. If God should preserve the pitiable plunder, in the heavenly archives, which we have deposited as collateral for His mercies, it would be the chief curiosity in the museum of eternity.

Genuine faith has no proposition to make, no bargain to drive; it ascends above the commercial, worships, and commands what it wills. It worships whether God answers or not. It knows that He knows best, hence it worships without conditions. (Job on the ash-heap.)

NOTE HER ARGUMENT.—Faith carries the mightiest arguments, its logic is the trip-hammer to crush obstacles. I have seen a rock crusher which by simply pressing two blocks of steel together could crush the hardest granite and deliberately chew up a rock quarry. Faith can clench its hands and crush out obstacles as if for passtime.

Christ now speaks to her for the first time. And what words! "It is not meet to take the children's bread and cast it to dogs." The original says, "little female dogs." Could anything have been more withering? A weak faith would have risen up and left his presence with indignity and disgust, but she answered, "Truth Lord." True faith always consents to God's statements; it never controverts His word, but accepts what He says and makes that the basis of its argument. She made no effort to prove she was no dog, but accepted the situation. You are correct Lord, I am unworthy as a dog, but for this reason, because I am a dog, I claim that which belongs to the dogs, I claim the crumbs, and that on your own statement. Here is faith in its majesty. Not driving a bargain, but standing in its place and demanding its rights.

Faith has great thoughts of God. Our thoughts of God are too low and little. We depreciate Him, and deal with Him as if He were a small God. Nothing is so pleasing to Him as a faith that deals in large things. He bids us "ask largely," fling ourselves out on His mercy with the abandon of childhood; plunge in and do business in deep waters, go below the surface, down! down! to where we may disturb the quiet coral forests in the sea-beds of His compassion!

Faith is not foolishly sensitive. Abnormal sensitiveness rests on weakness or selfishness. Faith has the strength which is free from this, it is willing to take its right place and be called by its right name. This woman did not wilt under the fearful sarcasm of the Son of God.

That spirit that falters when it doesn't meet every courtesy, takes a back seat and quits the church if it fails to get a surfeit of social attention; that hesitates in duty because somebody has remarked about it. That is not the faith that commands what it wills. True faith doesn't care what it is called so you stand out of its way. You see a grand mogul engine coming, you may call it a baby-wagon, go-cart, or what not; you will get out of its way, it will have the track. That is true faith. It claims the track and pays no attention to what is in the way, but drives for its goal.

THE TRIUMPH OF FAITH.—The battle has

been long and hard, but the moment of triumph
has come. Christ has had His way with her.
Faith can be tested no further. She has met all
that can chill a sensitive nature or wound a proud
spirit. She has carried the last ditch between
her and the heart of God, and now, heart to heart,
she presses her claim, her submission is absolute
and her triumph complete.

Now it is as if Christ Himself surrenders, as
He exclaims, "oh, woman, great is thy faith; be
it unto thee even as thou wilt!" He did not tell
her He would heal her daughter, nor did He so
much as mention her; have your way! I turn over
to you the keys of the store-house of grace. Thou
art a queen in the realm, and "all that I have is
thine."

Have you long prayed and sighed for a certain
thing? Has God had His way with you? Can
you go down at His feet and hear what this woman heard, and endure what she endured? Then
your hand is even now on the latchet of the gate
that opens to the riches of God. Soon you will
hear what she heard, "Be it unto thee even as
thou wilt."

IT IS FAITH THAT MAKES HISTORY.—
Real history is made only in touch with the supernatural. It takes that touch to make it immortal. No man ever immortalized himself who
did not get above the material. The material will
perish with the men who belong to it, but this
woman has gotten beyond all material, and is now
in touch with God and making history, history

that will never perish, history that is helping us today.

We make history in coming over odds and obstacles to get to God. Daniel made history in the den, Job on the ash-heap, Paul in ship-wreck. If you are bleeding at heart under trial for which there is no relief, yet standing—Gibraltar like—you are making history..

THE SCENE WILL CHANGE.—It changed with this woman. It changed with Joseph, from the dungeon to promotion. It changed with Daniel from the den to the palace. It changed with Job, from the ash-heap to affluence, so will it change with you. Suddenly, some sweet day, the sunlight of heaven will flash in, and, caught up to God, you will hear the glad surprise, soul, heaven is thine! "Be it unto thee even as thou wilt," and that forever!

CHAPTER XLII.

THE DIVINE DECREES.

"Wherefore, the rather brethren, give diligence to make your calling and election sure, for if ye do these things, ye shall never fall."—2 Pet. 1:10.

THE DOCTRINE OF ELECTION IS A BIBLE DOCTRINE.—This doctrine has given rise to much controversy and has led many into error. There are THREE great facts decreed of God, and they involved the Redeemer and the redeemed. They are the three pillars that prop the whole Christian system. They stand out clearly before us in Scriptures and are planted in divine love.

The first decree rests upon Christ. "The seed of the woman shall bruise the serpent's head." This decree was consummated in the crucifixion. "God so loved the world that He gave His only begotten Son," and He, by the grace of God, tasted death for every man." While this decree rests on Christ it reaches every man. Death for him, but possible life for the race.

THE SECOND DECREE.—This decree is over on the right-hand of the first. "He that believeth shall be saved." The third decree is upon the left-hand of the first. "He that believeth not shall be damned." There stand the decrees and the foreordination of God, as laid down plainly in the Scriptures. Upon these decrees our destiny hangs, and by these will our eternity be determined.

Christ the central figure, dying under the first decree. On the one hand is belief and heaven, on the other unbelief and hell. The immutable SHALL is linked with each. Christ SHALL bruise the serpent's head. "The believer SHALL be saved, the unbeliever SHALL be damned.

Here we see that predestination rests upon CHARACTER and not upon personality. Unbelief is reprobate ground, while belief is elect ground. This is illustrated by the colored man who said, "Dar is two powers after me. De Lord he wants me, and de debil he wants me, so when de test comes, I votes on de Lord's side, and dat gibs de 'jority in my favor."

Believing brings change of heart and this changes the character, and therefore changes the relation to God, and the soul comes from the darkness of reprobation into the light and liberty of election.

OBSERVE THE ETERNAL VERITY OF THESE DECREES.—The first decree has been fulfilled upon the person of Christ. "God spared not his own Son." Then, if the first and greatest has been fulfilled must not the least decrees be unequivocally met? So sure as "Christ suffered by the will of God," so surely will you and I enter heaven, or plunge the pit, by these decrees. The atonement is real, heaven and hell are real, and our election is made sure by our faith in Him "who loved us and gave himself for us."

THE CANDIDATE FOR PUBLIC OFFICE.—
To make this subject practical let us observe one
who is trying to make his election sure with men.
The first thing with the candidate for office is
to announce his candidacy. He comes out publicly
and prominently before the people and lets the
facts be known. He tells it himself, puts out his
cards and pays for the announcement in the papers, and gets his friends to give it publicity.
No man ever attempts a secret race, and the idea
would be simply absurd. The candidate goes before the public knowing that he will be publicly
picked. If he has ever done any meanness now is
the time it will come out, and he knows he must
suffer the criticisms and misrepresentations common to candidates, and all for the sake of being
elected to office.

So when a man becomes a candidate for election to eternal life he must announce himself, let
it be understood at all times and places that he is
standing up for Christ. There is nothing better
than to be always and unequivocally on the Lord's
side. I have great confidence in the final election
of the out-and-out Christian—the man who lets
it be understood by his very manner of life that
he is on that side, regardless of the criticisms,
jeers, or persecutions of those whose business it
is to war against those who are living for Christ.

THE CANDIDATE'S RACE AFFECTS HIS
ENTIRE BEING.—His hope of election fills his
thought from which his life and conduct proceed.
Everything else is secondary. He becomes polit-

ically pious, and will neither do nor say anything that will militate against his election. All his nobler nature is awakened, and he feels an interest in his fellow-men that he never felt before. He is even interested in the "common people" and "minds not high things but condescends to men of low estate." He comes into a sort of sacrificial state, and takes the woes and wants of all the men (over twenty-one) on his moral feeling. He studies and plans for success and seeks the help of those whom he thinks will be most helpful.

Thus should a man's religion affect his whole life and take possession of his entire inner being; everything else should be secondary. His entire life should trend toward that one thing, doing and saying nothing that would militate against his success in the things of God. He should have one chief desire which should be manifest in his bearing toward his God and his fellow-men. He should become a "living sacrifice." In a word, his life is to be, from sincerity and principle, what the life of a candidate is, many times, from policy and self-interest.

THE CANDIDATE GIVES MUCH THOUGHT TO HIS ELECTION.—Did a candidate ever become so engrossed with other things as to forget he was on the track? Who ever heard of such a thing? Yet persons become so taken up with the world that they forget they are in the service of God. Some people think very little on this matter and never very seriously, unless it is under some pungent point from the pulpit or some imminent danger or heavy judgment of God. Others, late in life, and when death is about closing the probation polls, wake up to the fact that they have neglected their opportunities and lost their election. There is no time to be lost. God has made your election possible and laid down his life to secure to you that possibility. Now it is left to you, and to you *only*, "to make that election sure."

THE CONVERSATION OF THE CANDIDATE.—In this his election is first. He may talk to you of other matters but will bring that in before he quits. He will tell you of his prospects, difficulties, and hopes of success, and will draw you, if possible, to his support. He associates with men for their help and will talk by day and by night; and I have even had the matter brought to me while in the pulpit.

Brethren, is not an eternal election of more moment than the election to a petty office? Shall it not sufficiently engross the mind as to cause us to talk about it? Shall we not bring this matter into the conversations of life? And is it not the wise policy to associate with such people as can, and will, help us in this campaign? Shall we not electioneer with such as have influence at the throne of grace and get them to cast their prayer-ballot in our favor? Let us use the zeal, the energy and the persistence of a candidate. Let them be a living lesson to us, teaching us how we may make "our election sure."

THE CANDIDATE HAS PERSISTENT EN-
ERGY.—There is very little fag in the candidate
for office. He goes all day and borrows a part
of the night. Many the poor, tired, candidate who
trudges the streets of the city, who otherwise
would be at rest in the bosom of his family. Indeed he has no rest until he is satisfied and sure
of his election. Such zeal and such sacrifice are
worthy of imitation. If the honors of a petty
office in this life elicit such effort, shall we not,
in the race for glory contest every inch of ground
and use every hour of time? Shall we not be
ready to sacrifice ease, confort, rest and money?

If his election requires money (as it generally
does), he will use it if he has it. If I had ten per
cent of the money spent in some cities in the last
ten years on elections, I could endow your church
for all time to come. Give to this church in which
I am now speaking the zeal and self-sacrifice of the
candidate for office, and it could send the biggest
delegation to heaven, in proportion to its membership, that ever went from the church on earth
to the church on high.

THEN LET US WORK FOR EACH OTHER.
—I heard a man say, "I quit business for a whole
day to work for a friend who was a candidate,
and I secured seven votes for him that day." I
wonder if he ever turned seven men to Christ in
one day. When you associate with a man find
out—in a wise manner—whether or not he is for
Christ? And if he is not, then get him over on the
Lord's side if possible. You can influence men

in politics, then influence them in religious life also "He that converteth the sinner from the error of his way shall save a soul from death, and hide a multitude of sins."

THERE IS NO FAILURE WHEN WE INVEST ALL.—Men sometimes run for office and invest all, and are beaten and financially ruined, but in the race for immortality there is no such failure to him who invests all. There is not a failure on record where all was invested. It is the partial investments that fail—such as wish to be saved but are not willing to pay the price. The text gives the guarantee, "For if ye do these things ye shall never fall." Our election to eternal life will just cost us all, whether that be little or much, whether the fortune of Zaccheus or Peter's old fish-nets too rotten to mend, but when we give all we get all. Let us calculate on nothing less than ELECTION. We may think of failure on some lines, but never, never think of it in the matter of the soul and its destiny!

DO YOU EXPECT TO BE ELECTED?—The forces against us are strong I know, but he that is for us is mightier than all that are against us." I expect to be elected, and my prospects are better than they were fifty years ago. I have some forces drawing me heavenward which were not there when I first started, and some things which bound me to this world have lost their hold and dropped away. Christ is more real and personal and I feel the grasp of the divine hand more firmly than in earlier years.

Brethren, when the ballots are counted and the election is over shall we be among the elect? There will be no "second count." No fraud can be practiced where Christ is judge. Shall we be at the final great installation where Christ himself shall install us "kings and priests unto him forever?" To this end we were born, to this God has called us, let us therefore "give diligence to make our calling and election sure."

CHAPTER XLIII.

SHINING LIGHTS.

"Let your light so shine before men, that they may see your good works, and glorify your Father which is in heaven."—Matt. 5:16.

Darkness makes light visible, and the density of the darkness is in proportion to the brilliancy of the light. The tapir that lights the room at mid-night is scarcely visible in mid-day. The lesser stars are not seen in the moon-light, and even the brightest of them fade out at noonday. So in the moral universe. This world is well adapted to the shining of lights. Sin has made the background black enough and the darkness dense enough to bring out all the force of a burning light. God has put us in the best possible place for the light-shining—better than heaven itself. Carry the brightest Christian light to heaven and its luster is lost in the divine glory.

But here is this world there is so much darkness that every little light has a chance. The dark nights are the nights for the little stars, and if you are one of the least of His little ones there is darkness enough to bring out your light. And he bids us use our advantage, while he makes sin and the very darkness to be our servants.

SHINING PRESUPPOSES LIGHTING.—The tapir must have a touch from an extraneous fire before it has power to shine. All adjustments for lighting are worthless without this. In this

371

text we are supposed to have been in touch with the Holy Spirit. He is the great Lamp-lighter going through the streets, lanes, and highways of earth.

I come to a street at cloudy night-time and try to look down it, but the darkness is impenetrable, but I hear the footsteps of the lamp-lighter who touches each lamp as he passes, and soon the darkness is broken. There are times when the church seems as an unlighted street at moonless midnight, but if the Holy Spirit does but pass by and touch the spirit of each member, how quickly the darkness passes and Zion shines forth with "the beauty of the Lord." The church revived is God's highway with her lamps burning. Have you had this divine touch? Have you been "born of God and made a new creature in Christ Jesus?" If so, then

LET YOUR LIGHT SHINE.—Christ was preaching to a mixed multitude, just as I am today, but He said nothing of the size, character, or style of the lights, but simply fixed the fact of personal responsibility upon everyone. Let YOUR light shine. That is the light for which you are responsible, whether it be in a palace or hovel; whether you are high-priest or servant in a heathen kitchen. No matter what your sphere or position let your light shine.

The magnitude of responsibility depends on your position, but the fact of responsibility is not affected by the position. No intelligent soul can get so little or so low as to be free from responsibility. God has need of lights of all sorts and sizes. Not a place on earth where He does not want a light There are places where the light is not appreciated, but God wants it to go into those places. "Ye are the light of the WORLD." That means all the dark places, secret recesses, gloomy corners and neglected portions. Not a place outside of hell in which God does not want a light.

THE DIFFERENT LIGHTS.—The visible heavens are studded with stars of different magnitude; yet every star is a light, and all alike let their light shine. This world is filled with accountable beings differing in heart, brain and features; yet each is to be a light, and let his light shine.

The twelve apostles were the great planets in the gospel heavens, yet they differed in magnitude. And while Peter and John are yet shining, Bartholomew and others are scarcely seen. Our size as pulpit lights does not affect our responsibility. Some of us will never reach the magnitude of a Luther, or a Wesley. Your light may not be powerful enough to reach the coming generation, still we are to do our full duty and let our light shine however small it may be.

Bartholomew let his light shine, although there was no glory to him. The people followed Peter and sought to have his shadow fall on the sick, and thousands now think it a great privilege to kiss the great toe of incarnate presumption sitting in Peter's chair. The people also tried to worship Paul and Barnabas, crying, "The gods have come down among us!" But Barnabas did his work and left his name unsung and even seldom mentioned. I doubt not that he healed the sick, gave sight to the blind, and cast out devils; and men glorified God through him. As preachers we must have the grace of Bartholomew, to work and wear out in the vineyard and pass from sight and be forgotten, if only God be glorified.

THE BUSINESS LIGHT.—You may be active and influential in business circles; perhaps at the head of some department, having men under your direction. A sort of great light at the corner-crossing in the city where men are perpetually passing. Just that many, perhaps more, are walking in your light. Then you have need to be careful; let your light so shine that men may see that it comes from God and glorifies Him. Religion doesn't go into business to take every advantage of wind and weather and stuff its pockets, even at the cost of the poor. There are times when the poor and dependent look to the prominent and influential for help, and if that looked-for light be darkness "how great is that darkness!"

Winter was howling in the distance; the coal-grates of God's poor were empty, but it was in the power of the men controlling supplies to meet the emergency. Stewards of God in a Christian city, they had a chance to let their light so shine as to warm the shivering children of the poor. A cart-load of coal—not as a charity, but at a reasonable price—would have been a benediction. But alas! it was fixed at a price the poor could not reach, and they had to suffer. And while they suffered, religion blushed and hid her face, and the city received a scar which will disfigure it at the judgment; while the coal kept from the poor will intensify the heat of a hell that is hungry, and weary of waiting for those guilty of such greed and unmitigated meanness.

IS YOURS SIMPLY A STORE OR GROCERY LAMP?—Then let it so shine that men may see God in its light. God has stock in every Christian man's office or business house as well as in every preacher's pulpit. And if you do not let your light shine in your trade it cannot shine anywhere, because you are all your time in that work.

It is surprising what a diffusive thing religion is. It gets into everything a Christian man has anything to do with—the dry goods that prove to be just as represented, the barrel of apples or potatoes as large down in the bottom and middle of the barrel as on top. An honest beefsteak or a full weight pound of butter has more influence often than a long prayer or flowery sermon.

I know that my success depends largely on my conduct when out of the pulpit; and your light in the church depends very much on your light in your office or your store. We once knew a jeweler who had wonderful influence in his church. He was modest and unpretentious, and the basis of his great influence was not in his prayer meeting or his church, but in his store. His integrity was such that it was reflected on every piece of jewelry that went out from his store, and as far out as his wares went just that far his light was shining.

PERHAPS YOURS IS JUST A MODEST HOUSE-LAMP.—Then yours is the sphere of all spheres. There is no light so cheering and so inviting as the light in our home You remember, when you were a boy, and returning in the cold and darkness of night to your country home you saw the light afar off, with what a peculiar beauty it shone. And now in the populous city, when you return after the nightfall worn and weary with business, and perhaps discouraged, the light in your home-window dispels the shadow from your spirit and seems to shine into your very soul. You pass the lights in a hundred windows but none shine with the brilliance and beauty of the one in your own window.

Ye wives and mothers-house-lamps to shine in every department of home—in parlor, family room, nursery and kitchen. You know not the power of your light. Yours is more powerful than the mightiest electric light. Your light goes with your child to the school-room and helps him in many a dark problem. It perhaps helps the boy to master the first great difficulty which becomes the key to his future success.

Many the lad who has become discouraged and morose in spirit simply because there was no light in his home, and he felt that his mother cared more for society than for him.

The home-light goes with a man into his business battles and into his studies and toils, and lights him through difficulties where without it he would fail. When a man in the battle of life sees nothing but darkness in his home, "how great is that darkness!" How many fair prospects in life have been wrecked for want of the home-light!

It is a privilege to be set in this world as a light in a dark place. Lights along the shore of the great surging sea of humanity And whether the light be the prince of the planets or the least of the little stars, whether seen by a nation or only a household, let it shine for God. And men shall see it "and glorify your Father which is in heaven."

CHAPTER XLIV.

THE UNIVERSE IN OUR SERVICE.

"And we know that all things work together for good to them that love God."—Rom. 8:28. "For all things are for your sakes."—2 Cor. 4:15.

Some people use this text as a sort of specific for the ills and misfortunes of life. They keep it, as our mothers used to keep salve for the children in case of a burn; as if God were running a calamity line through the life of His child, and only using his misfortunes for his good. But there is a broadness here. It is not merely the ills of life, but ALL THINGS are at work for our good.

God is not in so small a business as the running of a thread of calamities through our experience, but He is engineering the universe in our behalf. All things—material and immaterial—visible and invisible, things in heaven and things in earth. Like the millionaire managing his millions for his children, God manages the universe for them that love Him.

ALL THINGS ARE AT WORK.—Inactivity is not a property inhering in the economy of God. Idleness finds no warrant in God's vast universe. The earth is never still, and the heavens above us are in perpetual revolution. Even the fixed planets are ever energetically expending their force, driving their light-beams through the unmeasured darkness.

We are shut up in this marvelous and ever-moving organism, and we can never be still; we cannot spend two hours in the same condition. "God has beset us behind and before." We can neither check nor change the forces that bear upon us, we can neither retard the sun nor quicken the seasons. Time presses us mercilessly, whitening the hair, furrowing the brow, and shortening the steps; ever forcing us on toward the shadowy valley. We are incorporate with all things. The seasons change us, commercial happenings affect us, domestic changes make us other than we were; death in the home transforms us, causing what is left of life to seem so weird and strange.

DIVINE THINGS ALSO BEAR UPON US.— The Holy Spirit convicts and reproves. Memory calls up the ill-used past while conscience condemns and remorse consumes. The soul bleeding inwardly, and the body failing outwardly, we are sometimes ready to cry, Is there no release from this twofold conflict—this inward and outward war? Is there no way by which the soul may find rest?

They tell us "there is absolute rest in the cyclone's center" And there is rest amid the universal restlessness. And this text finds that rest, it solves the problem, "All things work together for good."

The soul at enmity with God is out of harmony with God's universe. Every jot and tittle in God's law is against that soul, every inch in His universe is against it, every holy intelligence is at war with such a soul. That soul meets a dagger in the hand of everything that is loyal to God. For such a soul there is but one hope, and that is in its absolute surrender to God.

Sin is the element of disharmony in man. Sin is the only thing in this universe that is not under law. Sin is lawless. Sin is the defiance and the transgression of law. God hates it, and can never harmonize with it. He will harmonize with our weakness, our ignorance and our helplessness, but never with our sins.

There is but one thing God can do with sin, and that is to DESTROY it. That was the mission of Christ to this world, "To destroy the works of the devil." Sin is the work of the devil, and God will destroy it, and He will destroy the soul that clings to it. Like Joshua, hunting the camp until he came to Achan's tent, and searching that tent until he found the hidden "Babylonish garment and the golden wedge;" God will hunt sin even unto the doorways of hell, and will destroy every soul that secretly conceals and refuses to give up sin. Sin must perish by the decree of the living God; and it is for us to decide whether we will give it up, or cling to it in moral madness until we perish with it.

SURRENDER OF SIN BRINGS HARMONY. —When we give up sin we come into harmony with God, and the moral universe comes into harmony with us. It turns all things to going our way and working for us. We may not understand the process, but the fact we know.

I stood, when a lad, in the middle story of a

grand merchant mill. Every story was full of moving machinery, but I could see only what was in the one story. I could not see the French burr millstones that crushed the grain, nor the machinery that whirled in the stories above me. Neither could I see the ponderous turbine wheel far below, turning in the water and propelling all, yet I knew it was all connected and under control and working for good; because I saw the snow-white flour as it poured down into the bins before me.

Thus we stand in the middle-room of a united universe. We see one element adjusting itself to another. The animal and vegetable kingdoms at work together; the animal taking up the oxygen and giving off the carbon, while the vegetable is taking up the carbon and giving off the oxygen. —Heaven and earth co-working together. The clouds come with waters to slake the thirst of the earth, while the over-flooded earth sends back its surplus burden through the river channels to the sea; the sea receiving it only to salt it and send it up through the sunbeams, giving purity to the atmosphere and health to mankind.

I can see and understand all this, but there are stories in the great merchant-mill of God's economy that we cannot see. We do not see the guiding Hand that is over all, nor can we detect the invisible hands that connect us with the higher and invisible departments. Nor can we even hear the rustle of unseen wings as the messengers come to "minister to those who are heirs of salvation." But while we cannot see the wheels nor the bands that unite them, yet we know that God is presiding over all, and that all is right, because we see the fresh-made blessings which, like the snowy flour in the mills, are ever pouring at our feet. "He loadeth us daily with benefits."

THE CENTER OF THE SYSTEM.—The sun is the all-controlling center of the solar system. His radiance reaches our world and the other worlds, His power draws from the surface of every stream and pool and lake and sea. He draws all waters unto Himself.

The cross of Christ is the great center of the moral universe. "All power in heaven and in earth is given to that center." All that is right is centripetal to that cross, and all that is wrong is centrifugal to it. All that is holy moves toward the magnetism of a suffering Christ. "I, if I be lifted up, will draw all men unto me."

That matchless sun in the moral heavens is drawing humanity to himself Like the natural sun, he is drawing from all fountains and streamlets of earth; from its cess-pools and from its places of stagnation, from its high places and from its low places, from palace and from hovel, from hunger-pinched poverty and from luxury-bloated wealth—He is drawing all men. The power of that cross shall be felt as far as the sun shall shed his light.

THE NATURAL SUN WIELDS A PERSONAL POWER.—His light and warmth fall directly upon me. I sit in the morning by the open window, while he sends his life-giving rays to warm

my blood and lend new life-force, and with gratitude I receive the sun-bath which is given me as a
blessing from heaven.

He also works for me indirectly, through the
grapevine, and through the orange bough, and
through the wheat stalk, and through a thousand
media to reach me with blessings. But when that
sun is darkened and his mission ended, Christ
shall still be the moral center from which all
things will be made to "work together for our
good." In the countless cycles of the coming life
He will be the attractive center. "The lamb
which is in the midst of the throne shall feed us,
and shall lead us to fountains of living waters."
He who is drawing us in time shall draw us in
eternity, while we shall be ever pressing on to
know the Lord." Brother, do you feel that magnetic force drawing you today? Then abide in
Him, and He will draw you in eternity.

ONE QUESTION SETTLES ALL.—If "all
things work together for good to them that love
God," then, DO I LOVE GOD? Is He first in my
heart and life? If so, this turns all the forces to
going my way. This sets the universe to work for
me. I may not understand this wonderful fact.
My little child cannot understand my affairs as a
father. He wonders why I am sometimes so long
absent from him, why I give him lessons so hard
to learn, why I refuse him things he so much desires. This is all mystery to him. But his understanding has nothing to do with my plans and
procedure. I am trying to work all things for

his good I don't try to explain it; he will understand it all later.

Our Father is working all for our good. We
don't understand why He sometimes seems gone
from us so long, while we without joy, have to
walk on in the dark by stubborn faith. We don't
understand the bitter lessons when we have to sit
in the ashes and look up through our tears to study
them, but we shall know later. "Now we know in
part." Our Father is working all for our good.
How He does this will be knowledge to come to us
in the other life, when the light falls upon us from
that side where there is "no need of a candle or
the light of the sun."

SURVEY YOUR DOMAIN.—"Now are we the
sons of God." Yes, the children of the King of
kings. Then look forth and survey your realm.
Read the text, "All things working for your good."
Read it on every object in the universe. Burning
in the sun, breathing in the zephyrs, and thunder-
ing in the ocean. Read it in the ashes of your
ruined fortune, read it in your own failing health
and shortening step, read it on the brow of your
darling dead; read it, believe it, rest in it, and you
will understand it when you are wise in the things
of eternity.

Misfortunes and calamities are but your servants, they are the black slaves which are at work
down in the deep things of God, where we cannot
see—the sooty miners, far adown the shafts of
his providence, sending up the fuel to feed the
fires which melt and purify and beautify our hardened natures.

The air about us and the earth beneath are co-working for us, maturing the corn, tinting the flowers and ripening the grain. Above these are the filmy clouds, servants sent from heaven, with velvet movement, balancing themselves in air as the caterers of the skies, waiting to fill the cups when God's princes and princesses are athirst.

Beyond these are the heavenly bodies in rythmic procession keeping step with creation in our service. Beyond these are the angel hosts on ready wing, and moving in ministry to "those who are to be heirs of salvation." Nor does the service end here. With "shoes off the feet of the soul" let us say it—when beyond all; when we come to the Eternal City, and enter in through the gates, and into the household of God; even there the only Son of the Highest shall "gird himself and serve us." Stupendous statement! "All things are for your sakes!"

THE UNIVERSAL STAMP.—Here we find one and the same stamp on every material thing. —God's distinctive mark of nobility on heaven and earth; on heights above and depths beneath; on nature's hands and angels wings—Service! Service! Service! and all in service for us.

What of the man, with this marvelous panorama before him—a universe in his service—and yet he doing nothing for God or humanity? What of such a man? Ah! not a man, but an ingrate! selfishness incarnate! an immortal parasite on the bosom of divine beneficence! a breathing SPONGE!

God's order echoes through all being, "Go work today in my vineyard!" A race to be rescued and the universe in action! Shall I be inert? Shall I stand all the day idle? Is sin to be destroyed and humanity restored while I have no part in the mighty achievement? Shall I be simply a clog in the co-working wheels of the universe—the only inactive thing in all God's realm? Nay! Nay! Let me serve. Let me fit in and fill my place in the universal service, and be not an obstruction, but a factor in the processes of salvation!

CHAPTER XLV.

THE HIGHEST KNOWLEDGE.

"Yea doubtless, and I count all things but loss for the excellency of the knowledge of Christ Jesus my Lord."—Phil. 3:8.

ALL KNOWLEDGE RESTS ON THE UN-KNOWN.—God has ever kept human inquiry under curb. Man is reined in. Turn which way he may, he finds the unknown guarded as the tree of life. He can never reach extremes. Go downward with the microscope, and the infinitesimals become so small that we cannot apprehend them. Rise with the telescope, and the magnitudes become so vast we cannot grasp them. At all points we reach the line of the unknown. We are insphered, enskyed, shut in. What we know is but the island on the bosom of the unknown. Like the water-spider in mid-ocean, reaching but an inch or two toward the compass-points with its slender limbs, man must be content to live and die in the middle of things with no power to reach extremes.

The agnostic says, "I will accept nothing as truth that I cannot grasp with my reason." Whereas, we have to accept the very foundations of all reasoning by simple faith before we can begin to reason at all. Would you reason astronomically of the relation and inter-influence of the spheres? On what would your reasoning rest? On SPACE. What is space? It is a first principle. How do you reach it? Not by your reason. It is beyond your reason, it is a revelation, it comes to your consciousness, it grasps you, and you simply accept it as from the unknown.

Now having accepted the fact of space, you can then begin to reason of height, depth, and extent. Would you reason geologically of the record of the rocks? On what will you base the process? On duration. What is duration? It is another first principle, another voice from the unknown. Accepting this, you can then reason inside of it, you can then talk of cycles, aeons, years and days. If you would reason on the higher and ethical, of the rightness and wrongness of things, the process would rest upon the great first principle of RIGHT. And that is a revelation upon which all moral teaching rests.

Here we see the folly of "Accepting nothing but what the reason can grasp." Instead of faith being the product of reason, all sound reason is dependent upon faith. *By faith do we reason.*

Then if the foundations of all knowledge are in the unknown, He must have the highest knowledge, who is familiar with that unknown; and who came out from that realm to manifest God unto us, and show us the way of salvation.

JESUS CHRIST IS FROM THE UNKNOWN. —The eternal, the supernatural, is His home. He came out from it and returned to it, "He was in the beginning with God." Present when the universe was founded. "By him were all things made." The visible is but the interplay of His power, as if He had carved His name on the beech-bark of the material, which passeth away.

Christ comes to us, camps with us for a time, tells us of that unknown realm, "His Father's house of many mansions," and then returns to that realm to "prepare a place for us."

CHRIST EXPRESSES GOD TO US.—Knowledge of God is the highest knowledge. It was the divine aim to express Himself both to the mind and to the heart of man. Nature puts God before our thought. It puts man on inquiry, speculating, philosophizing, investigating. But "The world by wisdom knew not God." He could not fully reveal Himself in this way. He must show to humanity, not what He *has done,* but what *He is.* Hence He must approach another and deeper side of humanity. God in nature made known His *power.* God in Christ made known His *heart.* Only Christ could show us what God is; this He did when He revealed God's heart of love, and the proud intellect must wait, while the loving heart receives him. "With the heart man believeth unto righteousness."

This is as true of the infant Christ as of the Christ in manhood. The faith stream is as deep at the shore as in mid-channel. That Bethlehem babe is either miracle or scandal. There in the stable He must be worshipped or rejected. Reason must do one of two things: reject Him as scandal, or kneel, with the wise men, and worship at His feet.

THE UNIVERSE WITNESSES TO HIM.—
All things are prospective. A mighty river in its
flow will diverge and turn, now settling in the
quiet bay, now eddying in the whirlpool, then
dashing amid the rocks or leaping the cataract,
but over all is the dominating impulse, *onward*.
Everything yields to this; the bushes along the
shore bend that way, the driftwood points that
way, even the rocks are worn in that direction.

So this universe is prospective. There may be
disharmonies, cross-currents, jarring elements,
and sometimes the breakers of a mighty Niagara
in the vast channel of things, but over all is the
irresistible onward impulse, as if the breath of
God were blown that way. The willows along
the shores of time swing toward the future, while
the driftwood of the dead centuries is pointing
that way.

Such is the prospective force and tendency of
things that the universe has never dared—like
Lot's wife—to halt and look back. Its index
hand is ever pointing forward, and its divine motto is, "Reaching to things which are before."

THE HAND WRITING IN MAN.—The proph-
ecy and proof of a futute state, are stronger within man than they are without, and the man who
learns to read his own innner self has learned to
read the hand-writing of God.

The idea of another life beyond this is held
by mankind the world over. The lowest have
crude notions of a higher power and a future
state. So deeply is this truth ingrained into the

heart of civilization, that to destroy it would be to paralyze progress and destroy all interest in life. Moveover, the very structure of our nature and being is in accord with this universal faith and feeling.

OUR THINKING IS PROSPECTIVE.—The general current of human thought does not turn back toward the past. We think but little in that direction, we hear sentimental sayings about "sad memories" and "buried hopes", but there is more of that on tombstones and in old albums than in the real life of the living.

Our thinking powers lean toward the future, and our thoughts are born with wings set in that direction. When we cannot see the future we make imagination pioneer and light the way while we follow, and the most of our mental touring is toward that "great West" of the future.

LIFE IS PROSPECTIVE.—We are not situated today just as we desire, but our plans are laid, and we expect to be better situated after a time— not living just as I should right now, some duties neglected, some indulgences practiced which I will regulate after a time. Our intentions are like gangplanks which lie with one end in the water, their larger ends lying out in the fogs of to-morrow; the powers of the mind are taken up in the anticipative.

Memory, with most of us, is a sort of dove which we send out occasionally to note the floods we have passed on the life voyage, and happy is he whose memory-dove, returning, brings the olive-leaf, token that he is at peace with all his past.

THE IMPULSES.—These strange nervous children of the heart are ever in motion, and reaching their hands toward the future, clamoring for things to come. The tot longs to be large like his elder brother, the lad longs for manhood, and old-age yearns for the future. How few wish to return and live life over again; no impulse in that direction. Though suffering, dissolution, and the grave be before us, yet over all is the onward impulse.

THE AFFECTIONS.—That adhesive chapter in our constitution, which connects us with other souls, and other things, and sometimes so closely that the soul would perish rather than relax its grasp. You will find this writing in a leaning hand, inclining toward the future. We do not love backward, there is no object back there to love. We parted with loved ones back in the past, but they are not there now. It was only a divergence of the paths, we had the consciousness they would meet us again when the ways converge in the future.

Hence we think of them, not as back there, but as "gone before." We talk of them that way, love them that way, and long for them that way. The affections are God's sign-boards in the soul pointing us to things to come."

THE CONSCIENCE.—That greatest writing in the immortal nature, written in God's own hand and pointing us to a coming judgment—that which made Felix tremble at a thought of the judgment. That is in a leaning hand, and that toward the future. Why all this? Why are all things prospective? Why is everything leaning toward the future? Is it that all these index hands in concert mean nothing? Is it that the whole universe is one huge and confederated falsehood? Are all her hands lifted in a lie and pointing to nothing? Why everything in man, and the universe, yearning the same way? WHAT DOES IT MEAN? It means that GOD HAS GONE THAT WAY! It means that He and the eternal verities are there. Christ himself has passed that way, and the forward trending of things is but the brushing of His skirts as He passed. "All things were made by Him," and all things trend toward Him. Can we not understand this universal yearning for things to come!

CHRIST MEETS THE DESIRE OF HUMANITY.—As the fin calls for the water, and the wing for the air, so the very constitution of the soul cries out for God. Humanity has ever had a sense of God. and has sought Him in almost every object, and bitterly cried, "Oh, that I knew where I might find Him." In darkness, yet consciously near the light. Lost, yet near the Father's house. The world could see intimations and get glimpses of God, but could not find Him. Nature, prophecy and promise could tell that God was nigh, yet He could not be seen, until "The word was made flesh and dwelt among us." Then they "beheld the glory of the Lord in the face of Jesus Christ".

This is the God that men want; a God in their own likeness, a God who looks like they look, feels as they feel, and suffers as they suffer.

KNOWLEDGE OF CHRIST TRANSFORMS MEN.—A man may be educated to the highest possible in the intellect, and still be unchanged in his moral nature. Men grow wiser without growing better. They may press research to the ultimate and rise to mental altitudes unapproached, and all may be a walk amid glaciers without a warm breath to quicken the moral nature. The greatest students—without Christ—are coldest and farthest removed from humanity.

But in coming to the knowledge of Christ, there is a point at which the heart warms and worships —a point where Christ communicates God to us, a point where the whole being is revolutionized, the man made a "new creature" and initiated into a new life; a life as different from the old life, as the cocoon in its wintry grave is different from the spring-day butterfly in its new-born glory; as unlike the old life as the uncouth eaglet, powerless in the nest, and the bold proud bird sporting with the storms and soaring toward the sun.

THIS KNOWLEDGE EMPOWERS MEN.— It is only soul-power that can control men. It is not given to things, but to souls, to have absolute dominion over men. The intrepid commander, whose spirit dominates his men, can carry them into the very jaws of death. We once saw a small painting of Cæsar and his hosts when they had just crossed the Rubicon. Cæsar was mounted, sword drawn and pointing forward, while his spirit seemed to clothe his whole army, and the very tiger-skin thrown across his saddle seemed strangely alive. That host was ready to follow him, to go anywhere Caesar went, fight where he fought, and if need be, to die where he died. It took the soul-force of Christ to dominate humanity before it could be awakened and saved, His Spirit dominating the church will lead her to the conquest of the world.

The soldier is calm, brave, and self-poised when dominated by the spirit of his commander. In Christ we have a personal force so mighty, so magnetic, so inspiring, and so gentle, and yet so omnipotent, that when under His gracious domination, "we can do all things."

The man who is thus corporate with Christ is not only mighty in leading men upward, but there is a silent and saving influence going out from his life and character. His influence exhales as the odor of flowers; He makes men broader and better by his very presence among them. There are men whom we might well employ to walk the streets that we might catch their inspiration.

THIS KNOWLEDGE PERFECTS MEN.—Perfection inheres in God, and we reach it only when we get back to Him and partake of His nature. However beautiful the character and broad the attainments, there is no perfection until it partakes of the divine nature. Perfection is impossible except in unison with God. Highest consecration gives highest communion and knowledge of Christ. Whatever keeps us from entire consecration, will keep us from the highest knowledge of Christ. "Therefore, let us lay aside every weight, and the sin that doth so easily beset us, that we may run with patience the race which is set before us."

A captive eagle was held by a tiny silver chain, and when he would spread his wings and endeavor to rise and escape that small silver chain held him a prisoner. How many are there who might rise to sublime heights in spiritual life, but for some sin, indulgence, or habit, which holds them as the silver chain held the king of the air! Let us, by the help of God, break the last tiny chain, give up everything that prevents our perfect freedom, and let Christ set us free! 'If the Son shall make you free, you shall be free indeed!"

CHAPTER XLVI.

THE GRACE OF UNSELFISHNESS.

"Freely ye have received, freely give."—Matt. 10:8.

Strange instruction to men who had neither gold nor silver, nor even brass, in their purses, but their condition gave them fine opportunity to trust in the Lord: their possessions belonged to that higher class of things which are not bought or sold.

THE TWO REALMS.—These are the material and the immaterial, the perishable and the imperishable, the purchasable and the unpurchasable. Things in the lower realm are priceable—food, raiment, houses, lands, merchandise. In the higher realm are things beyond price—our faith, family ties joys, friendship and the higher joys. Price finds no place in this realm; all here are free gifts, and benevolence, generosity, and gratuity govern all.

Nature types this higher domain in things without price. The air, light, heat, dew, and rain are without price, and yet are the elements by which we live, and without which we cannot live. Thus God aims to keep us mindful, that the things essential to the life of soul and body, are His free gifts.

THE HIGHER PLANE IS ONE OF MUTUAL DEPENDENCE.—Where nothing can be bought or sold, we are dependent entirely upon what we give to each other. A man may become a hermit, and dig a living out of the ground, but he cannot dig society, friendship, and sympathy out of the earth. If he enjoys these things he must receive them as free gifts from others. Nature also types this mutual dependency. The atmosphere is dependent upon the ocean for moisture, and the ocean upon the atmosphere for its supplies. The boughs are lonely without the birds, and the birds are lost without the boughs. The tree does not selfishly say, "No bird shall rest in my boughs;" nor do the birds declare, "No bough shall be vocal with my songs." But the tree says, "I will shade you with my foliage," and the bird says, "I will warble my richest notes through your branches." Thus it is as if the tree itself were singing, and there are melody and gladness as far as you can see the tree or hear the bird.

These are God's types in nature by which we are to print out our lives. We have received "freely" of a love that is pure, unselfish, and everlasting. Christ gave himself to, and for us, and we are to give our love and ourselves to Him, and to humanity in this way, and in this way only can we minister unto Him, by ministering unto "His little ones.' And we shall meet the Master more frequently in the huts and garrets of poverty than in the walks of pleasure.

THE GOSPEL OF NATURE.—This is a gospel of unselfishness. Nature seems in one universal effort to give itself away. The sun—strongest object in nature—has been pouring itself out in one golden gush through all the ages, flooding the universe with light, but has never shot a ray for himself. The raincloud, moving with thunderous tread, like the draft-horses of heaven, pours its watery burden upon the thirsty earth and retains no drop for itself. The birds sing out all the songs they know, and the flowers breathe out all their store of fragrance. The old apple tree, which has brought forth its fruity burden for a score of years, has never produced an apple for itself. If there be no child to pluck the last apple from its boughs, it benevolently drops that one to feed some hungry worm that crawls beneath its shade.

Even the wild untutored forest gives its foliage, takes off its own wrapping to cover earth's bare form in winter's cold; nature gives all and reserves nothing. No sunbeam glitters for itself, nor dewdrop distills for itself, nor flower unfolds its beauty for itself. The perpetual movement of nature is an effort to give itself away.

The tree retaining its leaves or fruit beyond its time, refusing to give them up, when all other trees are bare, is diseased, and perhaps dying. And the soul that lives for itself, and clings to all within its grasp, and selfishly surrenders nothing, that soul is spiritually diseased and dying, like the miser who "sat among his bags of gold and died of utter want".

THE ONE GREAT WORK OF LIFE.—For the soul to give itself away, is the one great all inclusive lesson which God would teach. First, by his word, and then by nature. "Son, give me thine heart." "Love me with all thy heart, soul, mind and strength." This gospel he would shine into the soul by the sunbeams, and sing it in by the bird-song, and breathe it in by the breath of the flowers.

The happiest one on earth is that one who is most completely divorced from self and given away to God. We favor this kind of divorce, and no other. Oh, that we could all procure a full and final divorce from self! How good it is to get rid of yourself, even in a ten-minutes afternoon nap.

The happy pair are those wholly given away to each other. The happy home is the one in which every member of the circle is given away to the rest. The happiest church is that in which every member is loving and seeking the good of all the others. There is no perfect happiness until we are free from self, and the only way to get rid of self is to give it away or work it to death for God and humanity. The sanctified soul is that one who is sanctified into the lives of its fellowmen, to love them and sympathize with them as Jesus did, and not sanctified above and beyond them, and ready to ostracise and excommunicate them when they are unable to utter a certain shibboleth. May God sanctify us into humanity, and not over and above it!

THE MANNER OF GIVING.—"Freely give." Not alone in the sense of Largeness, but also of WILLINGNESS. How much this affects what we give and what we do! The huge sunflower lifts its head proudly in the autumn sunlight and is seen afar off, but it has no fragrance. The tiny violet, that peeps from beneath the rosebush without pretence, gives out its rich and delicate perfume. The large gift, without the heart in it, is the sunflower without fragrance, while the lesser kindness, done with all the heart, is the violet running over with sweetness and life

All nature seems to be giving—not alone as a charity—but as a relief to itself, as if it would suffer and almost die if it did not get relief by giving. Should the sun repress and retain all his fire within himself, he would consume with his own self-excess. The fountain must flow and strengthen the streamlet as a relief to itself. The rosebud cannot be repressed, but must burst forth in sweetness and beauty, or die and rot of its own self-retention.

THE HIGHER GOSPEL.—Redemption—the higher gospel—carries the same lesson of unselfishness. "In the fulness of time God sent forth His Son." What does this fulness mean? Fulness of time? Yes. But does it not mean more than this? Does it not mean that the mighty tide of divine love must break upon the world at that time, and in the person of the Lord Jesus Christ? The birth of Christ was but the breaking in of God himself upon the world, like a glorious sunrise after the gloom of the night. We ask the question with uncovered head, Could God have waited longer? Was it now "the fulness of time" and the fulness of the Godhead with that redeeming love that could no longer wait for expression?

HERE GRACE AND NATURE TEACH THE SAME LESSON.—The beneficence of nature is from its own fulness; and redemption is from the fulness of God. Redemption is the overflow of God's heart upon humanity. "God so loved the world."

We are effective only when we serve on the same principle. Hence the Apostle prayed, "that we might be filled with all the fulness of God." Only this fulness will impel us to give ourselves freely in His service. It is a fulness which makes us restless when not at work for God and humanity. We have to work to find relief from our unrest. There is no fulness of God with us when we are doing nothing; lazy, listless, and indifferent. The river leaves no rich alluvial deposits on its shores when its volume is low and simply creeping in its channel; it is the overflow that enriches.

The Church does little for humanity when her life tides are low—it is the full tide that brings salvation. "There is a river, the streams whereof make glad the city of God." And this gladness comes only when those streams rise and flood, and overflow, then they make Zion to be fruitful in the things of God.

THE EXCESSES.—We live from the excesses. The daylight is but the excess of the sun; more light than he can hold, and we dwell in that excess. The rain that refreshes the thirsty earth, is the excess of heaven's wealth of waters, more than the heavens can contain, and that more is poured out upon us. The fruits and flowers are but the excess of life in the earth, thrown up and out at our feet to make the world beautiful about us.

Herein is the glory of our redemption. It is no meager or labored effort, no measured work on God's part, but the excess of His infinite benefi- cence, the abandon of His divine nature in its impulse toward us. It is that love which is "from everlasting to everlasting," breaking in its over- flow upon humanity—a tide which never ebbs— a river that never runs down—a flood that never abates!

The gospel, preached for ages, is as rich now as at first. Souls have found comfort from the Bi- ble for thousands of years, and its resources—like the ocean—are as full and exhaustless as before. The Holy Spirit has been leading and laboring with men through all ages, and "there is no wear- iness with him." He is as gentle and patient with us as He was with the Patriarchs, and He now "maketh intercession for us with groanings that cannot be uttered."

HAVE WE NO EXCESSES?—With all this world-wide teaching, with heaven and earth and the living God as instructors, living off of the excesses of infinite beneficence, have we nothing to serve but self? Surely, surely these lessons shall not all be in vain. Surely we will not dis- appoint that God whose "thoughts are ever to usward."

Have we no overflow of sympathy that might help some helpless soul? no excess of FAITH to inspire some faltering fellow-spirit? no excess of LOVE to enrich some unfortunate one who has lost confidence in all things? Have we no heart to minister to Christ by ministering to "the least of his little ones?" shall not the sentiment of the sacred poet be our sentiment from this day to the end of life?

> Since from His bounty I receive
> Such proofs of love divine,
> Had I a thousand hearts to give,
> Lord, they should all be thine."

CHAPTER XLVII.

SIMPLICITY OF SALVATION.

"The love of God is shed abroad in our hearts by the Holy Ghost which is given unto us."—Rom. 5:5.

Here we have the inspired definition of experimental religion. This tells us what it is—"The love of God." Where it is—"In our hearts." How it gets there—"By the Holy Ghost."

There are many who do not think intensively or extensively on religious matters, and much that is thought is misty and indefinite. The familiar expression, "getting religion," suggests the idea that a veritable something is to be procured, that a mysterious process is to be passed, and new power added to the moral being. That this process is dark and fearful, as the soul grasps after something that is ill-defined, and comes out at last—as the pearl diver from the watery deep—with all his forces expended, but holding the precious pearl in his grasp. All this is misconception. There is no power of the mental or moral being added or removed. It is a "resurrection." The moral powers, long dead in sin, are awakened. It is the same old powers—in veritable identity—raised from the dead and invested with a new life. When the Scriptures speak of the converted man as a "new creature," they simply mean that his moral powers are filled with a new life.

TO ILLUSTRATE.—You speak of "giving your son an education." You do not mean that you

will send him to school with the idea that he will,
in his mental researches, find a veritable something. Surely not. You expect him to develop
his mental powers. That is the meaning of the
word "educere," to lead out, to develop. And
that developed state we call "education."

There is a house with its doors and windows
closed, the light excluded, while darkness, dust
and disorder are within. But the owner comes
and opens the doors, and throws back the shut-
ters, and the sunlight streams in, and the darkness disappears. The dust is brushed off, furniture
is arranged, fire kindled, dampness driven out,
and light and warmth make it cheery and inviting—the same house, but full of new light and
life.

The moral powers come into this world in a
state of darkness and hopeless disorder. The soul
has its windows closed, and the divine light shut
out. And by becoming religious we mean the opening of the doors and windows of the immortal nature, and the letting in of the divine light. Then
the soul has light and warmth, and like "a city on
a hill, it cannot be hid."

IT IS GOD'S LOVE THAT SAVES.—Everywhere in the Scriptures it is the prominent idea
that salvation depends on God's love. His love
has the power of awakening our love. "We love
him because he first loved us." Our love is the
response—the echo—of His love.

It is not an effort on our part to grasp and get
hold on God. That is what we call "trying." It

is not that we are to try and struggle to love God. You couldn't love your wife, or your child if it required trying. Loving is an involuntary thing; we love because we cannot help it. Loving God is but the opening of the soul's doors and windows and allowing the Saviour to come in. "If any man will open the door, I will come in and sup with him, and he with me."

WE BAR OUT THIS LOVE.—Whether intentionally or unintentionally, consciously or unconsciously, we fortify against its advances. This love spirit pervades the universe, and seems to fill all space. There is everywhere a spirit of gladness, as evidence of this love-spirit. The heavens are bright, and the earth seems glad and joyful. There is a bewitching beauty in the landscape, as if the face of earth was in a broad smile, and you look over it and smile, and feel as if you were somehow akin to it; while over that landscape animal life is frisking and rollicking as if wild with the joy-spirit. Even the streamlets—away down in their little channels—and bedfast forever, are yet full of joy and cannot keep quiet; and we hear their music coming up all the day and all the night. Even the winds are full of joy, and whisper the softest melodies in nature's music, while the very motes—animated atoms—float in the sunshine, intoxicated with the spirit of gladness. This love-spirit is everywhere, and barred out of nowhere except the human heart. It does not have to knock at nature's doors for access; those doors are ever open, but when it comes to the human heart "the door is shut." "He came unto his own and his own received him not." Shut out of His own house, He stands and waits and knocks.

WHY DO MEN SHUT OUT THE LOVE-LIGHT?—It is because there is much in the heart which they do not want exposed. Go down the street at midday when the world is full of light, and you will find every house where they do an honorable business, is thrown open to the public and as full of light as they can get it. A clear glass front, with the dust rubbed off, and perhaps a great sky-light in the roof, as if they were willing that God should look down upon their work.

But note the red-light tenement, the gambling hell, and the rum shop, where they do dark work, where men kindle a hell within themselves, and when the fires are under way they gulp down their wages, their family supplies, their reputation, and their own souls, into that self-made hell; and leave wife and little ones to be tortured with their memory. Notice these houses. There is no sky-light above nor clear glass in front; but the front glass is heavily frosted, and a screen inside the door to obscure and shut out the light. There are deeds of darkness within that shrink from the light.

Thus it is with the heart that is full of sin. Full of uncleanness, it is not willing to admit the light of God's love—so pure and clear and searching; not willing that it shall flash upon its selfishness, worldliness, and evil passions which lie in their respective places, like slimy serpents coiled in their snaky retreats.

STUBBORNNESS OF THE HUMAN HEART. —Such is the stubbornness that people sometimes refuse to allow themselves to be loved. There may be a multitude of love forces pressing upon them, yet they fortify against all of them. Sometimes the man will not allow his wife or child to love him, though their purest natures may be yearning for his appreciation. Still they are repulsed at every advance, while he moves on in his miserable majesty and cruel selfishness—a being of too much importance to allow himself loved.

It is thus with God's love. It is ever making advances toward us, storming the heart with all the tender influences which make up the artillery of love; and only to be repulsed, and to fall back upon itself grieved and wounded. How often we "grieve the Spirit of God!" How often do we open the Savior's wounds afresh!

BUT THIS LOVE WILL NOT LET US ALONE.—When the prodigal has fallen into disgrace he can bear anything better than the thought of his mother's knowing his shame. That is his first request, "Don't let mother know it." But mother-like she will know it, and will pray for him, and pity and love him and cling to him. And the moral power of his mother's love is his strongest support; and when he becomes truly penitent he confesses his guilt and rests on that mother's love and prayers.

Such is the soul in its sins. Not willing for God

to love it or to know its condition. It keeps as
far away as possible from God, away from the
church, away from religious society, away from
influences that would bring it close to God. It
doesn't want to be brought close to Him, doesn't
want to unbosom itself to Him, doesn't want to
weep over its sins and fall into the arms of His
mercy for help.

But the Holy Spirit—like the mother—still
loves, and follows, and pities, and warns, and
woos and "makes intercession with groanings
which cannot be uttered." If the Holy Spirit
would only let man alone in his sins, the work of
ruin would be complete. But He ever follows,
waking from sleep, pulling the coat when going
into danger, and trying to get us to consent to
let God love us, to let His love come into the heart
and drive out the serpents and the unholy things;
to get the heart's door open to God, to get us to
slide back the royal WILL-BOLT and allow the
heavenly messenger to come in and flash the light
of His love into every room of the moral being.
This is CONVERSION. This is RELIGION.
And what is it after all? It is "The love of God
shed abroad in the heart by the Holy Ghost."

And what have we done after all? Simply con-
sented to let God love us, that is all. We have
done nothing, grasped nothing, but have only con-
sented to let the love-spirit—which is everywhere
and in everything—come into our nature. Now
we are in harmony with all things and we understand why all things are so full of joy; it is because they are full of God.

THE CLOSED DOOR.—Dear sinner, there is but one door closed between you and God, and that is neither the gate of grace nor the gate of heaven, it is the door of your own HEART. When you would secure yourself against the night thief, you trust to neither latch nor lock, but to the strong bolt fastening on the inside, that the door may not be opened unless you open it.

When God made the human heart and placed His chief treasure within,—powers that are imperishable—He established man's royalty over himself. He placed a bolt on the inside which only the man could move. That bolt is what makes the man, that bolt is the royal WILL. None but yourself can move that bolt. God will not move it, and all the forces of the church cannot. Hence, ye are not saved, because "Ye will not." The love of God is not in your heart, because you bar it out That love is at the door, but the old will-bolt shuts it out. That will-bolt is the grandest gift of God to man, and to give it back to God is the grandest act of the soul. That act on your part will cause a jubilee among the angels. "There is joy in heaven over one sinner that repenteth." We drew back this bolt and admitted God's love while in boyhood, and we want that bolt to lie back in its brackets, the rusty relic of our consecrated royalty.

Oh, that some blood-bought spirit may throw back the will-bolt and open the door, and thril the celetstial batteries, and create a jubilee in heaven at this Sabbath hour!

CHAPTER XLVIII.

DEATH.

Text: "And I looked, and behold, a pale horse; and his name that sat on him was death, and Hell followed with him."—Rev. 6:8.

We have here a thrilling picture of the great conqueror of conquerors. The monarch is mounted and moving. The horse indicates speed, a speed from which none may escape; his pale color is significant of his mission. The magnitude of his conquest is seen in his following. Hell, or Hades, followed with him, the receptacle of departed spirits, with its countless millions as his escort.

He finds his victims everywhere. He takes his captives from every home and at all times, at sunny noon and solemn night. We have heard and will hear again the relentless hoofs of the pale horse until, one by one, the loved ones are all in his captivity; his conquests will increase until time shall be no more, until a mightier than he shall command his surrender. Death shall then dismount, his captive millions be liberated, and Death and Hades shall give up their dead; the pale horse and rider shall perish, and there shall be no more death.

THE NATURE OF DEATH.—Since death is real and we, with our families, are to meet it, how important that we should have all the knowledge of it possible! What is death? and what is its effect upon us? Death is a change, solemn, absolute, complete. The natural functions and

forces cease, the gates of the senses all close simultaneously, and the curtain falls. The tableaux
of time dissolve and pass from sight. Death ends
the old relations and surrounds us with new ones;
the eyes close on earthly scenes, the ears die to
earthly sounds, and the hands are folded from
earthly toil.

Disembodied, we step upon a new shore, where
life is upon new principles. It is a second conversion. "Old things pass away, and all things
become new." Death is not more wonderful than
life, it is only another change added to the changes through which we are ever passing, only this
is the last. It closes a sort of embryo being in
which we see darkly and introduces us into an
enlarged and elevated state where we shall "know
perfectly what we now know in part."

Your birth was your first change, and that gave
you consciousness; the nursery your first world,
from which you gradually took in a world that
was higher, and now in your maturity the spin-
ning-top and hobby-horse days are like a long
past dream. The difference between that world
and your world of today is what life has done. If
life has wrought such wonders with us, is it any
more wonderful that death should bring great
changes? To die is but to pass into a higher and
clearer life.

The unhatched birdling is in the midst of the
scenes of its future being. It is not the distance
that shuts out the air and the sunlight, it is only
the thin shell, and the breaking of this crystal is
not a change of place but of conditions.

Thus while living we are as much in eternity as we shall ever be. Eternity surrounds us now, and supernatural things press about us, and we often catch glimpses of them. It is not distance, but it is this shell of clay that hides from us the sunlight of eternity. Death will break this chrysalis of clay and open the door to the imprisoned spirit. It is death that brings the supernatural into view. May it not be that when death unbars the door and the loved one comes into newborn liberty, it may linger in the room to look on while we weep and wring the hands and, were it possible, would gladly comfort us in our grief?

DEATH THE GREAT SPECIALIST.—We often carry the suffering loved one a long way to have some specialist treat his malady. Death is the great specialist whose practice is as old as time and as wide as the world. He comes without summons when all other physicians and remedies have failed, and his touch gives rest and sleep. Like the affrighted babe among strangers, whose cry is incessant and whose anguish is untold until the mother comes, then on her bosom it sobs itself to sleep and forgets its distress. Thus hurting humanity, with agonies too grievous to be borne, when past human aid or comfort, when the death angel comes, then on its bosom the groans cease, and they forget their anguish and sweetly sleep.

There is somewhere a picture of a frightful face, livid and ghastly, from which one would turn away with horror but for a hideous fascination which draws one toward it. But on approaching, the fearful face is changed into the face of an angel—it is a picture of death.

Walk over the battlefield after the conflict. The smoke has gathered into a cloud above, horses and men mangled, groaning, and bleeding in helplessness; men begging for water and praying for mercy, while the brutes by piteous moans tell out in their own way of what they suffer, and that peculiar and sickening odor common to the battlefield, adds faintness to the horrors. Surgeons cut and bind, chaplains pray and seek to comfort, but no mortal ministry can bring relief to hundreds of the fallen. Yet when the death angel passes silently over the scene the groans are hushed, the blood staunched, the pains cease, and the sufferers sleep as sweetly as the loved ones they have left in the old churchyard.

Death never brings an added pain, but relieves the pain already too grievous to be borne. Think of a world groaning and travailing in pain, and of the relief that death has brought to the hopeless millions, then tell us if his is not a mission of mercy.

Death comes only in hopeless cases. He does not intrude when the trouble is slight and only temporary, but comes only when disease has proved too much for skill and remedies. But when the sufferer is given up to suffer forever unless some deliverer comes, then death comes to the rescue. Death is king over all diseases. Like the eagle king, ever on watch for the fishhawk's prey, the death angel, mightier than all diseases, is ever on watch for the sufferer hopeless of recovery.

Sometimes we long for his coming. When the loved one has passed beyond the possibility of recovery, and every hour and moment is only anguish, to think of their remaining in that state forever, doomed to suffer thus perpetually, is too awful to contemplate. Yet this would be the doom of every hopeless sufferer but for the kindly ministry of death. Hence, after all our dread of death and fighting against it, it is our best friend, next to Him who is Conqueror of death.

Eliminate every disease from the catalogue, and what would the world *in sin* be without death? Time would soon lay on the couch of helpless age, to become a ceaseless burden upon others, our fathers, grandfathers, and the previous generations, as helpless babes on our hands; the world become a nursery of babes a thousand years old, while we would be worn with the crushing and ever-increasing care. How the world would cry in anguish for the return of death! Next to the blood of Christ, this poor world while sin remains needs the ministries of death.

THE REALIZATION OF DEATH.—In this we cannot have the benefit of experience, either our own or that of others. Others can help us by giving us their experience in every form of suffering, but none have ever given us their experience in death. We have reason to believe that when disembodied, our powers of perception will be increased. "Sown in weakness, raised in power." God is without body or physical parts, yet He perceives in a higher and broader sense than is possible to us. Hence when we are like Him, free from cumbrous mortality, we shall perceive in a higher and more perfect sense than now.

You have felt the exhilaration of the balmy air on a bright spring day when carried into it from the sick room. I remember when, after confinement for five long months, I was carried for the first time into the open air. It was a revelation, a new life, and like paradise to my spirit. What then must be that transition from the sick room into the paradise of God?—the restful tranquility of that home which He is preparing for His faithful children who suffer here?

THE EXPECTATION OF DEATH.—When the mind is wound up and set for some important event, some unusual trial which has taken up our thought and solicitude, when it has come and gone; then we have a strange reverse of feeling. So when death has come and gone and with it all lassitude, dullness, and disappointment, then will come the happy, heavenly realization of the disembodied spirit, as if it said to itself, "So now all is over. This is what I have looked and waited for. I spent life getting ready for this, fasting, praying, working and trusting, and now it is over. How light it seemed at last! I had anticipated it, and when I came to it I found it was only the 'shadow of death.' Christ had taken the substance away. Now I am beyond death, have crossed the strange dark river and am in the land which has been in mind on all the life journey.' Then will come the sweet, strange reverse of feeling that comes with the first experience of disembodied being.

CHAPTER XLIX.

THE RESURRECTION AND FINAL JUDGMENT.

"For the Lord himself shall descend from heaven with a shout, with the voice of the archangel, and with the trump of God; and the dead in Christ shall rise first."—1 Thess. 4:16. "For we must all appear before the judgment seat of Christ."—2 Cor. 5:10.

THE JUDGMENT A DIVINE FIXTURE.— There are things absolute and things contingent in the economy of God. He sent Jonah to cry against Nineveh, "Yet forty days and Nineveh shall perish." But Nineveh repented and her repentance turned the contingency and the city was spared. Heaven with its joys and hell with its horrors hang upon a contingency. "He that believeth shall be saved, and he that believeth not shall be damned." Believing turns the contingency.

But the final judgment is absolute and the day is set. "The Lord hath appointed a day in the which He will judge the world." He appointed a time to come into the world and lay down His life for sinful men, and He met that appointment, and He will come again to meet His appointment for the judgment of men.

There will be a vast contrast between His first and His second coming. The first was in weakness, the last will be in power; the first in dishonor, the last in glory. He came first as man, He will

418

come last as God. The first utterance was the birth-cry of infancy, the final utterance the shout of an all-conquering God. Compare the shout of the descending God with the feeble cry of Bethlehem's babe, and you have the contrast between His first and His second coming.

Wrapped then in swaddling clothes and laid among the beasts of the stall; wrapped now in the clouds of heaven and attended by the angels of God. Mark the apposition. Swaddling clothes against clouds, beasts against angels, servitude against dominion, and the manger against the throne.

THAT DAY IS FIXED IN HUMAN CON-SCIOUSNESS.—Saint and sinner have an inner consciousness of this coming day. That imperial power which we call CONSCIENCE, which resides and presides in every human breast, has its being in that coming judgment. To that day the pure conscience looks for its reward, and the guilty conscience for its doom.

The unrest of guilt is in view of that judgment. Felix could sit unmoved while Paul reasoned of "righteousness and temperance," but when the thunders of a "judgment to come" broke upon his conscience "Felix trembled." Guilt can bear anything better than a coming judgment. The judgment day is conscience day, it is the last door between the sinner and his doom, and conscience unlocks that door and lets hell into the heart of guilt, tormenting the sinner before his time. Conscience and the judgment are counterparts standing the one over against the other. Conscience in the human soul and judgment in the plan of God, co-working throw the impenitent into wretchedness to drive him to Christ. Oh, that they might accomplish their work in every impenitent soul present at this hour!

EVERY DAY IS A DAY OF DOOM.—The day of judgment will not affect my destiny, but this day will. This day is a factor making up the verdict that will be made known on that day. Judgment day is simply the receptacle of all other days, the ocean into which all the life-streams flow. Hence each day bears its part in making up that momentous day, and how sadly we fail to realize it!

How deceptive is a running account! You purchase a few trifles of minor cost every day, but think nothing of the account until called to settle, when you are astonished at the amount; yet the articles are all on the book. What will be the horror of the impenitent when called to final settlement? Not an account of a few days or weeks, but of twenty, thirty, fifty years; yes, of a lifetime. Dear sinner, look back today to childhood and come down, day by day, through all the years you have lived in sin—sins of omission and sins of commission, day after day—they are on the imperishable register. All there. How long, dark and overwhelming the list, and no farthing paid! God has borne with you. Amazing grace! But He will call you to settlement on the day "when the books are opened."

HIS COMING WILL BE UNEXPECTED.—As a thief in the night and at such an hour as ye think not. Whether tomorrow or in the coming centuries, whether at midnight, the third watch, or the morning-dawn, no man knoweth. Busy life will halt in a moment, the Bible lie closed on the desk, its work done. The merchant's counter forsaken, the banker's vault unguarded, the mechanic's shop silent and the hum of business hushed and still.

Godless mirth from the halls of revelry betakes itself to prayer. The husband pale with fear hastens to home and loved ones, where little children have left their sports and are clinging close to the mother, who is transfixed with awe and dare not ask what meaneth? A strange portentous spell is on the world when God is nigh.

Should judgment fires flash about us at this moment what a scene! Pale faces, wringing hands, clinging to loved ones, crying for mercy! How unexpected! Just that unexpected will it be when the Son of man shall come in the clouds of heaven."

THE THREE VOICES.—The text announces three distinct voices. The shout of God—the voice of the archangel—and the trump of God. In which of these is the resurrection power? Not in the voice of the archangel. The tones of an archangel's voice are not strong enough to reach and wake the dead. "An angel's arm can't snatch me from the grave. Legions of angels can't confine me there." Angels have ever had intense interest in man, they sang for joy when God built our earthly home. On snowy wings, with messages of mercy, they have beaten the air-lines twixt heaven and earth until they are more familiar with the ethereal tracks than we with the dusty highways of earth. They have been "ministering spirits" for us while living, then when God shall call us from the dust shall not those angel guardians witness the triumph with an interest that is intense? Is not this the purpose in "the voice of the archangel" to summons the angel hosts under His command to witness the scene?

"The trump of God" is the third voice named, but the power of resurrection is not in this. This will be heard after the dead have arisen calling them together for the final judgment. The ancient use of the trumpet was to assemble the multitudes. The trump of God will call the risen millions together into one place, while the voice of the archangel will assemble the angels.

THE SHOUT OF GOD.—This is the power that shall wake the dead. In that shout *alone* is resurrection power. Men express their mightiest impulses with a shout. The shout of an army in battle-advance is something unearthly, and you almost feel your flesh creep upon the bones. But then will be heard—not the shout of an advancing army—but the shout of God. What words! Words not found elsewhere in all the holy Book. What does it mean? Has the magnitude of the occasion unsettled the divine equilibrium and thrown the Godhead into excitement? Not so. But that shout will indicate the reserves of power in the divine Being. We know but little yet of God. "The visible heavens declare His glory" as the pioneer cuts his name in the bark of the beech to be seen a hundred years afterward. The visible universe is only the touch of the Eternal, the divine name cut in the beech-bark of being to indicate God to us. But that final personal shout which awakens a world of the dead, that will give us some conception of the reserves of His power.

IT WILL BE A TIME OF VICTORY.—Wars have arisen and then subsided, nations have struggled and then made peace, but the war between the "Lion of the tribe of Judah" and the "Dragon of the pit" has known no cessation. They will have fought over every mountain and valley from Eden to the resurrection. The line of history is marked with blood, but this will be the culmination, the Actium, the Waterloo of Christianity. The enemy driven from the last ditch and all recovered but the dust and bones of his saints. Like Michael and his angels contending over the body of Moses—God's last battle will be over the bodies of his saints. Descending with a shout that wakes the dead, He carries the last intrenchment and leads captivity captive. Then shall follow the shout of triumph and "death and hell shall be cast into the pit."

LET US CONTEMPLATE THAT HOUR.— God's purposes complete and creation no longer to stand shall become unsteady and reel as a drunken man. Her rivets loosen and her joints fall apart, revealing the distant perspective Godhead.

The living, with upturned faces, are pale and breathless while He halts His angel armies in the air. A moment's pause, the universe in awe, and then the SHOUT OF GOD—that shout which thrills all being. Earth hastens to uncover her dead, throw open her graves, and roll back the stones from her sepulchre doors. Old ocean gathers her treasured dead and flings them living into the populous air. Lazarus like—the race rises from the dead and answers to the shout of God in "Hosannahs in the highest!"

I see the graves of the great as they surrender their dead. Warriors who slept in Christ—Abraham, David, Joshua, and our own Washington and Lee. Spiritual warriors mightier still—Noah, Jeremiah, Paul, Luther, Wesley and Knox; with voices long used to answer to the roll-call of the church, they now shout responsive to the voice of God!

Then I see the lesser graves as they give up their treasures. "Suffer the little children to come unto me." Now I know what those words foretold as I see them coming! Coming by millions, as frightened birds that fly up from the earth and rustle the leaves and darken the heaven! The air populous with risen and immortal infancy. Among them your own darling one, fluttering up from its rust-eaten casket and adding its bird-note to the universal anthem.

THE UNDERTONE.—The resurrection is not a time of universal joy. There is a deep discordant under-tone. The wicked also have been made alive. The hosts who hated God are now alive forever in all the hell of their bad character. The tyrants who have let the blood-hounds of war loose upon men—Herod, Caesar, Alexander, Nero, and the host of their like. They are now immortal in their own lusts. Blood was their glory and now it shall ooze from their fingers and drip from their skirts, only to be lapped by hell-hounds forever on their track. The human beast-like Henry the VIII and Wilhelm the II—are now immortal in all their beastliness They fed only on the animal while living, and now the beast in them is alive forevermore. Their passions on fire and the soul a walking flame. The covetous man whose God was gain, now has his greed, an undying hunger with naught to gratify it; an endless gnawing without mitigation.

WE MAKE OUR OWN RESURRECTION CHARACTER.—The grave works no change. We reap what we sow. Tell me how a man lives in time and I will tell you how he will appear in eternity. The man whose lustful life has photographed itself on his facial outlines will look the beast when raised from the dead. Heaven knows no retrogression. Hell knows no moral advance. Look on your life today and see what it will be in eternity. Look on your loved ones and see what they shall be forever. Are you willing to be and see them forever what they are now? If not, then seek a change and seek it speedily, for as ye are so shall you be.

THE SENTENCE WILL BE JUST.—That sentence will be just what we make it. You and I decide our own destiny. Mercy never met an appointment beyond this world. This is the only world that has an atmosphere of grace. Heaven has the white atmosphere of life, hell the black atmosphere of death, and earth the blood-red atmosphere of redemption and grace. Earth is covered with rendeeming blood and God looks through that blood when He looks on us. This earth is mercy's hospital and works under the blood, ever calling, "Come all ye ends of the earth and be ye saved." Mercy will carry us to the final edge of life and there lay us down—as Hagar laid her child under the bramble to die. We pass this life under cover of the blood, but beyond this there is no covering. When we cross the death-line we enter the clear white light which penetrates the soul through and through and drives the impure soul to "its own place."

The only hope is to be washed and made pure while we are under the blood. Then and only then can we stand the clear cold light of the judgment where the secrets of all hearts shall be made known. Let the saving work be done today! Today is the day of salvation! The night cometh when thy soul shall be required of thee!

CHAPTER L.

ENDLESS RETRIBUTION.

"And these shall go away into everlasting punishment; but the righteous into life eternal."—Matt. 25:46. "—And if the tree fall toward the south, or toward the north, in the place where the tree falleth, there shall it be."—Eccl. 11:3.

We hear much of "The problem of the age." The problem of all the ages has been HOW TO GET RID OF GOD. God is a great inconvenience to men who wish to live as they list, and serve their lusts. And while they cannot cipher Him out of existence, they have done the next best thing for themselves, they have abolished hell, and say, "there is no future retribution."

The "Sermon on the Mount" has the range of destiny, and the difference in doom is as wide as the "fixed gulf." Jesus Christ is not a fallible ceature, but He is the CREATOR, and deals with the eternities. When we hear from Him we hear things worthy of God.

HIS UTTERANCES ARE DECISIVE.—He loves men and has suffered for men as no other has loved and suffered. Yet it is He who preaches this awful doctrine of endless retribution, He who came by the manger, the garden, and the cross, announces this appalling truth. This doctrine comes to us out of the tenderest heart and the purest life that ever dwelt among men. He who is uplifting humanity, and soothing and saving it, is the author of this teaching. We must accept

427

this doctrine or discard the only hope of humanity. With all the sweetness of the gospel anthem, it has a deep and awful undertone which paralyzes the soul that is out of harmony with God.

THE DIVINE APPOSITION.—There is a God-made apposition threading the universe. Every moral state has its opposite; light against darkness, vice against virtue, sin against holiness, and God and heaven against Satan and hell. Beware of the Commentator who is unwilling to take the Bible as it is. The devil was the first higher critic, and he was very modest. He simply inserted the little word "Not." "Thou shalt *"not"* surely die." That word ruined the race. And the old Adversary is still urging his emendations. "Everlasting does not mean eternal, but simply a long time." He is still at work at the translations, deceiving and damning the people through the Greek.

The original word is the same in both directions, hence if one is eternal the other is also. If the lost are sometime to be taken from hell, then the saved may be taken from heaven. If hell is to end, then heaven may end. Admit the future a state of change, and you have a chaotic eternity. One thing this age and another the next. Then your loved ones are you know not where, and situated you know not how. In heaven once, but where now you cannot tell. Hell is eternal, or heaven is an uncertainty and a caprice.

THE MAIN STOCK ARGUMENT.—The infidel says, "It is unjust to punish a soul eternally for a short life-time of sin." But time is not a factor in the case. It is the atrocity of a crime that gauges its punishment, and not the time taken to commit the crime. What matters it about the time it takes to throw a bomb, or pull a trigger, or sink a dirk to another's heart? The civil law sends a man to prison for life, for what he did in the twinkling of an eye.

What would be thought of an attorney who would stand up and say, "May it please the Court, it is not just to send my client to prison for life. It only took one second to kill the man which he slew. There is no justice in punishing a man a whole life-time for what he did in one second of time?" You would say, "That attorney had an indisputable right to an arch-dukedom among fools." And yet that is the main argument urged against endless punishment. Every man who is damned is SELF-DAMNED, and that in spite of all God could do to save him.

HELL IS A SEQUENCE.—It is the fruit and legitimate result of sin. Sentiment and sympathy have no effect upon inflexible law. So long as effect follows cause, that long will hell follow sin. As long as men sow sin, that long will they reap hell, and hell ripens here in this life. The sot, the murderer, the human beast, can say, "Where I am is hell." "Myself am hell"

How much of sentiment has gathered about this awful sequence of sin, seeking to disprove and dispel it. It is but the fogs hanging about the rock-reefs. They hide the fatal rock, but do not remove it. They only conceal it, while the doomed vessel drives upon it to destruction. Men theorize and sentimentalize over this doctrine, and cover it with their foggy fancies, but—reef like—it stands to receive and wreck the soul that dashes upon it.

FACTS ARE INVULNERABLE.—Opinions have no more effect on facts than moon-beams have on marble. The fact that men do not believe this awful truth does not affect the truth itself. To deny this doctrine it to deny the whole Christian system; without it the atonement has no meaning. Why the humiliation of the manger, the agony of the garden, and the ignominy of the cross? Why the death of a God, if there be no eternal issue at stake? If retribution be not eternal, then is the atonement a ponderous piece of divine fanaticism. A groaning God, a darkened heaven, and a reeling earth, and all for what? To save a sinner from a purgatorial hour? Nay! Nay! Christ's stupendous suffering is the exponent of the tremendous issues at stake.

Endless retribution is the dark back-ground to bring out the majesty and tremendous meaning of the crucifixion. Our sins and His suffering have the reach of the eternities, and the soul unsheltered by His blood "shall go away into everlasting punishment."

REVOLUTION IS THE LAW OF TIME.— Time is the MEASURED part of eternity, and nature is the clock-work for its measurement, hence men look at the sun to know the time. Nature is in circles, and revolution is her law. The earth is a sphere, and God made it to revolve. The atmosphere is in a circle around the earth, and the electric current is her invisible belt. The ocean is only the "great waters" in ceaseless revolution. The heavenly bodies move in circles, the seasons chase each other in perpetual procession, day and night are in a circle. We sleep, and rise, go forth to toil, then return and sleep and rise again, thus we live in a ceaseless circle; life itself is REVOLUTION.

PROGRESSION IS THE LAW OF ETERNITY.—Time is revolution—*round* and *round*. Eternity is progression *onward* and ever *onward*. The eddy in the stream whirls and swirls in a circle, while the stream flows on. Time is the eddy in the stream of eternity. While living we whirl in the eddy, when we die we float out into the stream.

We wish to rivet upon your minds the two laws of the two states—the CHANGEFULNESS of time, and the CHANGELESSNESS of eternity. These laws are *inflexible* and *infallible*. Even sin cannot change God's laws. It changes men, and nature, and society, and government, but can never change God's laws. The law of this world is change, therefore changes come whether we are ready for them or not.

We cannot repress the spring-time. When the sun touches the earth with resurrection power the sleeping millions respond, as Lazarus to the Master's call. Silently, grass and bud and bloom unfold on every hand We cannot prevent the summer's heat, or winter's merciless cold. It is the law that these shall come, and we can do nothing against law. Then if law is inflexible here, shall we not learn from this the inflexibility of it in the hereafter? Change here is the *law*, and we cannot prevent it. In the future, *no change* is the law, then how shall we produce it? There is a mighty gospel in the silent coming and going of the seasons.

THERE IS NOTHING BEYOND TIME TO PRODUCE CHANGE.—The very machinery which marks and governs change will have passed away. Like the nest, which goes to the winds when the birdlings take wing—when history is complete, and humanity has ascended to God, this fabric of nature shall dissolve. "The sun shall be darkened," the moon shall cease from its circuit, and the stars shall put out their lights. Nature's frame-work shall fall apart, and "the heavens and the earth shall pass away." The machinery by which nature kept up her rounds shall perish, and the law of revolution shall be no more.

Then we shall enter upon life on different principles. No alternating day and night. "There is no night there." No ebb and flow of the tides, "for there is no more sea." No revolution of the seasons, but eternal summer, and the trees "Yielding fruit every month." Progression is the *only law* of the future. In heaven, it is onward to grander heights, in hell, it is downward to darker depths.

ETERNITY'S LAW OF PROGRESSION RUNS THROUGH TIME.—The fallen tree in the text illustrates it. Suppose its life one hundred years. I draw a circle, and intercircle it with another and another, until ninety-nine circles are round the first. The tree begins life in the center circle. Both laws hold it. Revolution carries it round with the seasons, while progression moves it out one circle each year, making it taller, older, larger, as it moves toward the outer circle. But when it reaches that outer circle and falls, there its changes cease forever. "In the place where the tree falleth, there shall it be." The seasons continue their rounds, but it is outside the life-circle—no rising sap, nor budding leaf, nor ripening fruit. There were two laws holding it, but only one now. Progression is now its only law—from decay to decay. Thus is it with men. "The days of our years are three-score and ten." We begin life in the center of seventy annular circles, each year carrying us one circle outward, until we reach manhood and womanhood. Then driving us into the outer circles, the gray-haired circles, the short-step circles, the palsied and tottering circles, and at last, into that shadowy circle that laps the death-valley and there we fall.

WE ARE NOT WHERE WE BEGUN LIFE.— Progression has moved us outward Whether we have used the seasons or not, each season has used us. We are changed, the keen-edged taste and relish of childhood are gone, its sports and pleasures have dropped away, we have become men and "Put away childish things."

As the seasons change the tree, so they change

the spiritual man. The soul has its seasons. There comes a summer-time to every soul—a time when the divine warmth is felt, and the heart yearns for the higher and nobler life. Glorious growing summer-time of the soul! Would that it could last all the year! Again there are times when the heart is heavy, and the spirit bleak and lifeless as the chill of winter.

THE ROYAL PREROGATIVE.—It was not left for me to decide when I would come into life or when I would go out, but the royal choice is left to me as to *which way* I will go out—whether upward toward God, or downward toward Satan, whether from glory to glory, or from wretchedness to wretchedness..

DEATH ENDS ALL CHANGE.—"In the place where the tree falleth there shall it be." That tree has changed every season for a hundred years, but with its falling changes ceased, never again to unfold its buds in the morning light, or wave its limbs in the winds of heaven. It fell in decaying character, and progression is now its only law. From decay to decay, from rottenness to rottenness, from death to death, its last circle was its last change.

Death does not end all, but it does end all probationary change. Beyond death the very agencies of change are abolished. This awful truth is God's last utterance to man. In the last part of the last chapter of the last book of Revelation, this statement is made, "He that is unjust, let him be unjust still; and he which is filthy, let him be filthy still; and he that is righteous, let him be righteous still; and he that is holy, let him be holy still." This fallen tree is God's picture to impress this awful truth; its old trunk is full of the gospel of doom, it speaks with a voice to make men tremble. When they have made this old decaying trunk to live and bloom again, then may they talk of a time when the state of the lost shall be changed.

THE ULTIMATE DOOM.—The sinner rejecting the gospel, lives in sin, matures in sin, and hardens in bad character and then dies. He has passed the last life-circle, and gone into that state where progression is the only law. Naturally, scripturally, logically, he must "abide in death:" with him it is then from hell to hell.

The resurrection will not change character. "The wheat grain of today is the same it was when the pyramid builders flashed their trowels in the Egyptian sun-light. Six thousand deaths and resurrections that grain has passed with no change in identity.

The words of doom are, "Depart from me!" You have been going from me, and going downward through all your life history. Now have your way:—"and go forever!" Forever going into deeper and further "outer darkness." This is hell. To let the sinner have his way *is hell*.

THE FALLING IS DETERMINED BY THE LEANING.—See a tree hanging heavily and bending in a certain direction, you may easily tell in what direction it will fall. Human character falls by its leanings. The willows along the stream never lean backward, but bend toward the stream from which they draw their life. Sometimes the long graceful streamers droop upon the very bosom of the waters. The soul leans toward that from which it lives." Let me know a man's leanings; if his life and influence and his trendings are all toward Christ, then I can tell you how that man will die. When the tree has grown all its years and hardened in a certain leaning, you cannot change it and make it fall in another direction. All you can do is to get out of the way and let it fall as it leans.

I ask then, what of your leanings? There are eternal issues in our leanings. What of it? Is it toward the world or toward God? Dear sinner, only God can change the moral leaning. Conversion alone can make a "new man." The cross of Christ can change the gravitation. That cross can make the moral nature lean the other way. It will kill the carnal nature and cause things "belonging to the spirit to live and grow in us." It will bring the heart, the will, and the life, to bend toward Christ as the willows toward the stream. I beseech you, come into the Christ-life! Then will the crossing of the time circles be a continual joy. The whirling seasons then will only hasten you heavenward, and as you cross the last time-circle you may shout, "Thanks be unto God who giveth us the victory through our Lord Jesus Christ!" (Finis.)